T0305481

"During the last decades, many areas of the law have been tainted by simplistic economic analyses. Nowhere is this truer than in corporate law, where property rights and agency relationship have been identified when they are absent. Shareholders do not own corporations; they own shares. And Directors and officers are not the shareholders' agents; they are the agents of the corporation. Dennis Huber has written a serious book evidencing these contradictions and the need to bring back corporate law's lost logic. It is a must for business lawyers and for economists willing to address the complexity of the legal structure of the firm."

Jean-Philippe Robé, Sciences Po Law School

"Huber's book is one of the most interesting discussions of the relations between law and the economics of the firm to appear in decades. It asserts, in some key respects, the primacy of the law and argues that most of the economics of the firm literature pays too little attention to the law. I don't agree with everything in it, but the book is surely an impressive undertaking that should be of significant inspiration to economists and other social scientists."

Nicolai J. Foss, Copenhagen Business School

Corporate Law and the Theory of the Firm

Dozens of judicial opinions have held that shareholders own corporations, that directors are agents of shareholders, and even that directors are trustees of shareholders' property. Yet, until now, it has never been proven. These doctrines rest on unsubstantiated assumptions.

In this book the author performs a rigorous, systematic analysis of common law, contract law, property law, agency law, partnership law, trust law, and corporate statutory law using judicial rulings that prove shareholders do not own corporations, that there is no separation of ownership and control, directors are not agents of shareholders, and shareholders are not investors in corporations. Furthermore, the author proves the theory of the firm, which is founded on the separation of ownership and control and directors as agents of shareholders, promotes an agenda that willfully ignores fundamental property law and agency law. However, since shareholders do not own the corporation, and directors are not agents of shareholders, the theory of the firm collapses.

The book corrects decades of confusion and misguided research in corporate law and the economic theory of the firm and will allow readers to understand how property law, agency law, and economics contradict each other when applied to corporate law. It will appeal to researchers and upper-level and graduate students in economics, finance, accounting, law, and sociology, as well as attorneys and accountants.

Wm. Dennis Huber received a DBA in international business, accounting, finance, and economics from the University of Sarasota, Florida; a JD, an MBA in accounting and finance, an MA in economics, an Ed.M., and an MS in public policy from the State University of New York at Buffalo. He also has an LL.M. in homeland and national security law from the Western Michigan University Thomas M. Cooley School of Law. He is a certified public accountant and admitted to the New York Bar. He has taught at universities in the U.S., Canada, Mexico, and the Middle East.

The Economics of Legal Relationships
Sponsored by Michigan State University College of Law
Series Editors:
Nicholas Mercuro
Michigan State University College of Law
Michael D. Kaplowitz
Michigan State University

The Role of Law and Regulation in Sustaining Financial Markets
Edited by Niels Philipsen and Guangdong Xu

Law and Economics
Philosophical issues and fundamental questions
Edited by Aristides N. Hatzis and Nicholas Mercuro

Public Procurement Policy
Edited by Gustavo Piga and Tünde Tatrai

Legal Origins and the Efficiency Dilemma
Nuno Garoupa, Carlos Gómez Ligüerre and Lela Mélon

Law and Economics of Public Procurement Reforms
Edited by Gustavo Piga and Tünde Tátrai

Law and Economics as Interdisciplinary Practice
Philosophical, Methodological and Historical Perspectives
Péter Cserne and Magdalena Malecka

Extraterritoriality and International Bribery
A Collective Action Perspective
Branislav Hock

Economic Analysis of Property Law Cases
Boudewijn R. A. Bouckaert

Corporate Law and the Theory of the Firm
Reconstructing Corporations, Shareholders, Directors, Owners, and Investors
Wm. Dennis Huber

For a full list of titles in this series please visit www.routledge.com/The-Economics-of-Legal-Relationships/book-series/ELR

Corporate Law and the Theory of the Firm

Reconstructing Corporations, Shareholders, Directors, Owners, and Investors

Wm. Dennis Huber

Routledge
Taylor & Francis Group

LONDON AND NEW YORK

First published 2020
by Routledge
2 Park Square, Milton Park, Abingdon, Oxon OX14 4RN

and by Routledge
605 Third Avenue, New York, NY 10017

First issued in paperback 2021

Routledge is an imprint of the Taylor & Francis Group, an informa business

British Library Cataloguing-in-Publication Data
A catalogue record for this book is available from the British Library

Library of Congress Cataloging-in-Publication Data
Names: Huber, Wm. Dennis (William Dennis), 1951– author.
Title: Corporate law and the theory of the firm : reconstructing
    corporations, shareholders, directors, owners, and investors /
    Wm. Dennis Huber.
Description: Abingdon, Oxon ; New York, NY : Routledge, 2020. | Series:
    Routledge studies in the economics of legal relationships | Includes
    bibliographical references and index.
Identifiers: LCCN 2019059021 (print) | LCCN 2019059022 (ebook)
Subjects: LCSH: Corporation law—United States.
Classification: LCC KF1414 .H83 2020 (print) | LCC KF1414 (ebook) |
    DDC 346.73/066—dc23
LC record available at https://lccn.loc.gov/2019059021
LC ebook record available at https://lccn.loc.gov/2019059022

ISBN 13: 978-1-03-223657-5 (pbk)
ISBN 13: 978-0-367-89553-2 (hbk)

Typeset in Times New Roman
by Apex CoVantage, LLC

This book is dedicated to Vivian, Jennifer, and Justin.

Contents

Acknowledgments

Thanks to Dr. Dina Rady, Dr. Stephen Errol Blythe, Dr. Bob McGee, and Geoffrey R. Goldstein.

Thanks to Kristina Abbotts, Christiana Mandizha, and the production staff at Routledge.

Thanks to Vivian, whose comments, criticisms, and suggestions were invaluable.

Other publications by the author

PCAOB sanctions, sanction risk, sanction risk premiums, and public policy: Theoretical framework and a call for research. *Journal of Accounting, Ethics and Public Policy*, 14(3), 647–663. (2013). https://papers.ssrn.com/sol3/papers.cfm?abstract_id=2307559.

The history of the decline and fall of the American accounting profession. *International Journal of Economics and Accounting*, 4(4), 365–388. (2014). https://papers.ssrn.com/sol3/papers.cfm?abstract_id=2260594.

The structure of the public accounting industry – why existing market models fail. *Journal of Theoretical Accounting Research*, 10(2), 43–67. (2015). https://papers.ssrn.com/sol3/papers.cfm?abstract_id=2326297.

The research-publication complex and the construct shift in accounting research. *International Journal of Critical Accounting*, 7(1), 1–48. (2016). https://papers.ssrn.com/sol3/papers.cfm?abstract_id=2360378.

On the hegemony of financial accounting research: A survey of accounting research seen from a global perspective. *Journal of Theoretical Accounting Research*, 11(1), 14–29. (2016). https://papers.ssrn.com/sol3/papers.cfm?abstract_id=2444245.

Public accounting and the myth of the public interest. *Journal of Accounting, Ethics and Public Policy*, 16(2), 251–272. (2014). https://papers.ssrn.com/sol3/papers.cfm?abstract_id=2640375.

Guardians of the galaxy: Public accounting and the public interest. *International Journal of Critical Accounting: Special Issue on the Research Endeavours of Tony Lowe*, 7(5/6), 466–476. (2017). https://papers.ssrn.com/sol3/papers.cfm?abstract_id=2596373.

The SEC's *ultra vires* recognition of the FASB as a standard-setting body. *Richmond Journal of Law & the Public Interest*, 19(2), 120–152. (2016). https://papers.ssrn.com/sol3/papers.cfm?abstract_id=2662634.

Deep impact: Impact Factors and accounting research. *International Journal of Critical Accounting*, 8(1), 56–67. (2016). https://papers.ssrn.com/sol3/papers.cfm?abstract_id=2441340.

Accounting research productivity: More heat than light? *Journal of Theoretical Accounting Research*, 11(2), 28–62. (2016). https://papers.ssrn.com/sol3/papers.cfm?abstract_id=2444543.

The myth of protecting the public interest: The case of the missing mandate in federal securities laws. *Journal of Business & Securities Law*, 16(2), 401–423. (2016). https://papers.ssrn.com/sol3/papers.cfm?abstract_id=2605301.

Can a not-for-profit membership corporation be created as a "shell" corporation? *Liberty University Law Review*, 11(1), 1–32. (2017). https://papers.ssrn.com/sol3/papers.cfm?abstract_id=2361909.

On neo-colonialism and the colonization of accounting research. *International Journal of Critical Accounting*, 9(1), 18–41. (2017). https://papers.ssrn.com/sol3/papers.cfm?abstract_id=2548742.

Law, language, and corporatehood: corporations and the U.S. Constitution. *International Journal for the Rule of Law, Courtroom Procedures, Judicial Linguistics & Legal English*, 1(2), 78–110. (2018). https://papers.ssrn.com/sol3/papers.cfm?abstract_id=2835563.

Irreconcilable differences? The FASB's conceptual framework and the public interest. *International Journal of Critical Accounting*, 9(5/6), 514–523. (2018). https://papers.ssrn.com/sol3/papers.cfm?abstract_id=2789907.

The Supreme Court's subversion of the constitutional process and the creation of persons *ex nihilo*. *International Journal for the Rule of Law, Courtroom Procedures, Judicial Linguistics & Legal English*, 2(1), 53–72. (2018). https://papers.ssrn.com/sol3/papers.cfm?abstract_id=2841825.

The FASB's sabotage of congressional policy and federal securities laws. *Journal of Accounting, Ethics, and Public Policy*, 20(1): 31–75. (2019). https://papers.ssrn.com/sol3/papers.cfm?abstract_id=2841825.

The FASB's conceptual framework – A case of the Emperor's new clothes. (Forthcoming).

Social/Critical/Emancipatory accounting research: Its failure and prospects for redemption. In *Accounting, accountability and society*, Del Baldo, Baldarelli, Dillard, Ciambotti (Eds.), London: Springer. (2020).

Economics, capitalism, and corporations: Contradictions of corporate law, economics, and the theory of the firm. London: Routledge. (2020).

Prologue

This work is an exposé of the contradictions of contract law, property law, agency law, trust law, and corporate law and reveals how corporations, directors, owners of shares, and investors in shares have been legally and socially (mis)constructed by courts, legal scholars, economists, and society in ways that are contrary to property law, agency law, and corporate law.[1]

Part of the legal structure of society includes corporations and therefore corporate law. Corporate law is an amalgamation of state contract law, property law, and agency law (both statutory law and common law), as well as federal securities laws (although the latter are not relevant here). Agency law and private property law are part of the "foundation needed for the construction, growth and management of modern corporations" (Orts, 2013, p. 3). It is imperative, therefore, to understand property law and agency law and their relationship to corporate law.

As taught in every introductory economics textbook, economics is the study of the allocation of scarce resources. The allocation of scarce resources is a function of the legal structure of society (Banner, 2011), which therefore naturally includes corporate law. Corporate law thus determines the economics of the corporation which in turn determines the allocation of scarce resources. Yet economic researchers on the theory of the firm universally ignore corporate law.

The subject of law and economics is so important that the University of Chicago has, since 1958, published the *Journal of Law and Economics* and has come to be referred to as the "Chicago School" (Stout, 2012).

Berle and Means's *The Modern Corporation and Private Property*, first published in 1932, has been described as a "living classic" (Hessen, 1983). *The Modern Corporation and Private Property* is also credited by some with inspiring the New Deal and the securities laws of 1933 and 1934 (Hessen, 1983), although Stigler and Friedland (1983) see it as at most a "minor influence" given that the book was published in 1932 and the first securities law was passed in 1933.

Berle and Means are also considered by many as the originators of the theory of the separation of ownership and control[2] although that, too, is debated. The theory of the separation of ownership and control in turn led to the development of the modern "theory of the firm," grounded in economics and based on agency theory and agency costs (discussed in Chapter 11 and in *Economics, Capitalism, and Corporations: Contradictions of Corporate Law, Economics, and the Theory of the Firm*), and to the founding of the "Chicago School" (Stout, 2012).

Nevertheless, as with any classic, there are deficiencies with *The Modern Corporation and Private Property*. One deficiency Hessen (1983) highlights is Berle and Means's failure to provide a systematic discussion of private property or property rights or how such rights are established or forfeited or an analysis of types of property and types of ownership. However, that is not entirely accurate. Berle and Means devoted much of the book to a discussion of property in relation to shareholders and corporations. What they did not do was to analyze the law of property and property rights in relation to shareholders and corporations and therefore arrived at erroneous conclusions. Private property and property rights are the foundation needed for the construction, growth, and management of modern corporations (Orts, 2013).

Another deficiency noted by Hessen is the absence of an explanation of how a corporation differs from a partnership (Hessen, 1983). While partnerships are not directly relevant to corporations, the differences can inform our understanding of the relationship between corporations, directors, owners of shares, and investors in shares of corporations.

Jensen and Meckling's (1976) *Theory of the Firm: Managerial Behavior, Agency Costs and Ownership Structure* is considered the classic on the "theory of the firm." Jensen and Meckling's "theory of the firm," which is a product of agency theory, is considered to have originated in financial economics (Mizruchi & Hirschman, 2010). Jensen and Meckling attempt to "integrate elements from the theory of agency, the theory of property rights and the theory of finance to develop a theory of the ownership structure of the firm" (p. 305). While it was successful in launching an entirely new branch of literature on the economic theory of the firm, it was an abject failure in achieving its objective of integrating elements from the theory of agency, the theory of property rights and the theory of finance to develop a theory of the ownership structure of the firm. There is no integration in Jensen and Meckling's work because their premises are invalid, as proven in this work.

First, their approach was backwards. They (attempted to) use the theory of agency, the theory of property rights, and the theory of finance to develop a theory of the ownership structure of the firm rather than establishing the legal ownership structure of the firm as determined by agency law and property law to develop an economic theory of the firm. Property law determines the ownership of the firm, and agency law determines the relationship of directors and shareholders. It is only after the legal ownership structure of the firm and the relationship of corporations, directors, and shareholders are determined that the economic and finance theory of the firm can be developed. As it is, Jensen and Meckling had it wrong because shareholders do not own corporations, and directors are not agents of shareholders. Therefore, there can be no agency theory of the firm or agency costs on which the theory of the firm is grounded.

But second, the simple fact is Jensen and Meckling also completely ignored an analysis of property law and agency law, as did Berle and Means (although Jensen and Meckling were not lawyers, so that is somewhat understandable), choosing rather merely to rest on unproven assumptions and unjustified conclusions about the relationship of property law and agency law to corporations.

This book not only provides a rigorous, systematic analysis of property law, agency law, and partnership law, which Berle and Means neglected, but goes on to explain how they contradict contemporary legal scholarship of corporate law and almost all judicial opinions concerning corporations, owners of shares, directors, and investors in shares. Furthermore, it exposes how corporate law, property law, and agency law, as well as the theory of the firm, contradict each other. In doing so it undermines the entire premises on which the theory of the firm as promoted by the Chicago School is grounded.

Orts (2013) notes that while originating in law, economic theories have for a long time dominated the "theory of the firm."[3] Furthermore, "in law schools economic approaches have informed competing theories that emphasized principal agent relationships, transaction costs, the 'nexus' of contracts, or property rights as central to understanding the nature and purpose of the business enterprise." At the same time, "[t]he theory of the firm has been a neglected area of study in mainstream economics . . . and remains in the periphery of economic analysis" (Walker, 2016).

Orts (2013) endeavors to steer analysis of the theory of the firm back to its legal foundations using laws of agency, property, and contracts and emphasizes the corporation as a legal person. (See Chapter 10.) Walker (2016), on the other hand, hoped to move the analysis of the firm from the margins of economics to its center.

According to Orts (2013), economic theories of the firm are inadequate for providing an understanding of business firms. One reason, says Orts, is that economic theories often conflict with each other. But Walker (2016) believes that economics as a discipline has paid insufficient attention to the theory of the firm, to which Hart (2011) adds, "the theory of the firm is one of the less developed and agreed-upon areas of economics."

It is important, furthermore, to understand how the legal structure of corporations and the economics of corporations contradict each other. Not only do economic theories of the firm contradict the legal structure of corporations, legal theories of the firm also contradict each other. The reason for the contradictions is that both economic theories of the firm and legal theories of the firm lack rigorous, systematic legal analysis and logical validity.

In mathematics, proofs are arguments that sustain the truth of an assertion. In logic, valid conclusions can only be made based on valid premises. In legal reasoning, valid judgments can only be made based on the correct interpretation of law and facts. When attempting to apply property law and agency law to a corporation, for example, the arguments that shareholders own the corporation and that directors are agents of shareholders fall apart. Agency law and property law contradict each other when applied to corporations. While there is lively debate in legal literature on whether a corporation is or is not a "legal person,"[4] who owns a corporation, the relationship of shareholders to a corporation, and the relationship of directors to a corporation and its shareholders are questions that have not been subjected to rigorous legal analysis within the context of property law and agency law.

Similarly, as discussed in *Economics, Capitalism, and Corporations: Contradictions of Corporate Law, Economics, and the Theory of the Firm*, a companion to this work, attempting to apply economic theories of resources (factors) of production and production functions, securities laws, corporate financing, and capital and capitalism to corporations leads to erroneous conclusions because the premises are invalid when corporate law and securities laws are added to economic theories.

Separation of ownership and control pervades legal and economic scholarship as well as dozens of judicial opinions. But there is no legally valid argument based on facts, common law, or statutory law to support that doctrine. The separation of ownership and control is so infused in corporate law and the theory of the firm that it has ceased to be a theory and is now a doctrine, criticisms be damned. The belief that there is a separation of ownership and control is the result of assumptions handed down for decades; a result of inappropriate application of common law; a case of "if something is repeated often enough, people will believe it." However, shareholders are not owners of the corporation, as I prove in this text,[5] and if shareholders do not own the corporation, there can be no separation of ownership and control; there can be no shareholder-principals, no director-agents, and no fiduciary duties owed by directors to shareholders.

Virtually all textbooks used in the first course in accounting, typically called "Principles of Accounting" or "Introductory Accounting," include chapters dedicated to various parts of a corporate balance sheet beginning with the familiar equation assets = liabilities + equity, further divided into current assets, long-term assets, current liabilities, long-term liabilities (relevant here, bonds), and equity, with equity divided into common stock, preferred stock,[6] and retained earnings. The equity section is universally referred to as "Shareholders' Equity" or "Owners' (plural) Equity." Those labels are incorrect and misleading. If there are no owners of a corporation, which the evidence I provide in the following chapters proves, it cannot be "owners' equity" or "shareholders' equity." The equity of a corporation is not the shareholders' equity. It is the *corporation's* equity and is so recognized by at least a few courts (e.g., *Rhode Island Hospital Trust Co. v. Doughton*).[7]

The economic "theory of the firm" is grounded in agency theory (Jensen & Meckling, 1976), the result of the theory of the separation of ownership and control. The separation of ownership and control takes as axiomatic that shareholders are owners of the corporation. Corporate ownership is determinative of the economic theory of the firm. If shareholders own the corporation, then directors are their agents as taught by the economic theory of the firm. But if shareholders do not own the corporation, there are no owners to be separated from. If shareholders do not own the corporation, directors are not their agents, and 80 years of the economic "theory of the firm" falls apart.[8] The entire economic theory of the firm stands or falls on whether shareholders own the corporation.

When judges, legal scholars, and economists say that shareholders own corporations, there is a separation of ownership and control, and directors are the agents of shareholders, they assume that the reader not only knows what they are talking about but also agrees with them. They assume it is self-evident and needs no proof, or even an explanation, and therefore offer none.

While recently some researchers have correctly recognized that shareholders are not owners of a corporation (e.g., Robé, 2011, 2019; Stout, 2012), they failed to provide the necessary analysis of property law and agency law to sustain their (correct) legal conclusion. Likewise, when they say that directors are not agents of shareholders, they do not provide the necessary analysis of agency law to sustain their legal conclusion. My intent in writing this book is to buttress their conclusions with the evidence that they omitted.

The purpose of this book, therefore, is to present sufficient evidence, using a rigorous, systematic analysis of common law, contract law, property law, agency law, and the statutory language of corporate law, as well as authoritative court rulings of corporate law, that shareholders do not own the corporation, that directors are not agents of shareholders, that there is no separation of ownership and control, and that shareholders are not even investors in the corporation. Furthermore, the evidence presented herein demonstrates that property law, agency law, and corporate law are contradictory. The evidence exposes the false assumptions on which corporate law and the economic theory of the firm are based.

This book is neither praise nor critique of Berle and Means's classic *The Modern Corporation and Private Property* which is approaching its 90th anniversary. It is limited only to an examination of the separation of ownership and control and the contradictions of corporate law and the economic theory of the firm that have emanated from their work. In the following chapters I review basic principles of common law, contract law, property law, agency law, trust law, and partnership law, all neglected by Berle and Means, before proceeding to an in-depth analysis of corporate statutory and common law.

Obviously, corporate law is controversial, and the debate in legal scholarship is intense. But the legal structure of society is not governed by debates in legal scholarship. The legal structure of society is governed by actual law, whether common or statutory. Statutory law is purely within the purview of the legislative branch of government. However, it is the judicial branch that imports common law principles into its rulings and interpretations of corporate statutory law, and thus it is judicial decisions and interpretations that must be placed under the microscope to expose the contradictions in corporate law and which form the basis of the economic theory of the firm.

Before the critics say I neglected to include this work, omitted that author, or overlooked a certain case, I plead guilty. There are literally multiple dozens of books and research papers in law reviews and economic journals that could have been included but are not. First, there are space limitations to contend with, but more important, it is not necessary to include all of them, or even more of them. The arguments I make herein are sufficiently supported by a representative sample. Citing additional authors, books, articles, or cases would not make the arguments presented herein more valid or persuasive.

Notes on limitations and usage of terms:

1 The "firm" and the "corporation" are sometimes considered identical in the literature, but other times they are considered different.[9] Robé (2011) explains the use of the terms as follows:

> The notions of "firm" and "corporation" are very often confused in the literature on the theory of the firm. In this paper . . . the corporation is a legal entity entitled to operate in the legal system and in particular to own assets, to enter into contracts and to incur liabilities. . . . The firm is the economic activity developed as a consequence of the cluster of contracts connecting the corporation owning these assets to various holders of resources required in the firm's operations (p. 1).

> In this book and its companion, *Economics, Capitalism, and Corporations: Contradictions of Corporate Law, Economics, and the Theory of the Firm*, I consider corporations, firms, and enterprises to be identical. That is, I intentionally use the terms "corporation," "firm," and "enterprise" interchangeably since the legal entity, the corporation, and its economic activities, the firm, are inseparable when analyzing the contradictions of law and economics when applied to corporations. Furthermore, there can be no firm unless there is first a corporation. There are times and contexts when the terms "firm," "corporation," and "enterprise" should be used to mean different things, but not for the purposes of this book. There are also theories of the firm other than economic based theories (e.g., behavioral theories, organizational theories, management theories) (Walker, 2016). Fifty years ago, a survey found "at least 21 different 'concepts of the firm' in the literature of business and economics" (Orts, 2013) which is acknowledged. However, other theories are not relevant to the purpose of this book.

2 While corporations and social issues are important, in particular issues such as corporate social responsibility and sustainability, those issues are beyond the scope of this book.

3 Only publicly traded corporations are the subject of this book for reasons to be explained in the ensuing chapters.

4 The historical development of corporations, corporate law, and the theory of the firm is kept to a minimum. While important, most of the history and origin are not relevant to the purposes of this book. For readers who are interested in the historical development of corporations, corporate law, and the theory of the firm, there are dozens of books and articles that readers can consult.

5 The advantages and disadvantages of corporations compared to partnerships, joint stock companies, or limited liability companies are not considered here.

6 I use the terms "shares" and "stock" interchangeably, and sometimes "shares of stock," depending on context. Likewise, the terms "shareholders" and "stockholders" are used interchangeably.

7 All references to stockholders or shareholders refer to owners of common, not preferred, stock, unless otherwise stated.

8 The major emphasis is on U.S. corporate law but is also applicable to other jurisdictions based on Anglo-American common and corporate law, which have similar corporate statutes.

9 Many of the legal principles and concepts discussed in the first four chapters are basic and can be validated by legal encyclopedias such as *American Jurisprudence* or *Corpus Juris Secudnum*. Accordingly, *American Jurisprudence 2d* (Am. Jur. 2nd) is cited frequently.

10 In discussing the theory of separation and control, issues pertaining to control refer only to the board of directors, not to the officers or management. There are several reasons for this.

First, Berle and Means (1991) define the control of a corporation as "the power to select a majority of the board of directors." Second, Delaware General Corporation law defines control as

A person who is the owner of 20% or more of the outstanding voting stock of any corporation, partnership, unincorporated association or other entity shall be presumed to have control of such entity, in the absence of proof by a preponderance of the evidence to the contrary.[10]

Third, Stigler and Friedland (1983) argue that "The majority of the voting stock is the ultimate control over a corporation even if that stock is diffused among many owners." Shareholders only vote for directors. Shareholders do not elect managers or officers, and therefore managers and officers are not accountable to shareholders and not subject to shareholder votes.

Note on style:

This book, along with its companion, *Economics, Capitalism, and Corporations: Contradictions of Corporate Law, Economics, and the Theory of the Firm*, is intended for law students, lawyers, and judges, as well as economists and economics faculty, and researchers in law and economics. However, I am endeavoring to maintain a "Goldilocks"-style approach. That is, while there is a core of lawyers, judges, and legal scholars who have training in economics, and likewise a small cadre of economists and economics researchers who have training in law, there are many lawyers, judges, and legal scholars who have insufficient training in economics, and many economists and economics researchers who have no training in law. Thus, while it is not written as a legal brief trying to convince a judge or a law review article debating the finer points of law, my goal is to present a work that is sufficiently technical and accurate from a legal perspective to be meaningful to law students, lawyers, and judges but not so technical as to be irrelevant to economists and economics researchers. At the same time, although there are no charts, graphs, statistics, or econometrics, or even any equations (other than assets = liabilities + equity, which is the mainstay of economists), my aim is to make this work sufficiently technical and accurate from an economics perspective to be meaningful to economists and economics researchers, but not so technical as to make it irrelevant to law students, lawyers, and judges. A challenge at the very least, and I apologize in advance if I fall short in achieving that goal.

Notes

1 *Economics, capitalism, and corporations: Contradictions of corporate law, economics, and the theory of the firm* (London: Routledge, 2020) exposes the contradictions between economics (including finance, accounting, and investing), corporate law, and the theory of the firm.
2 Veblen (1923) suggests an embryonic theory of the separation of ownership and control.
3 Orts points out that while the "theory of the firm" is a popular title in economics and organizational behavior literature, there is no "theory of the firm." There are "*theories* of the firm.*" In this book the term "theory of the firm" is used to refer to the economic theory of the firm built on the theory that there is a separation of ownership and control and that directors are agents of shareholders.
4 There is no such debate in the literature on the theory of the firm.
5 While others have recognized that shareholders are not owners of the corporation, they failed to prove it with a systematic analysis.
6 Warrants and options may also be included but are not relevant for the purpose of this book.
7 Rhode Island Hospital Trust Co. v. Doughton, 270 U.S. 69, 81, 46 S.Ct. 256 70, L.Ed. 475 (1926).
8 Again, others have recognized that directors are not agents of shareholders; they failed to prove it with a systematic analysis.
9 Sometimes the word "enterprise" is used, especially in an accounting context, which means the same thing in this book unless otherwise stated.
10 Delaware General Corporation Law, § 203(c)(4).

Bibliography

Cases

Rhode Island Hospital Trust Co. v. Doughton, 270 U.S. 69, 81, 46 S.Ct. 256 70, L.Ed. 475 (1926).

Authors and publications

Banner, S. (2011). *American property: A history of how, why, and what we own*. Boston: Harvard University Press.
Berle, A.A., & Means, G.C. (1991). *The modern corporation and private property* (2nd ed.). New York: Routledge.
Hart, O.D. (2011). Thinking about the firm: A review of Daniel Spulber's the theory of the firm. *Journal of Economic Literature*, 49(1), 101–113. doi: 10.1257/jel.49.1.101.
Hessen, R. (1983). The modern corporation and private property: A reappraisal. *The Journal of Law & Economics*, 26(2), 273–289. Retrieved from www.jstor.org/stable/725101.
Jensen, M.C., & Meckling, W.H. (1976). Theory of the firm: Managerial behavior, agency costs and ownership structure. *Journal of Financial Economics*, 3, 305–360. doi: 10.1016/0304-405X(76)90026-X.
Mizruchi, M.S., & Hirschman, D. (2010). The modern corporation as social construction. *Seattle University Law Review*, 33(4), 1065–1108. Retrieved from https://digitalcommons.law.seattleu.edu/cgi/viewcontent.cgi?article=1011&context=sulr.

Orts, E.W. (2013). *Business persons: A legal theory of the firm*. London: Oxford University Press.

Robé, J-P. (2011). The legal structure of the firm. *Accounting, Economics, and Law – A Convivium*, 1(1), 1–85. doi: 10.2202/2152-2820.1001.

Robé, J-P. (2019). The shareholder value mess (and how to clean it up). *Accounting, Economics, and Law—A convivium*, 9(3), 1–27. doi: 10.1515/ael-2019-0039.

Stigler, G.J., & Friedland, C. (1983). The literature of economics: The case of Berle and Means. *The Journal of Law & Economics*, 26(2), 237–268. doi: 10.1086/467032.

Stout, L. (2012). *The shareholder value myth: How putting shareholders first harms investors, corporations, and the public*. Oakland, CA: Berrett-Koehler Publishers.

Veblen, T. (1923). *Absentee ownership and business enterprise in recent times: The case of America*. New York: B.W. Huebsch.

Walker, P. (2016). *The theory of the firm: An overview of the economic mainstream*. London: Routledge.

The ground floor
Jurisdiction, common law,
and contract law

Introduction

As I was writing this book, by the time I got halfway through Chapter 4, I was struck with the realization that half the intended readership – economics students, faculty, and researchers – may not be familiar with basic legal concepts. Therefore, it is necessary to begin with an overview of principles of jurisdiction, and common law and contract law. It will no doubt be rudimentary to law school students, faculty, and researchers, but it seemed appropriate to include this chapter to review the basic principles of common law and contract law in order to make sure that everyone is on the same page, so to speak. I encourage law school students, faculty, and researchers not to skip this chapter.

For the same reason, I provide a review of basic principles of micro- and macro-economics as well as financing considerations in Chapters 2 and 3 of *Economics, Capitalism, and Corporations: Contradictions of Corporate Law, Economics, and the Theory of the Firm*,[1] in order to provide a foundation for law school students, faculty, and researchers as well as economics students, faculty, and researchers in order to prove the invalidity of the economic theory of the firm. Economists will no doubt deem the review of economics and finance elementary, as indeed it is, but it also seemed appropriate to assume that the other half of the intended readership – law school students, faculty, and researchers – may not be sufficiently familiar with basic principles of economics. Economics students, faculty, and researchers may be tempted to skip Chapters 2 and 3 of *Economics, Capitalism, and Corporations: Contradictions of Corporate Law, Economics, and the Theory of the Firm*, but I urge economics students, faculty, and researchers not to skip those chapters so the material is fresh in their minds as they read the rest of the chapters.

That this chapter is referred to as "Chapter 0" does not mean it is less important but that it is more important. It is the foundation of Anglo-American law, like the first floor of American hotels, which is the 0 floor. Jurisdiction, common law, and contract law are three of the most important foundations of the Anglo-American legal system. Principles of jurisdiction, common law, and contract law are part of the curriculum of the first semester of Anglo-American law schools.

This chapter provides an examination of constitutional principles of jurisdiction and a review of the origin and function of common law and basic principles of contract law.

Furthermore, as this is a study in corporate law, it is important to understand the historical role and function of common law since common law was the major contributor to the development of corporations (Seymour, 1903; Morley, 2016).

Treatises have been written on both common law and contract law. The most well-known treatises on common law are Blackstone's *Commentaries on the Laws of England* (1765) and, in the U.S., Oliver Wendell Holmes, Jr's., *The Common Law* (1881), but there are others. Another treatise on American common law is Terry's *An Elementary Treatise on the Common Law for the Use of Students* (1898). One of the most well-known treatises on contract law is Samuel Williston's *The Law of Contracts* (1920). Readers who are interested in acquiring a more in-depth understanding of common law and contract law are urged to consult these and other treatises, legal encyclopedias such as *Corpus Juris Secundum* and *American Jurisprudence 2d*, or a series of *Restatements of Law* published by the American Law Institute.

While treatises are generally not necessary or useful for purposes of this book, I will on occasion refer to Terry's *An Elementary Treatise on the Common Law for the Use of Students* in this chapter, as well as *American Jurisprudence 2d* throughout Part I.

Law school students, faculty, and researchers may be tempted to skip this chapter, but I urge them to read it, so it is fresh in their minds as they read the remaining chapters to understand the contradictions in corporate law. Economics students, faculty, and researchers will benefit from reading this chapter in order to understand why the economic theory of the firm is invalid.

Jurisdiction

Prior to looking at common law, contract law, or any law for that matter, jurisdiction must be considered. In the United States federal courts have limited jurisdiction.

> The judicial power shall extend to all cases, in law and equity, arising under this Constitution, the laws of the United States, and treaties made, or which shall be made, under their authority; – to all cases affecting ambassadors, other public ministers and consuls; – to all cases of admiralty and maritime jurisdiction; – to controversies to which the United States shall be a party; – to controversies between two or more states; – between a state and citizens of another state; – between citizens of different states; – between citizens of the same state claiming lands under grants of different states, and between a state, or the citizens thereof, and foreign states, citizens or subjects.[2]

Under the Tenth Amendment of the Constitution

> The powers not delegated to the United States by the Constitution, nor prohibited by it to the States, are reserved to the States respectively, or to the people.[3]

Thus, contract law, property law, agency law, trust law, partnership law, and corporate law, whether statutory or common law, all fall under the jurisdiction of states. Accordingly, state courts hear cases pertaining to contract law, property law, agency law, trust law, partnership law, and corporate law. Federal courts can hear cases pertaining to contracts, property, agency, trusts, or corporations when the controversy is between citizens of different states, but unless the issue pertains to federal law such as securities laws, for example, or when constitutional issues are raised, federal courts must apply state laws rather than federal laws.

Common law

Why is an understanding of common law important to corporate law? For one thing, common law principles of agency and property are in conflict with corporate law when applied to corporations and in conflict with each other when applied to corporations. Yet courts continue to apply common law principles of agency and property laws to corporations in spite of the contradictions.

Common law encompasses many areas of law – contract law, property law, agency law, trust law, corporate law, and torts (injury to persons or property), for example. Principles of common law have been assembled into a series of "Restatements" of the law, such as *Restatement of the Law of Property*, *Restatement of the Law of Agency*, *Restatement of the Law of Contracts*, and so forth, published by the American Law Institute. This chapter is concerned with the origin and function of common law and how common law informs contract law; property law; and agency, trust, and partnership law and, importantly, how common law contributed to the development of corporations and corporate law. Accordingly, this chapter draws on several Restatements, as well as *American Jurisprudence 2d.*

Posner (2014) notes that common law, when viewed from an economic perspective, includes the law of property (creating and defining property rights) and the law of contracts (facilitating the voluntary transfer of property rights). The law of contracts is examined later in this chapter. Property law is examined in Chapter 1.

Common law principles of contracts, agency, trusts, and partnerships continue to have an important impact in modern judicial decisions. And, in spite of the comprehensive corporate statutory laws of most states, common law principles are still relevant and applied in modern judicial decisions involving corporations.

Property law, agency law, trust law, and partnership law are reviewed in greater depth in Chapters 1, 2, 3 and 4 and corporate law is examined in more detail in Chapter 5. Here, we need only understand how common law influences judicial decisions in cases involving property, agency, trusts, partnerships, and corporations.

Origin and function of common law

Legal regimes can be classified as either civil law regimes, common law regimes, or mixed. There is no pure civil or pure common law regime.

In simplest terms, civil law is code based or statutory while common law is court based as explained later. According to Bruncken (1920), in common-law countries, all statutes are modifications of the common law and must be interpreted with a constant regard to that underlying foundation. In the civil-law countries, on the other hand, every statute is basically an original statement of the law on the subject to which it relates.

The controlling principles in common law are judicial precedent and *stare decisis*. The two basically describe the same thing.

In judicial precedent, when judges issue opinions, they cite prior, relevant case law that guides their decisions in present cases. Common law depends on interpreting past cases to inform present cases. Judges follow the precedents of previous cases to guide, explain, and justify the decision in the present case, which then go on to become precedent for future judges to refer to and cite (Whalen, Uzzi, & Mukherjee, 2017).

Stare decisis "is Latin for 'to stand by things decided.'"[4] *Stare decisis* is the doctrine of precedent used by common law legal systems.[5] Bruncken's (1920) assessment of the importance of the consequences of common law in England was the establishment of the binding nature of precedents and *stare decisis*.

Origin of common law

Common law as found in the United States is centuries old, having originated in England in the Middle Ages (American Jurisprudence, 2nd (henceforth "Am Jur 2nd"), Common Law, §3). As they were derived from England, common law doctrines are thus found in countries colonized by England, including the United States, Canada, Australia, and New Zealand.[6] Thus, the American colonies settled by England are mostly common law states, while other colonies not settled by England, such as Louisiana, which was settled by France, are mostly civil law states. However, no state is purely common law or civil law.

In the United States, common law principles are found in most states to various degrees. In fact, the original 13 states explicitly recognized the presence of common law principles in their constitutions (Am Jur 2d, Common Law, § 11).

Since Delaware corporate law will be referred to frequently in Chapter 5, Delaware Supreme Court decisions provide a fertile background not only for understanding the origin of common law in America, but also for considering the role and importance of common law in modern American law.

In *Bridgeville Rifle & Pistol Club, Ltd. v. Small*,[7] the Delaware Supreme Court had occasion to visit the origin of common law in Delaware. The court stated,

> Article 25 of the original [state] constitution adopted by State of Delaware on September 20, 1776 stated
>
>> "The common law of England, as well as so much of the statute law as have been heretofore adopted in practice in this state, shall remain in force, unless they shall be altered by a future law of the Legislature; such parts

only excepted as are repugnant to the rights and privileges contained in this constitution and the declaration of rights, & c. agreed to by this convention.

The Delaware Supreme Court went on to state, "This Court has repeatedly held that Delaware law includes the English common law as it existed in 1776, except where it has been clearly modified by our statutory law." But the court did not stop there. Its historical review noted that

In 1792, the General Assembly made the anticipated changes and removed Article 25.43 The removal of Article 25 did not revoke the application of English common law in Delaware, but rather, reinforced the understanding that the Delaware General Assembly's creation of its own Constitution and statutes would take primacy over English law.

In *Sherman v. State Dep't of Pub. Safety*[8] the court stated,

[I]t is the duty of the courts to ensure that the common law is as fair and efficient as humanly possible, taking into account evolving societal conditions and the problems created by past rulings. See generally Oliver Wendell Holmes, The Common Law (1881). We should not adhere to all past common law precedent until such time as the General Assembly enacts a statute overriding a judicial precedent addressing a subject traditionally governed by judicially-determined common law, especially given the General Assembly's reluctance to intrude in areas of law it has chosen to leave to the common law to address.

Relevant to the purposes of this book are common law doctrines found in contract, property, and agency and partnership law. Contract, property, agency, and corporation law are matters of state law under the Tenth Amendment of the United States Constitution.

Function of common law

The function, perhaps even the purpose, of common law is to ensure that similar cases, i.e., cases that have similar facts and similar legal questions, are decided similarly. Stability and continuity of law are facilitated, and trust in the legal and judicial system is enhanced.

Since contract law, property law, agency law, and corporation law are matters of state law, understanding the function of common law in interpreting contract law, property law, agency law, and corporation law is important. The function of common law is seen in the meaning of common law. Common law, where it has not been overridden by statutory law, guides courts in their decision-making process such that decisions rendered today follow decisions in past cases where the issues are similar.

States may replace and have replaced common law principles with statutory laws. For example, the Delaware Legislature amended the Delaware Code to replace the common law of agency with statutory law of agency, which completely displaced the common law for persons in a relationship governed by statutory agency.[9] But unless replaced by statutory laws, common law principles will be relied on by courts. But even then, courts will rely on common law to interpret statutory law unless the statutory law was intended to completely replace common law. As stated by the Delaware Supreme Court, "Courts should, however, interpret statutory law consistently with preexisting common law unless the legislature expresses a contrary intent."[10]

Common law is law that does not derive its authority from statutes. Therefore, it is applied in the absence of statutes. Common law is created by the judiciary and is based on case law, rather than statutes (Am Jur 2nd, Common Law, §1). Thus, common law relies on judicial precedent and *stare decisis*. More importantly, state courts recognize the role and importance of common law when interpreting state statutory laws.

In older cases, for example, in Illinois, "It is a general rule in the construction of statutes that they are not to be construed as changing the common law farther than by their terms they expressly declare."[11] In New York,

> The general rule is that an intention to change the rule of the common law will not be presumed from doubtful statutory provisions; the presumption is that no change is intended, unless the statute is explicit and clear in that direction.[12]

However, that is not the view of some legal scholars today. Entrikin (2019), for example, sees the supremacy of statutory law over judicial decision-making in a democracy. Even when a court declares a statute unconstitutional, judge-made law is subordinate to statutory law. Her assessment is that for all practical purposes, American common law is dead, even though law schools continue to teach common law reasoning to law students. To claim the modern American legal system is a common law system perpetuates a legal fiction. Enacted statutory law is the driving force of modern American law: "the legal profession, the legal academy, and the judiciary together have been responsible for creating and perpetuating the common-law myth beginning in the last quarter of the nineteenth century" (Maxeiner, 2015).

Legal scholars differ as to whether the common law is worth preserving, with some claiming Anglo-American common law supports their statutory interpretation while others argue that the common law is obsolete (Pojanowski, 2015). But it is not only legal scholars who differ over the role of common law. Judges also dispute the importance and relevance of common law. The chief justice of the New York Court of Appeals sees her role as a "keeper of the common law" while the chief justice of the Michigan Supreme Court maintains that statutory interpretation is "not a branch of common-law exegesis" (Pojanowski, 2015).

Nevertheless, common law continues to play a significant role in the interpretation of statutory corporate law. Some corporate law statutes, e.g., New York Business Corporation Law, actually refer to common law interpretation.

Nothing in this paragraph shall create any duties owed by any director to any person or entity to consider or afford any particular weight to any of the foregoing or abrogate any duty of the directors, either statutory or recognized by common law or court decisions. (Emphasis added.)[13]

Corporate law is discussed in greater depth in Chapter 5.

Common law and property law, agency law, trust law, and partnership law

COMMON LAW AND PROPERTY LAW

Some principles of the common law of property were codified into statutory law, while others were not codified such that common law is still relied upon by courts in interpreting property law, including the rights of property owners. Property laws are discussed in greater depth in Chapter 1. For now, we will consider how common law informs property laws.

By the 15th century, English courts of common law had already developed rules pertaining to legal interests in land that were largely based on the feudal system of tenure.[14] A person has a possessory interest in land that exists in a person who has a physical relationship to the land, which gives the person physical control over the land, and the person has an intent to exercise control over the land by excluding others from occupying the land.[15]

"Property" denotes the legal interest a person has in, or the legal relationship a person has to, a physical object or the legal bundle of rights recognized in a non-physical object. "Property" is not the object itself,[16] and as will be seen in Chapter 5, a corporation, as an intangible object, is not the object of a bundle of rights as shareholders have no rights in or to the corporation; only to the shares.

Property rights consist of unrestricted rights to use, enjoy, or dispose of the object, subject to certain governmental restrictions discussed in Chapter 1. An object, whether tangible or intangible, is property only if the owner has the right to exclude others from using it. These rights originate in common law although some rights have been codified.

COMMON LAW AND AGENCY LAW

Agency law is discussed in greater depth in Chapter 2. For now, we will consider how common law informs judicial decisions involving agency relationships.

An agency is

the fiduciary relationship that arises when one person (a "principal") manifests assent to another person (an "agent") that the agent shall act on the principal's behalf and subject to the principal's control, and the agent manifests assent or otherwise consents so to act.

Fiduciary relationships are the product of common law[17] that has no statutory, or even universally agreed upon, definition.

For example, in *Estate of Eller v. Bartron*,[18] a 2011 case, the Delaware Supreme Court stated,

> The existence of an agency relationship empowers an agent to act on behalf of his principal [and] that relationship also imposes fiduciary duties on the principal. . . . This opinion [is] premised on the common law of agency as it has evolved over the course of centuries.

In addition to other duties specified by the agency contract, the court stated the agent owed the principal "traditional fiduciary duties." Citing *Restatement (Third) Agency*, the court went on to say,

> As a general matter, "[a]gency is the fiduciary relationship that arises when a person (a 'principal') manifests assent to another person that the agent shall act on the principal's behalf and subject to the principal's control, and the agent manifests assent or otherwise consents so to act."[19]

COMMON LAW AND TRUST LAW

Trust law is discussed in greater depth in Chapter 3. For now, we will consider how common law informs judicial decisions involving trust relationships.

As can be expected, the laws of trust are based on common law principles,[20] and therefore courts refer to common law in cases involving trust relationships. For example, the Delaware Supreme Court ruled

> the concept of a fiduciary relationship, which derives from the law of trusts, is more aptly applied in legal relationships where the interests of the fiduciary and the beneficiary incline toward a common goal in which the fiduciary is required to pursue solely the interests of the beneficiary in the property.[21]

COMMON LAW AND PARTNERSHIP LAW

As discussed in Chapter 4, partnership law is basically an extension of agency law. Therefore, it is also subject to common law principles even though many states have adopted the Uniform Partnership Act, including Delaware, a state that is the focus or my examination of corporate law and its contradictions.

In states where partnership law is governed by statute, principles of common law supplement the partnership statute. In states where partnership law is not governed by statute, common law principles determine the rights of partners and partnerships.[22]

Contract law

Am Jur 2nd notes that "a contract is not a law, nor does it make law: it is the agreement plus the law that makes the ordinary contract an enforceable obligation."[23]

Contract law is a product of common law,[24] much of which has been codified in the Uniform Commercial Code.

Contract law is the foundation for any purchase and sale and therefore highly relevant to purchasing shares in a corporation since purchasing securities from a corporation is a matter of contract. This section focuses only on the essential elements and requirements to create an enforceable contract in order to relate the elements and requirements of contract law to the purchase of securities from the corporation.[25]

Contracts create duties that are imposed by common law principles above and beyond the actual terms of the contract itself. Depending on the contract, a contract can create common law duties to act in a reasonable or prudent manner that are not actually stated in the contract, all the way up to creating fiduciary duties. For example, "An implied covenant or duty of good faith and fair dealing is also a longstanding fixture of the common law of contracts."[26] Citing its own previous rulings[27] in an example of *stare decisis*, the Delaware Supreme Court ruled in *Connelly v. State Farm Mut. Auto. Ins. Co.*,[28] "An implied covenant or duty of good faith and fair dealing is also a longstanding fixture of the common law of contracts."

The simplest definition of a contract is "an agreement to do, or refrain from doing, a particular thing."[29] That said, there are many additional requirements to create an enforceable agreement (contract). Creating an enforceable contract requires competent parties, offer and acceptance, consideration (mutual promises), mutual agreement, and legal purpose.[30]

Promises

Promises are the essential feature of a contract. (Am Jur 2d, Contracts, §3). A promise may be express or implied and may consist of mutual promises or a promise in exchange for an act.[31] Case reporters are filled with cases arguing over what constitutes a promise.

A bilateral contract is a promise in exchange for a promise (Am Jur 2d, Contracts, §8). I promise to pay you $20,000 for your automobile if you promise to sign the title over to me. That is an executory contract since neither promise is yet fulfilled (Am Jur, Contracts, §5). When I pay you the $20,000 and you sign the title over to me the contract is executed, i.e., completed (Am Jur 2d, Contracts, §5). The promises are fulfilled. If I pay you the $20,000 but you do not sign the title over to me, you have breached the contract, and I can sue you. If you sign the title over to me and I do not pay you the $20,000 I have breached the contract, and you can sue me.

A unilateral contract is a promise in exchange for an act (Am Jur 2d, Contracts, §8). I promise to pay you $25.00 if you mow my lawn. If you do not mow my lawn, I have no obligation to pay you. You have not breached the contract because there is no contract. You did not give me a promise. If you mow my lawn, I have an obligation to pay you $25.00 because you completed the act. If I do not pay you, you can sue me. I have breached the contract.

Purchasing shares from a corporation is a bilateral contract. I promise to give the corporation $20,000 for *x* number of shares; the corporation promises to give me *x* number of shares in exchange for $20,000. Of course, the promises and exchange of promises (consideration) are usually (relatively) simultaneous. I do not transfer $20,000 to the corporation in trust, to manage my money for me. (See Chapter 3.) The purchase of shares is a simple contract, an exchange of promises consisting of a mutual grant of certain rights from the corporation to me, cash being transferred to the corporation by me, and an agreement by me to surrender certain rights.

If I give the corporation $20,000 for *x* number of shares and the corporation does not give me the shares, the corporation has breached the contract. If I promise to pay the corporation $20,000 for *x* number of shares and the corporation gives me the shares, but I do not give the corporation the $20,000, I have breached the contract. In fact, by statute the corporation can sue me if I do not pay, as discussed in Chapter 5.

Offer and acceptance – agreement

An enforceable contract requires an agreement between the parties (Am Jur 2d, Contracts, §2). The agreement constitutes an offer by one party and acceptance of the offer by another party (Am Jur 2d, Contracts, §29). Case reporters are filled with cases arguing over what constitutes an offer, what constitutes acceptance, and what constitutes an agreement.

In order to create an enforceable contract, there must be an offer and acceptance. I offer to purchase your automobile for $20,000. You either accept my offer or reject it. If you accept my offer, an enforceable contract is created.[32]

A contract of adhesion is found in such things as credit card agreements or the terms of service of internet providers. It is one-sided – take it or leave it. The credit card or internet provider offers certain terms. The terms are non-negotiable. You agree to the terms, or they do not issue a credit card or provide internet service to you.

Consideration

Consideration is essentially a promise given by the promissor if the promise is accepted by the person to whom the promise is given (the promisee).[33] Case reporters are filled with cases arguing over what constitutes consideration and what constitutes adequate consideration. Here we will assume the promise is a promise to pay cash in exchange for a promise to receive an automobile. It could be a promise to receive shares of stock. In reality, the consideration given by each party is frequently simultaneous.

I offer to purchase your automobile for $20,000. The $20,000 is the consideration I give to you. If you accept my offer, an enforceable contract is created. The automobile is the consideration you give to me.

Consideration is normally set in terms of property (cash for an automobile), but consideration can also consist of surrendering rights or selling your rights. You write a book. I can purchase the rights to your book at a price mutually agreed upon. You then agree to surrender to me your rights to publish your book. I now own the exclusive right to publish your book.

When issuing securities, directors are empowered by statute to determine what is sufficient consideration for the securities. (See Chapter 5.) When securities are purchased in the market, the market determines the price of securities. (Note that none of the consideration goes to the corporation when securities are purchased in the market.)

In addition to cash, a purchaser of securities agrees to surrender to the corporation her rights to decide how to allocate the cash she pays for the securities. The corporation purchases her rights to decide how to acquire and allocate resources of production by issuing her the stock. The corporation now owns the cash along with the shareholder's rights to decide how to allocate the cash and, by extension, how to acquire and allocate the assets the corporation acquires with the cash received from the shareholder. The shareholder now owns the shares with certain rights attached to the shares such as the right (usually) to vote for directors and the right to liquidation proceeds. This is discussed in greater detail in Chapter 5.

Surrender of rights

Adequate consideration can consist of property, an act, or a return promise. A return promise can be a promise to refrain from a legal act, a forbearance to act, or a creation, modification, or destruction of a legal relation.[34] When a person purchases shares from a corporation, he is selling his rights to decide how to use the cash paid to the corporation for the shares and how to allocate the resources acquired with the cash paid for the shares. In exchange, the corporation gives the shareholder the right to vote for directors (usually), to vote on mergers (usually), to amend the articles of incorporation or the bylaws (usually), to receive dividends (if declared), and to receive a distribution of the net assets upon liquidation. The shareholders pay cash for the shares, which gives them only the expectation, but not the guarantee, of receiving cash in the future (dividends). This is discussed in greater detail in Chapter 5.

Capacity/parties

An enforceable contract requires that each party have the legal capacity to enter into a contract (Am Jur 2d, Contracts, §27). Case reporters are also filled with cases arguing over who is a party and whether a party has capacity to enter into a contract. Since the parties to a contract must have legal capacity, they may not be minors except in very limited circumstances not relevant here. They must have the mental capacity to understand the terms of the contract.

As discussed in Chapter 5, corporations are empowered by statute to enter into contracts; thus they are considered by law to have capacity even though they are artificial persons. "Artificial" (also called "fictitious" or "legal") persons are discussed in Chapter 10.

Purpose

An enforceable contract must be for a legal purpose. If a contract is not made for legal purposes, it is not enforceable. On the other hand, a contract may be made for a legal purpose (e.g., buying a house) but not be enforceable if it does not comply with certain statutory requirements, such as being in writing.[35]

The Uniform Commercial Code

Many doctrines and principles originating in common law were later codified into statutory law. The codification of some common law principles of contract law have been codified into the Uniform Commercial Code (UCC). The UCC governs contracts for both tangible and intangible property and property rights with the exception of real estate transactions. The UCC governs sales of goods, leases, negotiable instruments, bank deposits and collections, funds transfers, letters of credit, bulk sales, documents of title, secured transactions, and investment securities (Article 8). The relevant part of Article 8 is

> Uniform Commercial Code. ARTICLE 8. INVESTMENT SECURITIES. § 8–102 Definitions. § 8–102 Definitions. (a) In this Article . . . (9) "Financial asset," except as otherwise provided in Section 8–103, means: (i) a security . . . (15) "Security," except as otherwise provided in Section 8–103, means an obligation of an issuer or a share.[36]

The UCC also provides rules for determining if an obligation of an issuer is a security.

> § 8–103 Rules for determining whether certain obligations and interests are securities or financial assets. (a) A share . . . is a security.

The importance of the UCC's classification of shares of stock as investment securities, not as property or a proprietary interest in a corporation, will be discussed in greater depth in Chapter 5. For now, the UCC's classification of shares of stock as investment securities is important because classifying a share of stock as an investment security removes the purchase of stock from being classified as a trust and places it squarely within contract law. Shareholders invest in shares, not in the corporation.

Chapter summary

This chapter provided a review of the origin and function of common law and the principles and requirements of contract law. Understanding common law and contract law as two of the most important foundations of the Anglo-American legal system is necessary in order to understand corporate law and the relationship of property law, agency law, and trust law, the subjects of the next three chapters, to corporate law.

The importance of common law and its role in corporate law cannot be overstated. Since principles of common law are frequently referred to in legal literature and judicial opinions (rarely in economic literature), it is imperative to understand the meaning of common law, the principles of common law, and the function of common law in interpreting corporate law.

An enforceable contract requires

- An offer and acceptance, i.e., an agreement.
- A promise in return for a promise or in return for an act.
- Capacity of parties.
- Legal purpose.
- Consideration, which may consist of a surrender of a legal right or a promise to refrain from a legal act.

While contract law is rarely referred to in judicial opinions with respect to the relationship of shareholders, corporations, and directors, it is important to understand contract law to know whether or not contract law applies to the relationship of shareholders, corporations, and directors. The applicability of contract law to the relationship of shareholders, corporations, and directors is examined in Chapter 5.

Notes

1 *Economics, Capitalism, and Corporations: Contradictions of Corporate Law, Economics, and the Theory of the Firm* (London: Routledge, 2020) exposes the contradictions between economics (including finance and accounting), corporate law, and the theory of the firm.
 2 U.S. Constitution, Article III, Section 2.
 3 U.S. Constitution, Amendment X.
 4 Stare decisis. www.law.cornell.edu/wex/stare_decisis.
 5 Stare decisis. www.law.cornell.edu/wex/stare_decisis.
 6 Legal systems. www.law.cornell.edu/wex/legal_systems.
 7 Bridgeville Rifle & Pistol Club, Ltd. v. Small, 176 A.3d 632 (DE, 2017).
 8 Sherman v. State Dep't of Pub. Safety, 190 A.3d 148 (DE, 2018).
 9 Estate of Eller v. Bartron, 31 A.3d 895 (DE, 2011).
10 PHL Variable Ins. Co. v. Price Dawe 2006 Ins. Trust, 28 A.3d 1059, 2011; Kuehn v. Cotter, 77 A.3d 272 (DE, 2013).
11 Davis v. Abstract Construction Co., 121 Ill. App. 121, 129 (IL, 1905).
12 Rosin v. Lidgerwood Mfg. Co., 89 App. Div. 245, 47, 86 N. Y. Supp. 49 (NY, 1903).
13 New York Business Corporation Law Sec. 717.
14 Restatement of Laws, 1st, Property, § 6.
15 Restatement of Laws, 1st, Property, § 7.
16 American Jurisprudence, 2nd. 63C Property, § 2.
17 Restatement of Law, 3nd, Agency, § 8.01.
18 Estate of Eller v. Bartron, 31 A.3d 895 (DE, 2011).
19 Restatement of Law, 3nd, Agency, § 1.01.
20 Restatement of Law, 2nd, Trusts, § 2.
21 Crosse v. BCBSD, Inc., 836 A.2d 492 (DE, 2003).
22 American Jurisprudence, 2nd, 59A, Partnership, § 22.

23 American Jurisprudence, 2nd, 17A Contracts, § 1.
24 Contract. Legal Information Institute. www.law.cornell.edu/wex/contract.
25 Purchasing securities in the market does not involve the corporation and thus is not relevant.
26 E.I. DuPont de Nemours & Co. v. Pressman, 679 A.2d 436 (DE, 1996).
27 E.I. DuPont de Nemours & Co. v. Pressman, 679 A.2d 436 (DE, 1996); and Dunlap v. State Farm Fire & Cas. Co., 878 A.2d 434 (DE, 2005).
28 Connelly v. State Farm Mut. Auto. Ins. Co., 135 A.3d 1271 (DE, 2016).
29 American Jurisprudence, 2nd, 17A Contracts, § 1.
30 American Jurisprudence, 2nd, 17A Contracts, § 10.
31 American Jurisprudence, 2nd, 17A Contracts, § 3.
32 You can also make a counteroffer, but counteroffers are not relevant.
33 Am Jur, Contracts, § 101.
34 American Jurisprudence, 2nd, 17A Contracts, § 71.
35 Am Jur 2d, Contracts, § 6.
36 Uniform Commercial Code, §§ 8–102.

Bibliography

Cases

Bridgeville Rifle & Pistol Club, Ltd. v. Small, 176 A.3d 632 (DE, 2017).
Crosse v. BCBSD, Inc., 836 A.2d 492 (DE, 2003).
Davis v. Abstract Construction Co., 121 Ill. App. 121, I29 (IL, 1905).
Dunlap v. State Farm Fire & Cas. Co., 878 A.2d 434 (DE, 2005).
E.I. DuPont de Nemours & Co. v. Pressman, 679 A.2d 436 (DE, 1996).
Estate of Eller v. Bartron, 31 A.3d 895 (DE, 2011).
Rosin v. Lidgerwood Mfg. Co., 89 App. Div. 245, 47, 86 N. Y. Supp. 49 (NY, 1903).
Sherman v. State Dep't of Pub. Safety, 190 A.3d 148 (DE, 2018).

Authors and publications

American Jurisprudence, 2nd. (2009). *Vol. 63C. Property*. New York: Thomson Reuters.
American Jurisprudence, 2nd. (2011). *Vol. 15A. Common Law*. New York: Thomson Reuters.
American Jurisprudence, 2nd. (2015). *Vol. 59A. Partnership*. New York: Thomson Reuters.
American Jurisprudence, 2nd. (2016). *Vol. 17A. Contracts*. New York: Thomson Reuters.
Bruncken, E. (1920). The common law and statutes. *Yale Law Journal*, 29(5), 516–522. Retrieved from https://digitalcommons.law.yale.edu/ylj/vol29/iss5/4.
Entrikin, J.L. (2019). The death of common law. *Harvard Journal of Law & Public Policy*, 42, 351–487. Retrieved from www.harvard-jlpp.com/wp-content/uploads/sites/21/2019/04/Entrikin-Final.pdf.
Maxeiner, J.R. (2015). A government of laws not of precedents 1776–1876: The Google challenge to common law myth. *British Journal of American Legal Studies*, 4, 137–249. Retrieved from https://scholarworks.law.ubalt.edu/cgi/viewcontent.cgi?article=1755&context=all_fac.
Morley, J.D. (2016). *The common law corporation: The power of the trust in Anglo-American business history*. Retrieved from https://digitalcommons.law.yale.edu/fss_papers/5218.

Pojanowski, J.A. (2015). Reading statutes in the common law tradition. *Virginia Law Review*, 101, 1357. Retrieved from www.virginialawreview.org/volumes/content/reading-statutes-common-law-tradition.

Posner, R.A. (2014). *Economic analysis of law* (9th ed.). New York: Wolters Kluwer.

Seymour Jr., E.B. (1903). The historical development of the common-law conception of a corporation. *The American Law Register*, 51(9), 529–551. Retrieved from https://scholarship.law.upenn.edu/cgi/viewcontent.cgi?article=6409&context=penn_law_review.

Terry, H.T. (2013). *An elementary treatise on the common law for the use of students.* Tokyo: Nabu Press. (Original work published 1898).

Whalen, R., Uzzi, B., & Mukherjee, S. (2017). Common law evolution and judicial impact in the age of information. *Elon Law Review*, 9(1), 118–170. Retrieved from www.elon.edu/e/CmsFile/GetFile?FileID=946.

Part I

Foundations

Property law, agency law, trust law,
and partnership law

With the review of common law and contract law completed, we can turn our attention to the foundations of corporate law in order to understand the contradictions of corporate law. This part will review, in order, property law, agency law, trust law, and partnership law. While property law, agency law, and trust law are woven into the fabric of corporate law, partnership law is not directly incorporated into corporate law. However, property law, agency law, and trust law are inherent in partnership law, and it is therefore necessary to compare and contrast how property law, agency law, and trust law are applied to partnerships with how they are applied to corporations.

Corporate law is an amalgamation of contract law, property law, agency law, and trust law. It is a product of both state common law and statutory law. Corporations whose stock and other securities are publicly traded are also subject to federal laws with respect to the securities. Corporations are, of course, subject to a wide variety of state and federal laws and regulations pertaining to such things as the environment and workers' safety. While those issues are important, this book is concerned only with the laws governing the legal structure of the corporation and the implications of those laws on the economic theory of the firm.

In Part I, I perform a rigorous analysis of property law, agency law, trust law, and partnership law. This part serves as the foundation that exposes the logical fallacies and legally invalid arguments of the mantra of "separation of ownership and control" that undergirds the economic theory of the firm and exposes the contradictions inherent in corporate law.

Beginning with Berle and Means's *The Modern Corporation and Private Property* (first published in 1932) to Jensen and Meckling's *Theory of the Firm: Managerial Behavior, Agency Costs and Ownership Structure*, the doctrine of the separation of ownership and control and the economic theory of the firm based on the agency theory of the shareholder-director relationship has achieved a cult-like following, a secret society where admission is granted to law students and economics students after a period of indoctrination where questioning the legal premises on which the doctrine is founded is not permitted.

This part not only questions those premises but also proves that they have no legal validity.

1 Property and property law

Introduction

Economics, as defined by every introductory economics textbook, is the science of the allocation of scarce resources. Property in its various forms constitutes resources to the owner of the property. Property law is the legal structure that determines who owns the property (e.g., government or private persons), which resources are allocated and controlled (labor or capital), and how they are allocated and controlled (market or centrally planned by the government).

In this chapter, I review the basics of private property law, including types of private property and ways by which private property may be owned. Understanding basic property law is necessary to understand the relationship between corporations and property, shareholders and property, and shareholders and corporations. It is important to understand the nature of private property and property laws in order to understand the allocation of resources of production and the economic theory of the firm.

Private property in the United States

Our modern concept of private property[1] and property laws is centuries old, arising in common law. Private property, although not property law, is entrenched in the American Constitution. The Bill of Rights guarantees that "No person shall . . . be deprived of life, liberty, or property, without due process of law; nor shall private property be taken for public use, without just compensation."[2] The Fourteenth Amendment further guarantees that "[No] State [shall] deprive any person of life, liberty, or property, without due process of law."[3]

The Constitution never defines "property" or how property may be owned. Nor does the Constitution form the basis of property laws. Definitions of property and laws of property are left to the states and to common law. As the Supreme Court ruled in *Ruckelshaus v. Monsanto Co.*,[4] "[p]roperty interests . . . are not created by the Constitution. Rather, they are created and their dimensions are defined by existing rules or understandings that stem from an independent source such as state law." Only state law can define the legal parameters of ownership of private property as a result of the Tenth Amendment: "The powers not delegated to the

United States by the Constitution, nor prohibited by it to the States, are reserved to the States respectively, or to the people."[5]

State property laws are largely the product of common law, but also some statutory law, depending on the type of property. According to Posner (2014), common law, when viewed from an economic perspective, includes the law of property (creating and defining property rights) and the law of contracts (facilitating the voluntary transfer of property rights).

Prior to examining laws concerning private property, we must understand the various types of private property and methods of ownership. The method of ownership of private property depends on the type of property. There are various types of private property, each of which must be considered prior to examining private property within the context of shareholders and corporations. For example, the Delaware General Corporation Law[6] and New York Business Corporation Law[7] itemize the types of property a corporation may own, how it may acquire property, and what the corporation may do with the property. The Delaware General Corporation Law also declares that shares of stock owned by a stockholder are personal property.[8]

Furthermore, economics, as defined by every introductory economics textbook, is the science of the allocation of scarce resources. Property in its various forms constitutes resources to the owner of the property. Property law is the legal structure that determines who owns the property,[9] which resources are allocated to production, who controls the resources, and how they are allocated and controlled (Yuille, 2015). It thus behooves us to understand types of private property and laws of ownership of private property in relation to shareholders and property, shareholders and corporations, and corporations and property. Property law determines the ownership of resources and the ownership of the firm[10] while agency law determines the relationship of directors and shareholders, which is discussed in the next chapter.

Berle and Means's (1991) *The Modern Corporation and Private Property* failed to provide a systematic discussion of private property or property rights or how such rights are established or forfeited or an analysis of types of property and types of ownership (Hessen, 1983). A study of corporate law and the theory of the firm must begin with a study of types of private property and property law.

Types of private property

The term "property" has no universally accepted definition within Anglo-American jurisprudence (Yuille, 2015; Morales, 2013). Property refers to a legal interest in, or relationship to, either a physical or non-physical object, or a bundle of rights recognized in the object.[11]

Property describes the rights the owner has over a thing, rather than the thing itself. "[N]early everyone agrees that the institution of property is not concerned with scarce resources themselves ('things') but rather with the rights of persons with respect to such resources" (Morales, 2013, quoting Thomas Merrill, *Property and the Right to Exclude*, 77 Nebraska Law Review, 1998).

In rem rights attach to the thing, i.e., attach to the property itself, while *in pesonam* rights attach to the owner of the thing (Morales, 2013).[12] *In rem* rights are generally rights pertaining to real property[13] while *in pesonam* rights generally pertain to personal property (Morales, 2013).[14]

Am Jur 2d defines property as

> a collection of individual rights which, in certain combinations, constitute property and which can be divided in terms of dimension, duration, and scope. . . . Property . . . denotes the legal interest, or aggregation of legal relations, appertaining to a physical object or thing, not the object or thing itself.[15]

Most important, it includes the "unrestricted and exclusive right to a thing, the right to dispose of it in every legal way."[16]

The debate surrounding what constitutes property occupies a significant portion of legal scholarship (Yuille, 2015). Nevertheless, the basic types of private property, at least, are recognized in every jurisdiction, and there is general agreement that property has certain characteristics (Morales, 2013).

Private property is generally classified as either real property or personal property, although it is also classified as corporeal or incorporeal. "Corporeal" corresponds to tangible property, and "incorporeal" corresponds to intangible personal property.[17]

Real property

The first and most obvious type of property is real property, i.e., land and all that is appurtenant to the land, including buildings, trees, and that which is under the land such as minerals. Real property is naturally fixed,[18] immovable.[19]

Land is one of the three resources of production recognized by economists, the other two being labor and physical capital (i.e., human-made things such as tools, machines, and computer programs) used to produce either consumer goods or other physical capital (Krugman & Wells, 2008).[20] As a resource of production, it is important to understand land and all that land includes as well as the ownership of land. Resources of production are discussed in *Economics, Capitalism, and Corporations: Contradictions of Corporate Law, Economics, and the Theory of the Firm.*

Personal property

Personal property is any property other than real property and includes both tangible property such as automobiles and machines, and intangible property such as legal rights.[21] Personal property is classified as chattel property, choses in action, and intangible property.

Chattel property

Chattel property is any property not amounting to a freehold estate or fee in land (see Ways of owning private property in this chapter). Chattel property is personal property and is divided into "chattels real," which include things related to real property like leaseholds, and "chattels personal," which include any tangible movable property.[22]

Choses in action

A chose in action is something that the owner does not possess in tangible form as real property or chattel property, but to which the owner has a right of action for its possession such as a right to receive or recover a debt or damages on a cause of action, which cannot be made received without recourse to an action in a court of law.[23]

Intangible property

Morales (2013) comments that it is easy to recognize tangible objects as property; it is not as easy to recognize intangible things as property. Intangible property exists only as a right recognized in law.[24] Examples include shares of stock,[25] bonds, notes, and franchises, as well as intellectual property (copyrights, trademarks, and patents). The owners of such rights can enforce those rights in a court of law. A copyright, for example, means no one other than the owner of the copyright may publish the work that is copyrighted. If anyone else publishes the work, the owner of the copyright may sue for damages).

It is interesting to note that while Berle and Means (1991) may have concluded that ownership of shares cannot be called private property (Hessen, 1983), that is exactly how the Delaware General Corporation Law classifies shares of stock, as does the Uniform Commercial Code: "The shares of stock in every corporation shall be deemed *personal property* and transferable as provided in Article 8 of subtitle I of Title 6." (Emphasis added.)[26]

A right has no tangible, or even intangible, existence. Instead, the owner of the right obtains a piece of paper (usually) that is evidence of the right. The piece of paper may be given by a government (e.g., a trademark or copyright) or by another party by contract (e.g., a franchise).

Intangible property is only a right. Intangible property is a right in and of itself, nothing more. A share of a corporation, for example, is a right (explained in Chapter 5) or rather a bundle of rights such as the right to vote, but the corporation is not itself a right and a shareholder can exercise no right over the corporation. Therefore, a corporation cannot be owned.

There are other ways of classifying property. Heller (1999) classifies property as physical things, legal things, and legal relations. Physical things are those that can be physically divided. Physically dividing a thing may or may not make it more useful and may make it less useful. One can divide a parcel of land, which can then be sold separately. One can divide an automobile, but that would make it useless as an automobile (Heller, 1999).

Ways of owning private property

Ways of owning property go back hundreds of years (Posner, 2014). Ways of owning property, whether real or non-real, are the product of common law.

Ways of owning property depend on the type of property. Ownership means one has a legal or rightful title to the property.[27] Ownership rights in property include the right to the property's products (its fruit), increase in value, or rent.[28] One may also be a beneficial owner. A beneficial owner does not have legal title to or ownership of the property but has the right to the benefit derived from the property,[29] an important part of trust law as discussed in Chapter 3.

Estates

An estate is defined as "the degree, quantity, nature, and extent of interest that a person has in real property."[30]

Title to freehold estates are generally called "fees." A "fee simple" or "fee simple absolute" is a freehold estate of inheritance, absolute and unqualified. It represents the greatest and absolute interest in land, free of any condition or limitation other than government regulation. Its duration is infinite.[31]

A fee simple determinable is a freehold estate but less than a fee simple absolute. It is a fee that continues only until the occurrence of an event or expiration of time.[32] A fee simple conditional is also a freehold estate but refers to the devising of property to heirs.[33] A life estate is a freehold estate for the life of the tenant but is not passable by will.[34]

Non-freehold estates include leaseholds such as common leases in a landlord-tenant relationship. A tenant has the right by contract to possess or occupy the land (or apartment) for a certain time period.[35]

Real property ownership

A deed is a written contract that conveys title (ownership) to real property from a grantor to a grantee.[36] It is evidence that the property has been conveyed and the grantee has title and ownership of the property. In common law, a deed is a written instrument that is signed, sealed, and delivered and conveys an interest in property. Deeds must be recorded, usually in the county court or clerk's office.

Ownership of property is referred to as a "tenancy." In this context, tenancy does not necessarily refer to a leasehold or landlord-tenant relationship but to the type of ownership of real property. A tenancy in the context of ownership of property "is the possession of real or personal property by right or title, especially under a conveying instrument such as a deed."[37]

A husband and wife who own property together own the property as "tenants by the entirety."[38] Tenancy by the entirety is a product of common law. A tenancy by the entirety is reserved to a husband and wife.[39] Tenancy by the entirety means that if a husband and wife own real property as husband and wife, when one dies, the title and ownership pass immediately to the survivor with no further action necessary (e.g., a will). This is referred to as the right of survivorship.

Joint tenancy is an estate held by two or more persons "with equal rights to share in the enjoyment during their lives and having as its distinguishing feature the right of survivorship."[40] Each joint tenant has the right to possess the property. Each joint tenant owns 100% interest in the estate. When one joint tenant dies, title to the property passes to the other joint tenant(s) and not to the decedent's heirs. Property held by joint tenants is similar to a tenancy by the entirety except it applies to non-married owners of property. If two persons own property together but are not married, they own it as joint tenants. When one dies, the title and ownership pass immediately to the survivor with no further action necessary (e.g., a will).

In a tenancy in common, each co-tenant owns a fractional share of the estate. Each co-tenant has the right to possess the entire property, but there is no right of survivorship.[41] When one co-tenant dies, that co-tenant's share passes to her heirs, not to the other co-tenants. When property is held as tenants in common, there is no right of survivorship. When one owner dies, title and ownership do not pass to the other owner(s), but to the decedent's heirs.

Non-real property ownership

Ownership of personal property is evidenced by possession, title, or other document.[42]

Non-real personal property may have to be recorded, but not all non-real personal property must be recorded. Title and ownership of an automobile, for example, must be recorded. Ownership of your clothing has no title, and you do not need to record the ownership.

The law of private property

There is, of course, no "law of private property." There are laws that apply to different kinds of private property and different types of ownership of private property. The "law of private property" is generic and simply refers to the different laws of private property and property ownership and the legal theories that form the questions such as what constitutes property, who owns the property, and what restrictions are placed on the property and its ownership.

The nature and content of property define what Morales (2013) describes as the "normative plane," which includes the right to exclude others from the property or its use, the bundle of rights, autonomous interests, and economic interests. Relevant here are the right of exclusion and economic interests. As will be seen, partners have a right to enter or use partnership property. Shareholders have no right to enter or use a corporate property.

One of the most important aspects of private property is the right of exclusion, which some argue is "both a necessary and sufficient condition of property" (Morales, 2013). Thus, if, according to the law of a given jurisdiction,[43] I own land and you enter upon the land that I own without my permission, you can be arrested for trespass, fined, and imprisoned, depending on the jurisdiction.

As discussed in Chapter 4, a partner can enter onto the land owned by the partnership without permission because partners are joint tenants and, in fact, may use any partnership property for partnership business. However, as will be seen in Chapter 5, if a shareholder of a corporation enters onto the land owned by the corporation without permission or attempts to use the property owned by the

corporation, she can be arrested. This is an important distinction when considering whether shareholders own corporations.

A second fundamental aspect of private property is the exclusive right to use.
"Private property means that the right to make decisions regarding the uses (physical attributes) of a resource is vested exclusively in one individual" (de Alessi,
1973). If I own land, I have the exclusive right to use it as I want, subject to zoning
laws, etc. I can build a house on it, grow corn, or rent it to someone else. If I invent
a machine or computer program, I can be granted a patent or copyright,[44] which
gives me the exclusive right to use the machine or computer program. If you make
an identical machine or computer program, you can be fined and even imprisoned.

The right of exclusion and the right of exclusive use of private property play a
large role in Marx's economic theory, as discussed in *Economics, Capitalism, and
Corporations: Contradictions of Corporate Law, Economics, and the Theory of
the Firm* (Huber, 2020).

The third fundamental aspect of private property is the right to alienate the
property by selling it or otherwise disposing of it (Heller, 1999). Private property
means the right to voluntarily transfer the property or otherwise alienate the property (de Alessi, 1973), subject to certain restrictions.

In the economic interest definition of private property, property is the value of
something that is owned, and the property owner has a right to protect that value
(Morales, 2013). In 1922 the United States Supreme Court adopted a "bundle of
rights" theory of property ownership. In *Pennsylvania Coal Co. v. Mahon*, the
court stated "property is properly viewed as value, not physical possession" (Heller, 1999).[45] Two decades later, in *United States v. General Motors*,[46] the Supreme
Court ruled that "the constitutional provisions of private property apply to every
sort of interest a citizen may possess" (Heller, 1999). The following year, the
Supreme Court ruled in *United States v. Willow River Power Co.*[47] that

> not all economic interests are "property right;" only those economic advan-
> tages are "rights" which have the law back of them, and only when they
> are so recognized may courts compel others to forbear from interfering with
> them or to compensate for their invasion,

thus clarifying the *General Motors* ruling (Heller, 1999).

Owning property carries with it a responsibility and therefore limitations placed
by the government on the use of the property. I cannot use my property to harm
others[48] or to interfere with the rights of others to use their property.[49] If I injure
or cause damage to others with the use of my property, I am liable for the injury.
Furthermore, as discussed in Chapter 2, when my agent injures or causes damage
to another person with my property, I am liable for the injury.

Chapter summary

This chapter provided a review of basic property law. As we have seen, there are
many concepts of what constitutes private property, types of private property, and

ways of owning private property, an important consideration in the context of corporations and private property that was omitted by Berle and Means's (1991) in *The Modern Corporation and Private Property*, which laid the groundwork for the modern economic theory of the firm and the separation of ownership and control.

It is important to understand the types of private property and the forms of ownership of private property when considering partnerships, the relation of partners to the partnership and partnership property, and the relation of shareholders to corporations and corporate property.

Obviously, types of private property, types of ownership of private property, and private property laws are much more complex than the basics presented here and argued about in courts of law and legal journals. But the failure to understand how the types of private property, types of ownership of private property, and private property laws apply to corporations is the root cause of the contradictions within and between corporate law and economic theories of the firm.

Notes

1 Private property is here distinguished from government owned property and common property.
2 U.S. Constitution, Amendment V.
3 U.S. Constitution, Amendment XIV.
4 Ruckelshaus v. Monsanto Co., 467 U.S. 986, 1984.
5 U.S. Constitution, Amendment X.
6 Delaware General Corporation Law, § 122.
7 New York Business Corporation Law, Sec. 202.
8 Delaware General Corporation Law, § 159.
9 Private property forms a significant part of Marx's economic theories, as discussed in Chapter 10 of *Economics, Capitalism, and Corporations: Contradictions of Corporate Law, Economics, and the Theory of the Firm*.
10 It will be shown in Chapter 5 that shareholders do not own corporations.
11 Am Jur 2d, Vol. 63C, Property, § 1.
12 Am Jur 2d, Vol. 63C, Property, § 1.
13 Am Jur 2d, Vol. 63C, Property, § 1.
14 Am Jur 2d, Vol. 63C, Property, § 1.
15 Am Jur 2d, Vol. 63C, Property, § 1.
16 Am Jur 2d, Vol. 63C, Property, § 1.
17 Am Jur 2d, Vol. 63C, Property, § 9.
18 Land can, of course, be destroyed in a natural disaster.
19 Am Jur 2d, Vol. 63C, Property, § 9.
20 Resources of production, commonly known as factors of production, and their relationship to corporations are discussed in greater detail in Wm. Dennis Huber, *Economics, Capitalism, and Corporations: Contradictions of Corporate Law, Economics, and the Theory of the Firm* (London: Routledge, 2020).
21 Am Jur 2d, Property, § 21.
22 Am Jur 2d, Property, §§ 22–23.
23 Am Jur 2d, Property, § 25.
24 Am Jur 2d, Property, § 21.
25 Not all ownership of shares of stock are evidenced by a piece of paper. Both Delaware General Corporation Law, § 158, and New York Business Corporation Law, § 508, for example, allow corporations to issue uncertificated shares, i.e., no piece of paper.

Property and property law 27

26 Model Business Corporation Act, § 159.
27 Am Jur 2d, Property, § 29.
28 Am Jur 2d, Property, § 12.
29 Am Jur 2d, Property, § 29.
30 Am Jur 2d, Vol. 28, Estates, §§ 12–13.
31 Am Jur 2d, Vol. 28, Estates, § 1.
32 Am Jur 2d, Vol. 28, Estates, § 26.
33 Am Jur 2d, Vol. 28, Estates, § 42.
34 Am Jur 2d, Vol. 28, Estates, § 56.
35 Am Jur 2d, Vol. 28, Estates, § 130.
36 Am Jur 2d, Vol. 23, Deeds, § 1.
37 Am Jur 2d, Vol. 20, Cotenancy and joint ownership, § 1.
38 Am Jur 2d, Vol. 41, Husband and wife, § 18.
39 That may change with same-sex marriage laws.
40 Am Jur 2d, Vol. 20, Cotenancy and joint ownership, § 4.
41 Am Jur 2d, Vol. 20, Cotenancy and joint ownership, § 31.
42 American Jurisprudence, 2nd, Property, § 27.
43 Each of the 50 states and territories has its own laws regarding private property and penalties. While different, they are substantially similar.
44 Patents, copyrights, and trademarks are granted by the federal government.
45 Pennsylvania Coal Co. v. Mahon, 260 U.S. 393, 1922.
46 United States v. General Motors, 323 U.S. 373, 1944.
47 United States v. Willow River Power Co., 324 U.S. 499, 1945.
48 Am Jur 2d, Property, § 12; Am Jur 2d, Vol. 28, Estates, § 14.
49 Am Jur 2d, Property, § 38.

Bibliography

Cases

Pennsylvania Coal Co. v. Mahon, 260 U.S. 393, 1922.
Ruckelshaus v. Monsanto Co., 467 U.S. 986, 1984.
United States v. General Motors, 323 U.S. 373, 1944.
United States v. Willow River Power Co., 324 U.S. 499, 1945.

Authors and publications

Am Jur 2d. (2011). *Vol. 28, Estates*. Rochester, NY: Thomson Reuters.
Am Jur 2d. (2014). *Vol. 23, Deeds*. Rochester, NY: Thomson Reuters.
Am Jur 2d. (2015). *Vol. 20, Cotenancy and joint ownership*. Rochester, NY: Thomson Reuters.
Am Jur 2d. (2015). *Vol. 41, Husband and wife*. Rochester, NY: Thomson Reuters.
Am Jur 2d. (2018). *Vol. 63C, Property*. Rochester, NY: Thomson Reuters.
Berle, A.A., & Means, G.C. (1991). *The modern corporation and private property* (2nd ed.). New York: Routledge.
de Alessi, L. (1973). Private property and dispersion of ownership in large corporations. *The Journal of Finance*, 28(4), 839–851. Retrieved from www.jstor.org/stable/2978337.
Heller, J.A. (1999). The boundaries of private property. *The Yale Law Journal*, 108(6), 1163–1223. Retrieved from https://repository.law.umich.edu/articles/608.
Hessen, R. (1983). The modern corporation and private property: A reappraisal. *The Journal of Law & Economics*, 26(2), 273–289. Retrieved from www.jstor.org/stable/725101.

Huber, W.D. (2020). *Economics, capitalism, and corporations: Contradictions of corporate law, economics, and the theory of the firm.* London: Routledge.

Krugman, P., & Wells, R. (2008). *Microeconomics* (2nd ed.). New York: Worth Publishers.

Morales, F.J. (2013). The property matrix: An analytical tool to answer the question, "Is this property?" *University of Pennsylvania Law Review*, 161(4), 1125–1164. Retrieved from https://scholarship.law.upenn.edu/penn_law_review/vol161/iss4/5.

Posner, R.A. (2014). *Economic analysis of law* (9th ed.). New York: Wolters Kluwer.

Yuille, L.K. (2015). Essay: Toward a heterodox property law and economics. *Texas A&M Law Review*, 2, 489–499. Retrieved from https://scholarship.law.tamu.edu/lawreview/vol2/iss3/9.

2 Agency and agency law

Introduction

As explained in Chapter 5, just as common law and statutory laws of property determine the ownership of the firm and the firm's assets, the common law of agency, in addition to corporate common law and statutory law, determines whether there is an agency relationship between directors and corporations and whether there is an agency relationship between directors and shareholders.

Directors of corporations have been described in economic and legal literature as agents of the shareholders. (See Meurer, 2004.) Furthermore, dozens of judicial opinions have ascribed the role of agents and trustees to directors of corporations. (See *SEC v. Chenery Corp.*, 318 U.S. 80.)

A large body of academic literature, generally referred to as the "theory of the firm," has developed around the concept of agency law and agency costs in relation to corporations, directors, and shareholders. Agency theory, which informs the economic theory of the firm, is grounded in economics and finance (e.g., Jensen & Meckling, 1976; Fama & Jensen, 1983; Lan & Heracleous, 2010) and is the foundation of modern corporate governance research, policy, and practice.

Unfortunately, the literature on agents and agency with respect to corporations and shareholders has been content with merely making assertions and assumptions that such an agency relationship exists without formally proving the existence of such an agency relationship. More egregious is the fact that a myriad of judicial opinions have ruled that directors are agents of shareholders with no legal analysis of whether a shareholder-director relationship fulfills the requirements of a principal-agent relationship, merely relying on *stare decicis* and precedent. It is thus important to understand agency law before attempting to apply agency law and trust law to corporations, directors, and shareholders in order to understand why a director, either individually or as a body, is not an agent (or trustee) of shareholders.

This chapter reviews the fundamentals of agency law, which will then be placed in the context of corporate shareholders and directors in Chapter 5. Agency law will then be placed in the context of economics in Chapter 11 and in *Economics, Capitalism, and Corporations: Contradictions of Corporate Law, Economics, and the Theory of the Firm*,[1] to determine whether the assertions and assumptions on which corporate law and the theory of the firm are based are valid.

Definition of an agency relationship

Trusts and trustees are of ancient origin, whereas agents are more recent, appearing only at the end of the 18th century (Frankel, 1983). In general, agency relationships are governed by common law, although there are certain agency relationships that are also governed by statutory law.

The *Restatement of the Law Third, Agency* defines the agency relationship as a

> fiduciary relationship that arises when one person (a "principal") manifests assent to another person (an "agent") that the agent shall act on the principal's behalf and *subject to the principal's control*, and the agent manifests assent or otherwise consents so to act." (Emphasis added.)[2]

Fiduciary law, which is inseparable from agency law, will be examined separately in order to understand the nature and creation of a fiduciary relationship. However, keep in mind the requirement that an agent is subject to the principal's control.

Creation, duration, and termination of principal-agent relationship

Principal-agent relationships are mostly governed by common law principles of agency and contract law, although there are some exceptions that are subject to statutory law that are not relevant here. As a matter of contract, contract law applies to the creation of a principal-agent relationship including capacity, consideration, agreement, and purpose.[3]

Creation and duration of principal-agent relationship

As stated in the *Restatement of Law Third, Agency*, a principal-agent relationship is generally created by contract, either written or oral, although an agreement may be implied in law or by conduct of the parties.[4] Once created, the principal-agent relationship is presumed to continue in the absence of evidence to the contrary or until the purpose for which the relationship was created has been completed.[5]

In addition, the *Restatement of Law Third, Agency* goes on to state that

> an agency relationship arises *only* when the elements stated in the foregoing provision defining "agency" are present, and whether a relationship is characterized as agency in an agreement between parties or in the context of industry or popular usage is not controlling.
>
> (Emphasis added.)[6]

It is of the utmost importance to understand that there is no agency relationship in the absence of any of the elements contained in the definition. This is crucial in the context of corporations, shareholders, and directors and will be discussed at length in Chapter 5.

Termination of principal-agent relationship

In general, the principal-agent relationship is terminated upon the death of either the principal or the agent.[7] Furthermore, in general, the bankruptcy of either the principal or the agent terminates the principal-agent relationship.[8]

A principal-agent relationship may be terminated by the agreement of the parties to terminate the relationship, or it may be terminated by an act of law.[9] However, either the principal or the agent may terminate the agency relationship unilaterally, subject to any contract provisions that may give rise to breach of contract by either the principal or the agent for unilaterally terminating the relationship.[10]

Rights, duties, and liabilities of principals and agents

Since directors have been referred to as agents of shareholders, the rights, duties, and liabilities of agents and principals must be identified as created by the common law of agency and modified by statutory law.

Rights of principals and agents to each other

As a matter of contract, both principals and agents have certain rights. The rights of the principal correspond to the duties of the agent, and the rights of the agent correspond to the duties of the principal. As will be seen, if directors are agents of shareholders, then shareholders owe duties to the directors.

Duties and liabilities of principals and agents to each other

Duties of agent to principal

Agents owe greater duties to principals than principals owe to agents, and there is a large amount of literature on the duties of agents.

One of the most important and enduring aspects of agency law is that of fiduciary duty, although the concept of fiduciary has never been successfully defined or analyzed (Shepherd, 1981). A fiduciary is a person who undertakes to act in the interests of another person, and it is immaterial whether the undertaking is in the form of a contract or by operation of law (Shepherd, 1981).

Upon the establishment of a principal-agent relationship, a fiduciary duty of the agent to the principal arises as a matter of law.[11] That is, "an agent has a fiduciary duty to act loyally for the principal's benefit in all matters connected with the agency relationship."[12] A person who agrees to act as an agent is subject to common law fiduciary principles.[13]

Shepherd (1981) proposes a theory that

> a fiduciary relationship exists whenever any person [an agent] acquires a power of any type on condition that he also receive with it a duty to utilize that power in the best interests of another [the principal], and the recipient of that power uses that power.

But how that "power" is acquired is important. It must be understood that a principal-agent relationship is created in most cases by contract, and it is the principal who creates the agency relationship. That is, it is the principal who authorizes, hires, or appoints an agent to be her agent, i.e., to act on her behalf or to exercise a power on her behalf. The agent does not create the agency relationship; i.e., an agent does not authorize, hire, or appoint a principal to be his principal. Even non-lawyers understand this. "Bonding costs are the costs paid by the agent to induce the principal to hire the agent" (Brody, 1996; Jensen & Meckling, 1976).

This distinction is important to understand when we examine shareholder-director relationships in Chapter 5.

An agent must, of course, fulfill any duties created by the contract itself. Other duties an agent owes to the principal include the duty of due care, the duty to act with competence, and the duty to act with diligence.[14] But there is more.

Estate of Eller v. Bartron,[15] a 2011 case decided by the Delaware Supreme Court, provides insight into the duties owed by an agent to the principal. In *Estate of Eller v. Bartron* the court stated,

> Many forms of conduct permissible in a workaday world for those acting at arm's length, are forbidden to those bound by fiduciary ties . . . under elemental principles of agency law, an agent owes his principal a duty of good faith, loyalty and fair dealing. Encompassed within such general duties of an agent is a duty to disclose information that is relevant to the affairs of the agency entrusted to him. There is also a corollary duty of an agent not to put himself in a position antagonistic to his principal concerning the subject matter of his agency.

In addition to other duties specified by the agency contract, the court stated the agent owed the principal "*traditional* fiduciary duties." (Emphasis added.) Citing *Restatement of Law Third, Agency*,[16] the court went on to say,

> As a general matter, "[a]gency is the fiduciary relationship that arises when a person (a "principal") manifests assent to another person that the agent shall act on the principal's behalf and *subject to the principal's control*, and the agent manifests assent or otherwise consents so to act." (Emphasis added.)

The assent is the contract, whether express or implied, whether written or oral.

Liability of agent to principal

Whenever one party owes a duty to another, there is an accompanying liability for breach of that duty. An agent is liable for a breach of the contract that created the principal-agent relationship. However, an agent is also liable for a breach of traditional common law fiduciary duties and the duty of due care, the duty to act with competence, and the duty to act with diligence.[17]

If an agent breaches his fiduciary duty against conflict of interest, for example, or self-dealing, the agent is liable to the principal for any profit the agent made as a result of the conflict of interest or self-dealing.[18]

Duties of principal to agent

The duties of a principal to an agent are less than those of an agent to a principal (Frankel, 1983). The only duties principals have arise from the contract itself. Principals have a duty to fulfill the contractual duties, deal with the agent in good faith, reimburse the agent's expenses, and pay the agreed upon compensation or, if the contract is not express, then reasonable compensation.[19] Principals do not owe a fiduciary duty to agents.

Liabilities of principal to agent

The liabilities of a principal to an agent are also less than those of an agent to a principal (Frankel, 1983). Principals have a duty to fulfill the contractual duties, deal with the agent in good faith, reimburse the agent's expenses, and compensate the agent. Since principals do not owe a fiduciary duty to agents, a principal cannot be liable to an agent for breach of a fiduciary duty.

Duties and liabilities of agents and principals to third parties

Duties and liabilities of agents to third parties

In general, a principal is bound by and liable for the acts and representations of the agent to third parties, an important point to keep in mind when we examine the relationship of shareholders, corporations, and directors. There are exceptions to these general rules, but they are not relevant here.

When an agent commits a tort while acting within the scope of his agency, the acts of the agent are imputed to the principal (Terry, 2013), and the principal is liable for the acts of the agent as if the principal committed the tort herself. For example, if the agent causes an automobile accident during the course of acting as an agent, the principal is liable for the damages.[20] An agent may or may not be liable for his own acts committed while acting as an agent. The agent is often personally liable jointly with the principal for tortious acts committed while acting as an agent, such as causing an automobile accident during the course of acting as an agent.[21]

Duties and liabilities of principals to third parties

When the agent enters into a contract on behalf of the principal, the principal is bound by the terms of the contract as if the principal herself entered into the contract, and therefore the principal has a duty to fulfill the terms of the contract. Thus, when an agent signs a contract as an agent, the principal is liable if he breaches the contract.

More important, however, an agent may be personally liable in contract unless the agent discloses she is signing the contract as an agent and discloses the name of the principal.[22] Therefore, in order to avoid liability, an agent would sign a contract, e.g., "Jane Smith as agent of John Jones" if she wants to avoid personal liability. If the agent signs the contract only as "Jane Smith," the agent will be personally liable (Terry, 2013). This is an extremely important point to keep in mind when we look at corporate law. Directors do not sign as "Jane Smith, agent of shareholder John Jones." They sign as "Jane Smith, agent of ABC Corporation."

Fiduciary duty

Fiduciary duty has been alluded to throughout this section, but given the importance of the doctrine of fiduciary duty in agency law, trust law (discussed in Chapter 3), partnership law (discussed in Chapter 4), and especially corporate law (discussed in Chapter 5), a more focused examination is essential.

> [T]o say that a man is a fiduciary only begins analysis; it gives direction to further inquiry. To whom is he a fiduciary? What obligations does he owe as a fiduciary? In what respect has he failed to discharge these obligations? And what are the consequences of his deviation from duty?[23]

To begin, a century ago it was noted that the definition of "fiduciary relationship "is a matter of controversy,[24] and there has been no progress in defining either a fiduciary relationship or fiduciary duty.

> There are few legal concepts more frequently invoked but less conceptually certain than that of the fiduciary relationship . . . the principle on which that obligation is based is unclear. Indeed, the term "fiduciary" has been described as "one of the most ill-defined, if not altogether misleading terms in our law."[25]

Continuing, fiduciary obligations are one of most elusive concepts in Anglo-American law (DeMott, 1995), and

> Fiduciary relationships have occupied a significant body of Anglo-American law and jurisprudence for over 250 years, yet the precise nature of the fiduciary relationship remains a source of confusion and dispute. Legal theorists and practitioners have failed to define precisely when such a relationship exists, exactly what constitutes a violation of this relationship, and the legal consequences generated by such a violation.
>
> (Cooter & Freedman, 1991)

It could thus be said that fiduciary duty is like pornography as explained by Supreme Court Justice Potter Stewart: "I know it when I see it."[26] In other words, while it has no agreed-upon definition in either legal scholarship or judicial opinions within Anglo-American law, there are at least shared concepts of what fiduciary duty is and what it encompasses. In essence, the shared concepts of fiduciary duty that have been described by various courts include the duty of loyalty (including no self-dealing and no conflicting duties) (Shepherd, 1981; Cooter & Freedman, 1991) and the duty of good faith (including no secret profits and full disclosure of all pertinent information) (Shepherd, 1981; Cooter & Freedman, 1991).

Nevertheless, what we see is influenced by subjective factors. Beauty (or fiduciary duty) is in the eye of the beholder, but what is seen might be an illusion. That is, even if the shared concepts of fiduciary duty are understood (despite not being subject to agreed-upon definitions or easily applied in any given conflict), there are more serious problems that must be addressed: to whom fiduciary duties are owed and by whom they are owed. To whom fiduciary duties are owed may be more illusory than the duties themselves.

Fiduciary duties have been imposed on a wide range of relationships, not all of which are relevant here. (See Shepherd, 1981). The relationships in which fiduciary duties have been imposed that are relevant in this book are those of principal-agent; trustor-trustee-beneficial owner (discussed in Chapter 3); partnerships (discussed in Chapter 4); and the most important, corporation-shareholder-director (discussed in Chapter 5).

In order to impose fiduciary duties in a shareholder-director relationship, there must first be imposed, using common law principles, a principal-agent relationship between shareholders and directors, or a trustor-trustee-beneficial owner relationship (discussed in the next chapter) between shareholders and directors, which, of course, has been done in virtually every case. However, neither a principal-agent relationship between shareholders and directors nor a trustor-trustee-beneficial owner relationship between shareholders and directors fulfills the requirements of either a principal-agent relationship between shareholders and directors or a trustor-trustee-beneficial owner relationship. Therefore, when one sees a fiduciary duty existing between shareholders and directors, it is the result of the illusion that a principal-agent relationship exists between shareholders and directors, or a trustor-trustee-beneficial owner relationship exists between shareholders and directors. (This is examined in more detail in Chapter 5.)

Shepherd (1981) classifies fiduciaries into three categories, two of which are relevant here. The first is based on property, and the second is based on representation, which Frankel (1983) refers to as a delegation of power. A fiduciary duty based on the transfer of property from one person to another for the benefit of a third is the subject of trust law, which will be examined in Chapter 3. A fiduciary duty based on representation (power) is that of principal and agent.

Fiduciary duty is sometimes said to encompass a duty of loyalty, but at other times, a duty of loyalty is distinguished from a fiduciary duty. For example, under the Delaware General Corporation Law, a corporation's articles of incorporation may contain

> a provision eliminating or limiting the personal liability of a director to the
> corporation or its stockholders for monetary damages for breach of fiduciary

duty as a director, provided that such provision shall not eliminate or limit the liability of a director: (i) For any breach of the director's duty of loyalty to the corporation or its stockholders.[27]

Fiduciary duty also comprises a prohibition against conflicts of interest, self-dealing, and secret profits at the principal's expense (Cooter & Freedman, 1991).

Chapter summary

This chapter provided a review of basic agency law. Since directors of corporations are frequently referred to in legal and economic literature, as well as in judicial decisions, as agents of shareholders, it is imperative to understand what a principal-agent relationship is, how it is created, and the duties and liabilities of principals and agents. The importance of the legal requirements of a principal-agent relationship according to agency law and their application to corporate law cannot therefore be overstated.

In a principal-agent relationship, agency law requires, without exception:

- The appointment (or hiring) of an agent by a principal. Agents do not and cannot appoint (or hire) principals.
- The appointment of an agent by a principal is a matter of agreement, i.e., contract.
- Agents owe a fiduciary duty to principals.
- Absent an agreement to the contrary, a principal can terminate the agency relationship at any time.
- Absent an agreement to the contrary, an agent can resign as an agent at any time.
- Principals are bound by contracts entered into by the agent on behalf of the principal.
- Principals are liable for torts committed by the agent within the scope of their agency.
- Agents must disclose to third parties that they are agents or be personally liable on contracts.
- An agent does not have either legal or beneficial title to the principal's property, whereas a trustee, as will be seen in Chapter 3, does have legal title to the trust property.

Notes

1 Huber, W.D. *Economics, capitalism, and corporations: Contradictions of corporate law, economics, and the theory of the firm* (London: Routledge, 2020).
2 Restatement of Law Third, Agency, § 1.01.
3 Am Jur 2d, Agency, § 14.
4 Am Jur 2d, Agency, § 14–16.
5 Am Jur 2d, Agency, § 31.
6 Restatement of Law Third, Agency, § 1.02.
7 Am Jur 2d, Agency, §§ 49–51.
8 Am Jur 2d, Agency, § 53.

9 Am Jur 2d, Agency, § 31.
10 Am Jur 2d, Agency, § 42.
11 Am Jur 2d, Agency, § 192.
12 Am Jur 2d, Agency, § 192.
13 Am Jur 2d, Agency, § 193.
14 Am Jur 2d, Agency, §§ 198–225.
15 Estate of Eller v. Bartron, 31 A.3d 895 (DE, 2011).
16 Restatement of Law Third, Agency, § 1.01.
17 Am Jur 2d, Agency, §§ 198–225.
18 Am Jur 2d, Agency, §§ 198–225.
19 Am Jur 2d, Agency, §§ 226–242.
20 Am Jur 2d, Agency, §§ 243–246, 280.
21 Am Jur 2d, Agency, § 280.
22 Am Jur 2d, Agency, § 273.
23 SEC v. Chenery Corp., 318 U.S. 80 (1943).
24 Wells v. Skiver, 81 Okla. 108, 134, 197 P. 460, 484 (KS< 1921).
25 LAC Minerals Ltd. v. International Corona Resources Ltd., 61 D.L.R.4th 14 (Can. 1989).
26 Jacobellis v. Ohio, 378 U.S. 184, 197 (OH, 1964).
27 Delaware General Corporation Law, § 102(b)(7).

Bibliography

Cases

Estate of Eller v. Bartron, 31 A.3d 895 (DE, 2011).
Jacobellis v. Ohio, 378 U.S. 184, 197 (OH, 1964).
LAC Minerals Ltd. v. International Corona Resources Ltd., 61 D.L.R.4th 14 (Can. 1989).
SEC v. Chenery Corp., 318 U.S. 80 (1943).
Wells v. Skiver, 81 Okla. 108, 134, 197 P. 460, 484 (KS, 1921).

Authors and publications

Am Jur 2d. (2015). *Agency*. Rochester, NY: Thomson Reuters.
Brody, E. (1996). Agents without principals: The economic convergence of the non-profit and for-profit organizational forms. *New York Law School Law Review*, 49(3), 457–536. Retrieved from http://scholarship.kentlaw.iit.edu/cgi/viewcontent.cgi?article=1112&context=fac_schol.
Cooter, R., & Freedman, B.J. (1991). The fiduciary relationship: Its economic character and legal consequences. *New York University Law Review*, 66, 1045–1075. Retrieved from https://scholarship.law.berkeley.edu/cgi/viewcontent.cgi?article=2330&context=facpubs.
DeMott, D.A. (1995). Our partners' keepers – agency dimensions of partnership relationships. *Law & Contemporary Problems*, 58(2), 109–134. doi: 10.2307/1192148.
Fama, E.F., & Jensen, M.C. (1983). Separation of ownership and control. *Journal of Law Economics*, 26(2), 301–326. doi: 10.1086/467037.
Frankel, T. (1983). Fiduciary law. *California Law Review*, 71(3), 795–836. doi: 10.15779/Z38W45K.
Frankel, T. (2011). Fiduciary law in the twenty-first century. *Boston University Law Review*, 91(3), 1289–1299. Retrieved from www.bu.edu/law/journals-archive/bulr/documents/frankel.pdf.

Jensen, M.C., & Meckling, W.H. (1976). Theory of the firm: Managerial behavior, agency costs and ownership structure. *Journal of Financial Economics*, 3, 305–360. doi: 0.1016/0304-405X(76)90026-X.

Lan, L.L., & Heracleous, L. (2010). Rethinking agency theory: The view from law. *Academy of Management Review*, 35(2), 294–314. Retrieved from www.jstor.org/stable/25682413.

Meurer, M.J. (2004). Law, economics, and the theory of the firm. *Buffalo Law Review*, 52(3), 727–755. Retrieved from https://digitalcommons.law.buffalo.edu/buffalolawreview/vol52/iss3/8.

Restatement third of law agency. (2006). Philadelphia: American Law Institute.

Shepherd, J.C. (1981). *The law of fiduciaries*. Toronto: Carswell.

Terry, H.T. (2013). *An elementary treatise on the common law for the use of students*. Tokyo: Nabu Press. (Original work published 1898).

3   Trusts and trust law

Introduction

Just as common and statutory laws of property determine the ownership of property, including the ownership of a corporation and the corporation's assets, and the common law of agency and corporate statutory law determine whether there is an agency relationship between directors and corporations and between directors and shareholders, the common and statutory law of trusts determines if there is a trust relationship between directors and corporations and between directors and shareholders.

Directors of corporations have been described as agents of the shareholders, as discussed in Chapter 5. But directors of corporations have also been described as trustees of shareholders, also discussed in Chapter 5. Dozens of judicial opinions have ascribed the role of trustee to directors of corporations. Academic literature has also been developed around the theory of directors as trustees in relation to corporations, directors, and shareholders. Unfortunately, the literature on trustees in relation to corporations, directors, and shareholders, as well as judicial opinions, has been content with merely making assertions and assumptions that such a trust relationship exists without formally proving the existence of such a trust relationship according to the common law of trusts. It is thus important to understand trust law.

This chapter reviews the fundamentals of trust law and the grantor-trustee-beneficiary relationship, which will then be placed in the context of corporate law in Chapter 5 and in the context of economics and the economic theory of the firm in Chapter 11 and *Economics, Capitalism, and Corporations: Contradictions of Corporate Law, Economics, and the Theory of the Firm* to determine whether the assertions and assumptions on which corporate law and the theory of the firm are based are valid.

Trusts and trust law

Generally, trust law is considered a subcategory of property law (Sitkoff, 2003), although there is debate with some arguing trust law lies in contract law. The

Restatement of Law Third, Trusts classifies a trust as a conveyance of a beneficial interest in the trust property rather than as a contract.[1]

While there is disagreement over whether trusts are contract based or property based, a trust requires the transfer of property from one person to a second person for the benefit of a third person. A contract obviously does not require the transfer of property, although a contract can involve the transfer of property. Property may be transferred in trust by contract, by a last will and testament, or by operation of law. Regardless of how the property is transferred, trust law applies. If any one of the requirements for a trust is absent, then according to the law of trusts it is not a trust, and therefore trust law does not apply. If trust law does not apply, then it is because there is no trust – there is no trustor, there is no trustee, and there is no beneficial owner (beneficiary), as explained later in this chapter.

Like agency law, trusts and trust law are creatures of common law. Thus, trusts and trust law are matters of state law jurisdiction and state common law. However, as of September 2019, 34 states have enacted the Uniform Trust Code (UTC) with several more states adopting it in 2020 or later. Nevertheless, common law principles still apply to trusts.[2] Therefore, frequent reference will be made in this chapter to the Uniform Trust Code, supplemented by principles of common law.

Definition, creation, and termination of trusts

Definition and creation of trusts

The definition and creation of a trust are coterminous. The creation of a trust defines a trust. Several definitions follow.

A trust is a relationship involving three persons or entities wherein one person, the grantor (also referred to as a donor, settlor, or trustor), transfers legal title to property (the trust res, or trust corpus) to a second person, the trustee, for the benefit of a third person, the beneficiary (or beneficial owner), according to the terms of a trust agreement, also called the trust instrument.[3] The property is usually money or income-producing property, which the trustee invests or manages for the benefit of the beneficiary with the income, and sometimes the principal, distributed to the beneficiary pursuant to the trust agreement.[4] Thus, the grantor "trusts" the trustee to abide by and comply with the terms of the trust document.

While the trustor creates a trust by contract with the trustee, the beneficiary's interest in the trust is a property interest. There is no contract between the trustee and the beneficial owner. Contracts between two parties that merely convey property to a third party are not trusts.[5] However, by definition, the creation of a trust requires the conveyance of property by one party to a second party to be managed for the benefit of a third party. There is no such thing as a two-party trust.

A trust exists where the legal title to property is conveyed to another party who has an obligation "to convey, apply, or deal with such property for the benefit of other persons."[6] The obligation is a fiduciary duty; thus, a trust is "a fiduciary relationship with respect to property."[7]

It is important to note that an agency is not a trust,[8] and therefore, a trust cannot be an agency. A trustee is not an agent of the trust, the trustor, or the beneficial owner, and the trustee does not act on behalf of the trust, the trustor, or the beneficial owner as an agent acts on behalf of a principal. Neither the trustor nor the beneficiary is bound by the acts of or responsible for the torts of the trustee as a principal is bound by and is liable for the acts of the agent.

A requirement for a trust to exist is that there is a division in the ownership of the property. The trustee has legal ownership (title) while the beneficiary has an equitable ownership of the property. Unless there is a division of title, with the legal title belonging to the trustee and the beneficial title belonging to the beneficiary, there is no trust. The legal title must be vested in the trustee, not some other party.

The settlor (or trustor or grantor) is the person creating the trust. The trustee is the person who executes the terms of the trust and who has legal title to the trust property. The beneficiary is the person who benefits from the trust and who has a present or future interest in the trust.

The naming of a trustee by the grantor, and acceptance by the trustee, creates duties with which the trustee must comply.

A trust is created by contract, often called a "deed of trust" or "trust instrument." The contract creating the trust is between the trustor and the trustee. The consideration is the compensation given to the trustee by the trustor (often deducted from the income of the trust). The consideration given by the trustee is the promise to administer the trust for the benefit of the beneficiary.

Since the trustor "trusts" the trustee, the trustee has discretion as to how to manage or invest the trust property for the benefit of the beneficiary. Importantly, neither the trustor nor the beneficiary exercises any control over the trustee[9] as a principal exercises control over the agent.

A trust is created when a grantor executes a written declaration declaring (and naming) a trust, naming or appointing a trustee, and naming the beneficiary (or beneficiaries); transfers property to the trust (or arranges for the property to be transferred in the future); and specifies the purpose of the trust and the terms and conditions of the trust, which will normally include compensation to be paid to the trustee for services rendered.

A trust exists first, where the legal title to property is conveyed to another party who has a fiduciary "obligation to convey, apply, or deal with such property for the benefit of a other person,"[10] and second, when the trustee accepts the terms, although the trustee may not accept the position of trustee, in which case a court may have to appoint a new trustee.[11]

A trust agreement can be viewed as a contract since there is an agreement between the trustor and the trustee and consideration, which is the compensation paid to the trustee. But others do not consider the trust agreement to be a contract because a trust agreement imposes a fiduciary duty on trustees (discussed later) which is absent in a "normal" contract, e.g., the purchase and sale of goods and services governed by the Uniform Commercial Code.

Two other important points must be kept in mind. First, "A person who has the capacity to take and hold the legal title to property has the capacity to be the beneficiary of a trust of such property."[12] Therefore, if a person does not have the capacity to hold legal title to property, she cannot be a beneficial owner of the trust property. The importance of this requirement will be seen in Chapter 5. Directors do not have legal capacity to hold legal title to corporate property.

Second, "a trust cannot exist when the legal and beneficial interests are in the same person."[13] Thus, if a person has a legal interest in property, he cannot have a beneficial interest in the same property. Therefore, no trust exists, and therefore, there are no trustees. The importance of this requirement will be seen in Chapter 5.

Termination of trusts

Whether a trust is revocable depends in the first instance on whether it is created as revocable or irrevocable. A revocable trust may, of course, be terminated at any time by the settlor. An irrevocable trust may not be terminated. The terms of an irrevocable trust may not be modified. Except when they can. That is, while an irrevocable trust may not be terminated or modified by the settlor, it can be terminated or modified by a court.[14]

Types of trusts

There are various types of trusts, classified by how they are created, when they are created, and how long they last.

An *inter vivos* trust, also called a living trust, is created by the grantor during the grantor's life and is revocable during the life of the grantor. Trustors can also create *inter vivos* irrevocable trusts, meaning the terms of the trust cannot be changed at any time.[15]

A testamentary trust is created by the last will and testament of a decedent as part of the distribution of his estate. The decedent is the trustor. The will is the trust document, which names the trustee and the beneficiaries. The property is transferred to the trustee by operation of the will. It is an irrevocable trust[16] since the trustor has passed away.

Court-decreed trusts include "constructive trusts" and "resulting trusts." A constructive trust is not a legal trust. A constructive trust is created by a court to prevent unjust enrichment. There is no trustee.[17]

A resulting trust is also created by a court, but unlike a constructive trust, a resulting trust is an actual trust. A court creates a resulting trust when the terms of the original trust fails, or the trustee of the original trust does not comply with the terms of the trust.[18]

Rights, duties, and liabilities of trustors, trustees, and beneficiaries

As noted earlier, a trust relationship necessarily involves three parties. If only two parties are involved, then there is no trust and no trust relationship. If there is a trust relationship, then the parties may have rights, duties, and liabilities created as a result of the relationship.

Rights

Rights of Trustors. The rights of trustors are extremely limited since once the trust is created, unless the trust is revocable, the trustor no longer has an interest in the trust or the trust property. If the trust is revocable, the trustor has the right to modify or terminate the trust.[19]

Rights of Trustees. The rights of trustees are also limited. The only right the trustee has is to be compensated according to the terms of the trust instrument.[20]

Rights of Beneficiaries. Beneficiaries have the greatest rights since the trust was created for their benefit. The beneficiary has no rights to assert against the trustor. Since the trustee must manage or administer the trust for the benefit of the beneficiary, the beneficiary has rights that can be asserted against the trustee. Beneficiaries can sue trustees for breach of any of the trustee's duties as discussed next.[21] However, a beneficial owner has no rights to choose, name, appoint, or vote for a trustee, which is an important point to keep in mind when considering whether shareholders can be beneficial owners.

Duties

Duties of Trustors. Once the trust is created, a trustor has no duties to either the trustee or the beneficiary unless the trustee's compensation is not paid from the income from the trust property, in which case the trustor has a duty to compensate the trustee.

Duties of Trustees. As with agents, trustees have the greatest duties, but the duties are owed to the beneficiary, not to the trustor. A trustee owes a fiduciary duty to the beneficiaries. The trustee's duties are to carry out the trust according to the terms of the trust instrument and to act with the highest degrees of fidelity and utmost good faith.[22] "For centuries courts have required trustees to serve the interests of beneficiaries loyally – with the same devotion that the trustees dedicate to their own interests" (Easterbrook & Fischel, 1993).

The fiduciary duty a trustee owes is his greatest duty but differs significantly from the fiduciary duty of an agent.

> In an agency relationship the agent owes a fiduciary duty to the principal; i.e., the party who established the principal-agent relationship. In a trust, the trustee owes a fiduciary duty to the beneficiary, not to the trustor; i.e., not to the party who established the trust.
>
> (Shepherd, 1981)

Newman (2016) notes that "By definition, a trust is a fiduciary relationship." By common law, "the fiduciary nature of the relationship between the trustee and the beneficiary demands an unusually high standard of ethical or moral conduct." The Supreme Court of Utah has emphasized that "trustees are charged as fiduciaries with one of the highest duties of care and loyalty known in the law."[23]

In managing the trust, trustees must act with skill, due care, due diligence, caution, and prudence.[24] Furthermore, a trustee has a duty to the beneficiaries "to invest and manage the funds of the trust as a prudent investor would."[25]

The rule that governs trustees as informed by the common law of fiduciary duty is that trustees cannot take risks with the trust corpus. This rule must be contrasted with corporate directors, who are expected to take risks. A related rule by which corporate directors are judged is the "business judgment rule," discussed in Chapter 5, rather than the prudent person rule.

Duties of Beneficiaries. Beneficiaries have no duties. Since a trust is created solely for the beneficiary's benefit, there is no corresponding duty. The beneficiary is only a recipient of the benefit of the trust.

Liabilities

Liabilities of Trustors. Trustors have no liability other than to pay the agreed-upon compensation as set forth in the trust instrument. Thus, if the trustor does not pay the trustee, the trustor is liable for the compensation.

Liabilities of Trustees. Trustees have the greatest liabilities since they have the greatest duties. A breach of any duty owed to the beneficiary creates a liability on the part of the trustee.

Liabilities of Beneficiaries. Just as beneficiaries have no duties to trustees or third parties, they also have no liabilities to trustees or third parties.

Chapter summary

This chapter provided a review of the requirements and limitations of trust law. Since directors of corporations are frequently referred to in legal and economic literature as well as judicial decisions as trustees of shareholders, it is imperative to understand what a trust is, how it is created, who the parties are, and what the rights and duties of the parties are. The importance of the legal requirements of trust law and its role in corporate law cannot therefore be overstated.

The essential characteristics of a trust relationship relevant to corporate law are first, the transfer of property from one person to another for the benefit of a third person and second, the distinction between the legal ownership of the trust property. If any one of these elements is not present, then there is no trust relationship – no trustor, no trustee, and no beneficiary. If they are present, then trust laws necessarily and without qualification must apply.

A second important consideration is that a trust relationship is not an agency relationship. A trustee is not an agent either of the trust, the trustor, or the beneficiary, and an agent is not a trustee of a principal. Agency relationships and trust relationships are mutually exclusive according to both agency law and trust law.

A principal does not transfer property to an agent as a trustor transfers property to a trustee. An agent does not have legal title to the principal's property as a trustee has legal title to a trustor's property. Trusts and agency are antithetical to each other.

As will be seen in Chapter 5, none of the requirements are present in a shareholder-corporation-director relationship. Indeed, according to the *Restatement of Law Third, Trusts*[26] and *Am Jur 2d*, a corporation is not a trust.[27] If corporations are not trusts, then there are no grantors, no beneficial owners, and no trustees in a corporation-shareholder-director relationship.

Shepherd (1981) notes that the duties of agents and trustees are diametrically opposite. The agent has no volition, acting merely for the principal. The trustee, on the other hand, is a fully independent actor, and the law never limits that independence.

Notes

1 Restatement of Law Third, Trusts, § 197.
2 "The common law of trusts and principles of equity supplement this chapter, except to the extent modified by this chapter or another statute of this state." Uniform Trust Code, § 106.
3 Restatement of Law Third, Trusts, § 10.
4 Uniform Trust Code, §§ 65–66.
5 Restatement of Law Third, Trusts, § 5(i).
6 Am Jur 2d, Trusts, § 1.
7 Am Jur 2d, Trusts, § 1.
8 Restatement of Law Third, Trusts, § 2.
9 Am Jur 2d, Trusts, § 10.
10 Am Jur 2d, Trusts, § 1.
11 Am Jur 2d, Trusts, §§ 10,14, 66.
12 Am Jur 2d, Trusts, § 241.
13 Am Jur 2d, Trusts, § 241.
14 Restatement of Law Third, Trusts, §§ 61–69.
15 Restatement of Law Third, Trusts, §§ 20–26.
16 Restatement of Law Third, Trusts, § 17.
17 Restatement of Law Third, Trusts, §§ 169–205.
18 Restatement of Law Third, Trusts, §§ 7–8.
19 Am Jur 2d, Trusts, § 4.
20 Am Jur 2d, Trusts, § 565.
21 Am Jur 2d, Trusts, § 247.
22 Am Jur 2d, Trusts, § 334.
23 Pepper v. Zions First Nat'l Bank, N.A., 801 P. 2d 144, 151, 1990 (UT, 1990).
24 Am Jur 2d, Trusts, § 362.
25 Restatement of Law Third, Trusts, § 90.
26 Restatement of Law Third, Trusts, § 5.
27 Am Jur 2d, Trusts, § 9. Of course, a corporation may be formed for the express purpose of acting as a trust and may even be so named, in which case different statutes apply.

Bibliography

Cases

Pepper v. Zions First Nat'l Bank, N.A., 801 P. 2d 144, 151, 1990 (UT, 1990).

Authors and publications

Am Jur 2d. (2005). *Vol. 76, Trusts*. Rochester, NY: Thomson Reuters.

Easterbrook, F.H., & Fischel, D.R. (1993). Contract and fiduciary duty. *The Journal of Law and Economics*, 36(1), 425–446. Retrieved from www.jstor.org/stable/725483?seq=1#metadata_info_tab_contents.

Newman, A. (2016). Trust law in the twenty-first century: Challenges to fiduciary accountability. *Quinnipiac Probate Law Journal*, 29(3), 261–309. Retrieved from www.quinnipiaclawjournals.com/content/dam/qu/documents/sol/law-journals1/probate-law/volume-29/quinnipiac-probate-law-journal-volume-29-issue-3.pdf.

Restatement of law third, trusts. (2006). Philadelphia: American Law Institute.

Shepherd, J.C. (1981). *The law of fiduciaries*. London: The Carswell Company Ltd.

Sitkoff, R.J. (2003). An agency costs theory of trust law. *Cornell Law Review*, 89(3), 621–684. Retrieved from https://scholarship.law.cornell.edu/clr/vol89/iss3/2.

4 Partnerships and partnership law

Introduction

Having reviewed principles of common law, contract law, and property law, we are now in a position to consider partnership law prior to our main concern – corporate law. Although partnerships and partnership law are not directly related to corporations and corporate law as are property law and agency law, they are indirectly related. Understanding partnerships is important in order to compare and contrast partnerships with corporations and corporate law, the subject of the next chapter, and to understand the contradictions of property law, agency law, and corporate law.

This chapter reviews basic partnership law – creation and termination of a partnership, the rights of partnerships, ownership of partnership property, and the rights and duties of partners, as well as the relation of partners to the partnership and partnership property. Partnerships range from the simple two-person partnership to a partnership of many thousands of partners.[1]

Partnerships and partnership law are products of common law, but many states have also adopted statutes such as the Revised Uniform Partnership Act that govern the creation, governance, and termination of a partnership. I will therefore make frequent reference in this chapter to the Revised Uniform Partnership Act as adopted by Delaware.

Furthermore, in this chapter, I will only consider general partnerships. Limited partnerships are governed by special statutes.

Property law governs the ownership of the partnership and partnership property while agency law, in particular the fiduciary duty of agency law, governs the relationship of partners to each other and to the partnership. Indeed, a characteristic of partnerships is mutual agency.[2] Both property law and agency law have been incorporated into partnership statutes.

Creation, duration, and termination of a partnership

The following discussion assumes there is no explicit agreement to the contrary. Thus, both common and statutory partnership law apply.

Creation of a partnership

A partnership is a separate entity, i.e., it is an entity distinct from its partners.[3] Partnerships are formed by agreement, although the existence of a partnership may be imposed by law.[4] A partnership is defined in both common law and statutory law as an association of two or more persons formed for the purpose of carrying on any business, purpose, or activity with the intent of earning a profit.[5] Business includes "every trade, occupation and profession, the holding or ownership of property and any other activity for profit."[6] A partner is a person who is admitted to a partnership as a partner or member of the partnership.[7] "Person" is broadly defined and includes natural persons, other partnerships, or a corporation, among others.[8] The association of two or more persons to carry on as co-owners a business for profit forms a partnership, whether or not the persons intend to form a partnership.[9]

The creation of a partnership creates a partnership interest. A "partnership interest" or "partner's interest in the partnership" is defined as all of a partner's interests in the partnership, including the partner's economic interest in the partnership and all management and other rights.[10] The "economic interest" of a partner, as a subset of "partnership interest," means a partner's share of the profits and losses of a partnership and the partner's right to receive distributions.[11]

When a new partner is admitted to the partnership, a new partnership is created, unlike a corporation where the admission of a new shareholder does not create a new corporation. (See Chapter 5.) Also, as discussed in the next chapter, unlike a corporation, in order for a new partner to be admitted, existing partners must agree to the new partner joining the partnership. In a corporation, no agreement is necessary from existing shareholders in order to admit a new shareholder, who merely purchases the shares either directly from the corporation or from another shareholder. A new partner may be admitted either by expanding the total number of partners or by a new partner taking the place of an existing partner.[12]

Duration of a partnership

Absent an agreement, a partnership lasts only as long as the original partners remain in the partnership, unless the partnership is for a particular purpose or a specified period of time. Once the purpose is achieved or the time period expires, the partnership ceases to exist. An agreement, however, may extend the partnership for many generations, merely changing the members of the partnership.[13]

Termination of a partnership

A partnership may, of course be, dissolved by agreement of all the partners. However, unlike the creation of a partnership, which requires the agreement of all partners, the termination of a partnership does not require the agreement of the existing partners. A partnership can be terminated without unanimous agreement under certain circumstances.

A partner may disassociate herself from the partnership at any time, which terminates the partnership.[14] At the same time, while a partner may disassociate herself from the partnership at any time, a partner cannot just disassociate herself from the partnership without consequence the way a shareholder can leave the corporation by selling his shares without consequence. If a partner disassociates herself from the partnership without agreement from the other partners, she may be liable to the other partners for damages.[15] When a partner disassociates herself from a partnership, the partnership is terminated, and a new partnership is formed with the remaining partners.[16]

A partner is disassociated from the partnership when the partner files a voluntary petition in bankruptcy (or an involuntary petition is filed against him), which terminates the partnership.[17] A partner is obviously disassociated from the partnership upon the partner's death,[18] which also terminates the partnership.

A partnership may also be terminated by court order. An existing partner, for example, may petition a court for an order dissolving the partnership.[19]

Partnership existence, governance, and operations

While management and operation of a partnership differ depending on the number of partners (two vs. thousands)[20] and the type of partnership (professional vs. non-professional),[21] the common law principles of partnership and statutory laws of partnership are basically the same[22] (although state laws vary somewhat). Originating in common law, partnership law is built on agency law. The same common law principles that apply to principals and agents in agency law therefore also apply to partners. Although partnership law originated in common law, many states have adopted statutes to govern the formation, operation, and termination of partnerships, in particular the Revised Uniform Partnership Act as adopted by the State of Delaware.

Partnership existence

If there is a written agreement, a partnership comes into existence beginning on the date of the written agreement, the date specified in the agreement, or the date of filing the agreement. If it is implied in law, it begins on the date determined by the court.

Partnership governance

If a partnership is formed by a formal written agreement, the written agreement determines the governance structure of the partnership, subject to specific statutory or common law requirements and limitations. If there is no formal written agreement, common law principles apply to the operation of the partnership.

In all jurisdictions, each partner has equal rights in the management and governance of the partnership business and affairs.[23] Since all partners have equal rights to participate in management, each partner can vote on every transaction, not merely the transactions on which corporate shareholders can vote (Ribstein, 2005). However, partnerships, in particular large partnerships, may have committees that manage the partnership.[24]

Partnership operations

In all jurisdictions, each partner has equal rights in the management and conduct of the partnership business and affairs, and each partner has equal rights to use or possess partnership property on behalf of the partnership.[25]

Each partner is an agent of the partnership for the purpose of operating its business or activities. Therefore, an act of a partner for carrying on the partnership business in its ordinary course, including the right to buy and sell property on behalf of the partnership and incur debt,[26] binds the partnership and the partners.

Partnerships and agency law

As set forth in the Revised Uniform Partnership Act, mutual agency is a characteristic of partnerships (DeMott, 1995; Orts, 2013)[27]. Thus, according to the laws of agency, all partners are bound by and liable for the acts of other partners acting on behalf of the partnership. Even if a partnership is governed by statutory law, common law principles of agency will still be applied to the partnership, including interpreting the rights and duties of partners and the relation of partners to the partnership and to partnership property.

The law of partnership goes beyond simple agency because not only does a partnership involve multiple agents, it also involves multiple principals who jointly own the partnership (Cohen, 2017). Shared ownership of the partnership carries with it shared control over the partnership property (Cohen, 2017). Thus, e.g., as discussed in Chapter 1, when property is the subject of joint ownership, each joint owner has 100% rights to the use of the property.

Partnership rights, duties, and liabilities

Partnership rights

A partnership has the right to own property in the name of the partnership.[28] A partnership has the right to sue and be sued in the name of the partnership.[29] A partnership has the right to enter into contracts in the name of the partnership.[30] A partnership has the right to incur debts in the name of the partnership, with the caveat that each partner is personally liable for the debts of the partnership.[31]

Partnership duties

The duties of a partnership include fulfilling the terms of its contractual obligations, including paying its debts.

A partnership has a duty to credit partners' accounts with partnership profits or losses and give an accounting to each partner.[32]

Partnership liabilities

A partnership's liabilities correspond to its duties. A partnership is liable for a breach of contract and failure to pay its debts. The caveat is that each partner is personally responsible for breach of contract by the partnership or failure to pay partnership debts (DeMott, 1995).

Partners' rights, duties, and liabilities

Partners' rights

In all jurisdictions, each partner has equal rights in the management and conduct of the partnership business and affairs.[33] Furthermore, each partner has equal rights to use or possess partnership property on behalf of the partnership.[34]

Each partner is an agent of the partnership for the purpose of its business, purposes, or activities. Therefore, an act of a partner in carrying on the ordinary course of the partnership's business, including the right to buy and sell property on behalf of the partnership,[35] binds the partners.[36]

Of particular importance to partners' rights is that each partner must have a capital account that is

> (1) credited with an amount equal to the money plus the value of any other property, net of the amount of any liabilities, the partner contributes to the partnership and the partner's share of the partnership profits; and (2) Charged with an amount equal to the money plus the value of any other property, net of the amount of any liabilities, distributed by the partnership to the partner and the partner's share of the partnership losses.[37]

Furthermore, each partner has the right to an equal share of the partnership profits and is chargeable with a share of the partnership losses in proportion to the partner's share of the partnership.[38]

Partners' duties

Partners have a fiduciary duty to both the partnership and the other partners (Ribstein, 2005). Partners owe to one another, as trustees owe to beneficiaries and agents owe to principals, "the duty of the finest loyalty."[39]

However, the scope of those duties differs according to the common law of particular jurisdictions. The Delaware Revised Uniform Partnership Act considers fiduciary duty as encompassing the duty of loyalty and the duty of care, something that the Delaware General Corporation Law considers to be separate with respect to corporations, as explained in Chapter 5.

In Delaware, the only fiduciary duties a partner owes to the partnership and the other partners are the duty of loyalty and the duty of care.[40] A partner's duty of loyalty to the partnership and the other partners is limited to

> account to the partnership and hold as trustee for it any property, profit or benefit derived by the partner in the conduct or winding up of the partnership business or affairs or derived from a use by the partner of partnership property, including the appropriation of a partnership opportunity.[41]

The duty of loyalty is distinguished from, but still considered as a fiduciary duty, the duty of care.

> A partner's duty of care to the partnership and the other partners in the conduct and winding up of the partnership business or affairs is limited to refraining from engaging in grossly negligent or reckless conduct, intentional misconduct, or a knowing violation of law.[42]

Partners' liabilities

Because partners own the partnership, partners are personally liable for the contracts, debts, and torts of the partnership.[43] Partners' liability is not limited to their contribution to the partnership, their economic interest, or their partnership interest. Their liability for partnership contracts, debts, and torts is personal and unlimited.[44]

Partners and partnership property

While partners do not own the partnership property (i.e., its assets), each partner has equal rights to use or possess partnership property on behalf of the partnership,[45] and each partner has equal rights to buy and sell property on behalf of the partnership. Recalling the definitions of "property" from Chapter 1, the Revised Uniform Partnership Act defines "property" as "all property, real, personal or mixed, tangible or intangible, or any interest therein."[46]

A partner's partnership interest is the partner's personal property and includes her economic interest. The partner's economic interest may be transferred and therefore passes to the partner's heirs upon the death of the partner.[47] However, since partners own the partnership as joint tenants (sometimes referred to as tenancy in partnership),[48] ownership of the partnership itself passes to the surviving partners,[49] which would terminate the partnership absent an agreement to the contrary.

It is worth noting that by explicit agreement of all existing partners,

> Each person to be admitted as a partner to a[n existing] partnership . . . may be admitted as a partner and may receive a partnership interest in the partnership without making a contribution or being obligated to make a contribution

to the partnership. Each person to be admitted as a partner . . . may be admitted as a partner without acquiring an economic interest in the partnership.[50]

When a partnership is dissolved, any surplus property after all debts have been satisfied must be applied to pay in cash the net amount distributable to partners in accordance with their right to distributions in an amount equal to any excess of the credits over the charges in the partner's account.[51] However, if partnership assets are insufficient to satisfy the debts of the partnership, each partner must contribute, in the proportion in which the partner shares partnership losses, the amount necessary to pay or make reasonable provision to pay partnership obligations that were not known at the time of the settlement and for which the partner is personally liable.[52]

Partnerships and partnership property

A partnership owns property in its own name.[53] Property acquired by a partnership is property of the partnership and not of the partners individually.[54] Property is partnership property if it is acquired in the name of the partnership.[55] Property is acquired in the name of the partnership by a transfer of property to the partnership in the name of the partnership.[56] Property is presumed to be partnership property if purchased with partnership assets.[57]

Chapter summary

The purpose of this review of partnership law was to compare and contrast partners and partnerships with directors, shareholders, and corporations in order to understand the contradictions of property law and agency law inherent in corporate law. For example, as will be seen in the next chapter, partners have an economic interest in the partnership, but shareholders do not have an economic interest in the corporation; they only have an economic interest in the shares they own.

A partners' share of partnership profit is normally based on their percentage of original capital contributed, although other arrangements can be made. Each partner must have a separate capital account to which, as a matter of law, partnership profit (or loss) is added, and each partner has right, as a matter of law, to a share of the profit. But as explained in Chapter 5, shareholders do not have a separate capital account to which corporate profit (or loss) is added. Unlike partners, shareholders do not, as a matter of law, have a right to share in corporate profits. Their "right" to a dividend is discretionary with the board of directors. Shareholders do not have a separate capital account to which is added corporate profit or loss. Their share of profit or loss is based solely on the number of shares they own regardless of the price paid for the shares, which differs for each shareholder who did not purchase the shares in an IPO.

Partners have an ownership right in the partnership. As I prove in the next chapter, shareholders have no ownership right in the corporation.

Partners have a right to use partnership property on behalf of the partnership. Shareholders do not have the right to use corporate property on behalf of the corporation.

Shareholders are not joint tenants, or even tenants in common, of either the shares or the corporation itself. As owners of the partnership, partners could, but have a duty not to, appropriate firm property for their own use, including information and opportunities for their own benefit (Ribstein, 2005). Such appropriation would not be a crime, but it would be a breach of duty. If shareholders own the corporation, they could, but would have a duty not to, appropriate corporate property for themselves. Yet, if they attempted it, they would be arrested and charged with theft or trespass.

Shareholders of publicly traded corporations can sell their shares, although they must accept the market price. When partners disassociate themselves from the firm, their rights give them the power to insist on being paid their pro rata share of the asset value of the partnership as the price of agreeing to allow the other partners to continue the firm (Ribstein, 2005).

Notes

1 "Big Law" firms and the "Big 4" accounting firms, for example, have hundreds, even multiple thousands, of partners worldwide.
2 Delaware Revised Uniform Partnership Act, § 15–301.
3 Delaware Revised Uniform Partnership Act, § 15–202(a).
4 Delaware Revised Uniform Partnership Act, § 15–201(a).
5 Delaware Revised Uniform Partnership Act, §§ 15–101(1), (13).
6 Delaware Revised Uniform Partnership Act, § 15–101(1).
7 Delaware Revised Uniform Partnership Act, § 15–101(12).
8 Delaware Revised Uniform Partnership Act, § 15–101(18).
9 Delaware Revised Uniform Partnership Act, § 15–202(a).
10 Delaware Revised Uniform Partnership Act, § (17).
11 Delaware Revised Uniform Partnership Act, § 15–101(7).
12 Delaware Revised Uniform Partnership Act, § 15–203.
13 Delaware Revised Uniform Partnership Act, §§ 15–701, 801, 802.
14 Delaware Revised Uniform Partnership Act, § 15–602(a).
15 Delaware Revised Uniform Partnership Act, § 15–602(c).
16 Law firms and accounting firms continue when new partners are admitted or when existing partners leave because they have an explicit agreement that the partnerships will continue when new partners are admitted or when existing partners leave.
17 Delaware Revised Uniform Partnership Act, § 15–601(6)(b).
18 Delaware Revised Uniform Partnership Act, § 15–601(7)(i).
19 Delaware Revised Uniform Partnership Act, § 15–601(5).
20 Large partnerships such as accounting firms have management committees incorporated into the partnership agreement.
21 Professional partnerships are partnerships made up of licensed professionals such as physicians, lawyers, or public accountants.
22 Common law and statutory laws of professional partnerships are somewhat different due to the nature of professions (such as licensing requirements for physicians, lawyers, and public accountants) and differences in duties owed to the public. Only non-professional partnerships are considered here.
23 Delaware Revised Uniform Partnership Act, § 15–401.
24 Delaware Revised Uniform Partnership Act, § 15–401(l).
25 Delaware Revised Uniform Partnership Act, § 15–401.
26 Delaware Uniform Partnership Act, § 15–301.
27 Delaware Uniform Partnership Act, § 15–301.

28 Delaware Revised Uniform Partnership Act, §§ 203, 204.
29 Delaware Uniform Partnership Act, § 15–307.
30 Delaware Revised Uniform Partnership Act, § 15–202.
31 Delaware Revised Uniform Partnership Act, § 15–306.
32 Delaware Revised Uniform Partnership Act, § 15–401.
33 Delaware Revised Uniform Partnership Act, § 15–401(l).
34 Delaware Revised Uniform Partnership Act, § 15–401.
35 Delaware Uniform Partnership Act, § 15–301.
36 Delaware Revised Uniform Partnership Act, § 15–301(1).
37 Delaware Revised Uniform Partnership Act, § 15–401(a).
38 Delaware Revised Uniform Partnership Act, § 15–401(b).
39 Meinhard v. Salmon, 164 N.E. 545, 546 (NY, 1928).
40 Delaware Revised Uniform Partnership Act, § 15–404(a).
41 Delaware Revised Uniform Partnership Act, § 15–404(b)(1).
42 Delaware Revised Uniform Partnership Act, § 15–404(c).
43 Delaware Revised Uniform Partnership Act, §§ 15–305, 306.
44 Delaware Revised Uniform Partnership Act, §§ 15–305, 306.
45 Delaware Revised Uniform Partnership Act, § 15–401.
46 Delaware Revised Uniform Partnership Act, § 15–101(19).
47 Delaware Revised Uniform Partnership Act, §§ 15–101(17), 502.
48 Kay Investment Company, LLC. v. Brody Realty No. I, LLC. 731 N.W.2d 777 (MI, 2007).
49 This, of course, causes problems for both the partnership and the estate of the deceased partner, but a discussion of those problems is beyond the scope of this book.
50 Delaware Revised Uniform Partnership Act, § 15–205.
51 Delaware Revised Uniform Partnership Act, §§ 15–807(a), (b).
52 Delaware Revised Uniform Partnership Act, § 15–807(c).
53 Delaware Revised Uniform Partnership Act, § 15–204.
54 Delaware Revised Uniform Partnership Act, § 15–203.
55 Delaware Revised Uniform Partnership Act, § 15–204.
56 Delaware Revised Uniform Partnership Act, § 15–204.
57 Delaware Revised Uniform Partnership Act, § 15–204.

Bibliography

Cases

Kay Investment Company, LLC. v. Brody Realty No. I, LLC. 731 N.W.2d 777 (MI, 2007).
Meinhard v. Salmon, 164 N.E. 545, 546 (NY, 1928).

Authors and publications

Cohen, G.M. (2017). Law and economics of agency and partnership. In F. Parisi (Ed). *The Oxford handbook of law and economics: Volume 2: Private and commercial law* (pp. 399–422). Oxford: Oxford University Press.
DeMott, D.A. (1995). Our partners' keepers – agency dimensions of partnership relationships. *Law & Contemporary Problems*, 58(2), 109–134. doi: 10.2307/1192148.
Orts, E.W. (2013). *Business persons: A legal theory of the firm*. London: Oxford University Press.
Ribstein, L.E. (2005). Are partners fiduciaries? *University of Illinois Law Review*, 1, 209–243. Retrieved from www.illinoislawreview.org/wp-content/ilr-content/articles/2005/1/Ribstein.pdf.

Part II

Corporations, corporate law, and the contradictions of corporate law

Corporate law is an amalgamation of common law, contract law, property law, agency law, and trust law. It is a product of both state common law and statutory law. This section exposes the logical fallacies and legally invalid arguments of the mantra of "separation of ownership and control" that undergird the economic theory of the firm.

This section builds on the foundation of the rigorous analysis of common law, contract law, property law, agency law, trust law, and partnership law from the previous chapters to corporations and corporate law and exposes the logical contradictions inherent in judicial decisions concerning corporations, directors, and shareholders.

5   Corporations and corporate law

Introduction

Masten (1993) points out that economists either downplay or reject outright the role of the law in defining the firm. But those who ignore the relationship of basic property law and basic agency law to corporate law, including judges, economists, and legal scholars, do so at their own peril.

There are those who adhere to the economic theory of the firm who make a distinction between legal agents and economic agents. But that is a false dichotomy. The fact that one person, a principal, hires another person to be an "economic agent," i.e., to represent her in an economic transaction, necessarily and automatically makes the economic agent a legal agent. Thus, agency law must be applied to the economic relationship, which means that the principal-agent relationship is governed by the laws of agency as discussed in Chapter 2. An agent cannot be an economic agent unless he is first a legal agent, i.e., one who complies with the laws of agency.

The allocation of scarce resources is a function of the legal structure of society (Banner, 2011). Corporate law determines the legal structure of the corporation, and the legal structure of the corporation determines the economics of the corporation since corporate law determines the ownership of scarce resources and therefore the allocation of scarce resources. It is thus imperative to understand the relationship of property and agency law to corporate law and the legal structure of the corporation. When the relationship of property law and agency law to corporate law and the legal structure of the corporation is understood, then it is easy to understand how property law, agency law, corporate law, and the economic theory of the firm contradict each other.

In this chapter, I present sufficient evidence in the form of a rigorous analysis of corporate statutory and common law to resolve the debate whether shareholders own a corporation, whether directors are agents of shareholders, and whether directors have a fiduciary duty to shareholders. This chapter addresses the legal structure of the corporation (i.e., the firm, the enterprise), which necessarily determines the economic theory of the firm.[1] I provide sufficient evidence to sustain the truth of the assertion that shareholders do not own the corporation. I provide valid judgments based on the facts and the evidence of the relationship of property law and agency law to corporate law that directors are not agents of the shareholders and therefore do not owe a fiduciary duty to shareholders.

The state of corporate law and corporate legal scholarship

The current state of corporate law, as well as the legal and economic scholarship of corporate law, can be described as little more than chaos and confusion, filled with contradictions that are not just ignored by judges, legal scholars, and economists, but caused by them. Arguments over shareholders' rights; corporate governance; and relationships between shareholders and corporations, between shareholders and directors, and between directors and corporations are dogmatic, rather than being based on legal analysis.

One would think that something as basic as the ownership of a corporation would have long ago been resolved, but sadly, that is not the case. The question of the ownership of corporations remains unsettled in the legal scholarship and corporate law, with those arguing that shareholders do not own corporations in the minority, while judges continue to issue opinions that make no pretense of understanding the relationship of property law, agency law, and corporate law.

Velasco (2010) is quite correct in recognizing that

> As a theoretical matter, the issue of ownership [of a corporation] is necessary to a proper understanding of the nature of the corporation and corporate law. As a practical matter, it is an important consideration in the allocation of rights in the corporation: if shareholders are owners [of the corporation], then the balance of rights will tip more heavily in their favor, and against others, than if they are not. . . . Because the issue of ownership has the potential to shape all of corporate law and direct the very purpose of corporations, it is of utmost importance.
>
> (p. 897)

But obviously, the reverse is also true. If shareholders are not owners of the corporation, then the balance of rights will tip more heavily against them. That said, the question becomes, What rights would tip less heavily in favor of shareholders vis-s-vis corporations or directors as a function of ownership?

The confusion in the current state of corporate law and the legal scholarship of corporate law does not stop at ownership of the corporation, however. Not only is there no agreement on the ownership of a corporation; there is no agreement on the relationship of directors and shareholders, what directors' duties are, or to whom the directors owe duties. The basic reason for these disagreements is the absence of sufficient evidence on either side of the argument. It is essentially a debate based on ideology rather than a rigorous analysis of property law, agency law, and corporate law.[2]

Booth (2001) questions who owns a corporation. He notes that some theories are so widely accepted that it is forgotten they are theories. For Booth, one such theory is that a corporation is owned by its stockholders. This theory, he says, "has proved useful as a way of organizing our thoughts about corporation law. It has helped us define the duty owed by directors and officers to the corporation and to the stockholders." And that is precisely the problem. The theory has organized our thoughts with absolutely no proof. All theories must be proven true or false. No proof has, to this point, been offered that shareholders own, or do not own, corporations.

While the current state of corporate law and the legal scholarship of corporate law is one of confusion and contradictions, the economic literature on the theory of the firm is even worse. The economic theory of the firm is built on conjecture. Granted the economic theory of the firm was spawned by Berle and Means's *The Modern Corporation and Private Property*, beginning with Jensen and Meckling (1976), the economic literature on the theory of the firm extracted Berle and Means's thesis of the "separation of ownership and control" (which did not actually originate with Berle and Means),[3] augmented the "separation of ownership and control" with "agency theory," and magnified it into a cult-like doctrine. It subsequently infiltrated the legal scholarship of corporate law.

In reviewing the current chaotic state of corporate law and the legal scholarship of corporate law in this chapter, the contradictions of corporate law and the legal scholarship of corporate law will be briefly alluded to but will not be considered in depth. The contradictions of corporate law and the legal scholarship of corporate law will be examined in depth in Chapter 6. An in-depth examination of the contradictions of corporate law and the current state of the economic literature on the theory of the firm is reserved for *Economics, Capitalism, and Corporations: Contradictions of Corporate Law, Economics, and the Theory of the Firm.*

While reading the rest of this chapter, the reader should keep in mind that agency law and private property law are part of the "foundation needed for the construction, growth and management of modern corporations" (Orts, 2013, p. 3). Thus, with a background in property law, agency law, and partnership law, we are now in a position to examine corporate law in depth. This chapter is naturally the most important, with the previous chapters providing the background for an analysis of corporate law, which in turn provides a foundation for the remaining chapters and for *Economics, Capitalism, and Corporations: Contradictions of Corporate Law, Economics, and the Theory of the Firm.*

As explained earlier, we are concerned here only with publicly traded corporations. There is no issue of the "separation of ownership and control," the decades-old mantra of the "theory of the firm," in one- or few-person corporations. The corporation as an alter ego is created mainly as a means to reduce risk and limit liability for the owners who, unlike shareholders in publicly traded corporations, actually do own the corporation.

> It has long been possible for an individual to incorporate his business even though it still represents his own investment, his own activities and his own business transactions; he has in fact merely created a legal alter ego by setting up a corporation as the nominal vehicle.[4]
>
> (Berle & Means, 1992, p. 5; see also Stout, 2012).

The economic theory of the firm is only applicable to publicly traded corporations. The economic theory of the firm is built on agency theory and the separation of ownership and control, which is only seen in publicly traded corporations as a result of the wide dispersion of the ownership of the stock.[5]

It should also be kept in mind throughout this chapter that state incorporation statutes do not say that shareholders are the owners of the corporation. That shareholders are considered the owners of the corporation is a consequence of common law.

Concerning corporate ownership, agency, and directors' duties

How curious it is that Jensen and Meckling (1976) boldly declare

> Since the relationship between the stockholders and manager of a corporation fit the definition of a pure agency relationship it should be no surprise to discover that the issues associated with the "separation of ownership and control" in the modern diffuse ownership corporation are intimately associated with the general problem of agency. We show below that an explanation of why and how the agency costs generated by the corporate form are born leads to a theory of the ownership (or capital) structure of the firm.

They first define the relationship between the stockholders and directors of a corporation as a pure agency relationship. They then generate a theory of ownership. But as Masten (1993) tells us, the law defines the ownership of the firm, and therefore, "ownership itself is a condition sustained by legal rules and remedies."

But Jensen & Meckling freely admit that

> Many problems associated with the inadequacy of the current theory of the firm can also be viewed as special cases of the theory of agency relationships in which there is a growing literature. This literature has developed *independently of the property rights* literature. (Emphasis added.)

An example of literature that developed independently of property rights, and by no means the only example, can be seen in Masten (1993). Masten's purpose was to "explore in depth the . . . question of whether it even makes sense to talk about the firm as a distinct organizational form" (p. 196). But rather than examining property law, agency law, or corporate law, his paper was "devoted to exploring the status of the employment relationship in the legal system and a comparison of corresponding doctrines of commercial contract law" (p. 196), which has nothing to do with property rights laws concerning the ownership of the corporation that determine the organizational form.

It is perhaps doubly ironic that Masten himself ignores the legal basis of the corporation, given that he explicitly points out the irony that economics ignores the legal structure of the firm. "Ironically, economists have either downplayed or rejected outright the role of law in defining the firm [both of which are correct], divorcing the economic concept from the 'legal fiction.'"

If directors are agents of shareholders, that necessarily means that shareholders conferred upon directors the authority to act as their agents. But shareholders do not confer power on directors. A century ago, the New York Court of Appeals[6] ruled in *Mason v. Curtis*[7] "The stockholders do not confer, nor can they revoke those powers. They are derivative only in the sense of being received from the state in the act of incorporation."[8] (See also Suojanen, 1954.)

Economists might be forgiven for not knowing that shareholders do not own the corporation when they developed the "theory of the firm," not knowing that the law does not impose an agency relationship between shareholders and directors, or not knowing that statutory law does not impose on directors a fiduciary duty to shareholders. However, legal scholars and courts should have known better. Their errors cannot so easily be overlooked.

The modern economic "theory of the firm" is a product of the theory of the "separation of ownership and control," a.k.a. "agency theory," which is considered by many to begin with Berle and Means's 1932 classic, *The Modern Corporation and Private Property*. For more than 80 years, the "master problem for research" for legal scholarship on corporate law has focused on the separation of ownership and control (Reich-Graefe, 2011). The theory of separation of ownership and control evolved into the theory of the firm as espoused by economists.

Economists' "theory of the firm" will be discussed in greater detail in Chapter 11 and in *Economics, Capitalism, and Corporations: Contradictions of Corporate Law, Economics, and the Theory of the Firm*. Here, I focus on the legal scholarship and judicial opinions and their insufficient evidence and inadequate analysis of the law to support their positions that shareholders own the corporation, that there is an agency relationship between shareholders and directors, and that the law imposes on directors a fiduciary duty to shareholders. Legal scholars and courts should have provided sufficient proof in the form of valid legal arguments and analysis of the law to support their conclusions that shareholders do or do not own the corporation, that there is or is not an agency relationship between shareholders and directors, and that directors do or do not owe a fiduciary duty to shareholders. That evidence and analysis, which has been lacking, is provided here.

As a preface, it should be noted that first, state incorporation statutes do not say that shareholders are the owners of the corporation. That shareholders are considered the owners of the corporation is a consequence of common law. The actual shares (i.e., pieces of paper) are not the equivalent of a title to an automobile or a deed to real property.

Second, the essential distinction between common stock, preferred stock, and bonds is that common stock typically has voting rights as discussed later,[9] while preferred stock and bonds typically do not.[10] Those who argue that shareholders are the owners of a corporation are therefore essentially arguing that it is the existence of voting rights that confers ownership of the corporation on shareholders. However, there is neither a statute nor a court ruling that states that ownership of the corporation attaches to shares as a function of a right to vote. If that were true, there are common shares that have no voting rights, which would make shareholders not owners, and bonds that can have voting rights, which would make bondholders owners. And that is never the case.

Courts have been content with merely relying on *stare decisis* and precedents such as that directors are agents of shareholders and have a fiduciary duty to shareholders even when the precedents have no validity in law. Courts often merely parrot and reinforce each other and frequently rely on academics who also parrot and reinforce each other. But neither courts nor academics performed a legal analysis of property law and corporations, agency law and corporations, or fiduciary duty and directors.

Concerning ownership of the corporation

Arthur Levitt, Jr., former chairman of the Securities Exchange Commission, asserts, "The principle that shareholders own the companies in which they invest – and are the ultimate bosses of those running them – is central to modern capitalism" (Levitt, 2008).[11]

Putterman (1993) observed that, historically, "A basic preoccupation of the literature on the economics of organization has been the problem of the separation of ownership and control in the modern corporation" (p. 252). In most business firms, by which he means sole proprietors, he says, "decision-making rights are held by persons who are also financial risk-bearers and suppliers of funds. The holders of these rights are known as the owners of the firm," and the right of alienation of private property means that "the bundle of ownership rights may be transferred to another party or parties on mutually agreeable terms" (pp. 245–246). Bond holders and preferred stockholders are also risk bearers and suppliers of funds (Stout, 2003), but they are not considered owners of the corporation, even when they have rights to vote, as discussed later in this chapter.

Iwai (1999) proclaims outright, as if it were self-evident, that "the shareholders own the corporation" (p. 585). Velasco (2010) endeavors to provide an argument defending the traditional view that shareholders own corporations. Unfortunately, neither provides evidence that shareholders own the corporation. The evidence presented here proves they do not.

One reason why economists, the majority of legal scholars, and all courts latched onto Berle and Means's thesis of separation of ownership and control is explained by Mizruchi and Hirschman (2010).

> When the classics are read, they are subjected to selective interpretation as readers emphasize the parts that fit their preconceived notions of the world, while tending to minimize or ignore those that do not. As these selective interpretations are disseminated into an academic discipline, members of the field derive their views not from the work itself, but from interpretations of the work rendered by others. These interpretations then come to be accepted as the "correct" readings. The classic work thus develops a socially

constructed character, in which certain components of the original – those that fit with collectively accepted views – become the prevailing interpretation of the work itself.

(p. 1065; see also Mizruchi & Fein, 1999)

Mizruchi and Hirschman suggest that Berle and Means's *The Modern Corporation and Private Property* fits that description as one of the most important books on the corporation ever published. They speculate that "few works in the social sciences have been as often cited and as little read" and demonstrate that it was the subject of selective interpretation and outright misinterpretation.

Another reason the majority of legal scholars, economists, and courts focus on Berle and Means's thesis of separation of ownership and control can be found in Friedman. Although Friedman (1970) predated Jensen and Meckling's (1976) *Theory of the Firm: Managerial Behavior, Agency Costs and Ownership Structure*, Friedman's *The Social Responsibility of Business Is to Increase Its Profits* provided an impetus for the doctrine of maximizing shareholder value and director and officer compensation that both shareholders and directors latched on to although it had no basis in law.

It is both amusing and sad that Friedman assails discussions of the "social responsibilities of business" for its "notable . . . analytical looseness and lack of rigor" when he himself offered neither. Says Friedman,

> In a free-enterprise, private-property system, a corporate executive is an employee of the owners of the business. He has direct responsibility to his employers. That responsibility is to conduct the business in accordance with their desires.

But from whence cometh this? No doubt it was inspired by Berle and Means. Nevertheless, Friedman's "analytical looseness and lack of rigor" or, more appropriate, his lack of analysis and rigor, set the stage for Jensen and Meckling's (1976) *Theory of the Firm: Managerial Behavior, Agency Costs and Ownership Structure* and a deepening battle between shareholders' rights and directors' duties and further served as a catalyst for the power struggle not just between shareholders (shareholder primacy) and directors (director primacy), but more importantly between shareholders as a power class and society as a non-power class. (See Chapter 8.)

By "corporate executive is an employee of the owners of the business," Friedman means "directors are employees of the owners of the business" as proven by this statement: "The whole justification," according to Friedman, "for permitting the corporate executive to be selected by the stockholders is that the executive is an agent serving the interests of his principal." Only directors can be selected by shareholders. However, corporate executives, as he uses the term, are not employees (i.e., agents) of the owners of the business, by which he means shareholders, because, as I prove in this chapter, shareholders do not own the corporation.

Recently, some legal scholarship has begun to concede that shareholders do not own the corporation. Robé (2011), for example, maintains that "shareholders do not own . . . corporations" (p. 3). While correctly asserting that it is necessary to locate property rights with respect to owning corporations, he neglects to analyze property law to support his assertion that shareholders do not own the corporation. Easterbrook and Fischel (1983) acknowledge that "shareholders are no more the 'owners' of the firm than are bondholders [or] other creditors" (p. 396), but again, evidence is missing.

In any event, that shareholders do not own the corporation has not yet been accepted by the mainstream of legal scholarship or judicial decisions. Walker (2016) laments that "theories that attempt to incorporate real world features of corporations, partnerships and the like often lack precision and rigor, and have therefore failed, by and large, to be accepted by the theoretical mainstream."

Concerning agency relationships of directors and shareholders

Robé (2011, 2019) points out the common view that shareholders are the owners of the corporation and that directors are their agents. However, as seen in Chapter 2, in order for a principal-agent relationship to exist, both principal and agent must exist, and it is the principal who appoints or hires the agent.

State incorporation statutes do not confer upon directors the status or position of agent, nor does it confer upon shareholders the status or position of principal. That has merely been inferred by courts and legal and economic scholars, but as George Gershwin says, "It ain't necessarily so."[12]

Just as recent legal scholarship has begun to admit that shareholders do not own the corporation, it has also recently recognized that the law does not impose an agency relationship between shareholders and directors, but again, the argument has not been accepted by mainstream legal or economic scholarship. The proof that there is no agency relationship between shareholders and directors is absent.

Concerning fiduciary duties of directors

Berle and Means (1992) state in reference to shareholders and directors, "whenever one man or group of men trust another man or group with the management of property the second group became fiduciaries" (p. 295). But that is incorrect for at least two reasons. First, shareholders do not entrust directors with the management of their property (assumed to mean cash). Shareholders simply enter into a contract (Stout, 2012). They purchase shares for consideration in an amount determined by the directors (see the discussion that follows) in an arm's-length transaction. When you purchase a bond from a corporation, you are not entrusting the directors of the corporation to "manage your money" as fiduciaries. You are simply entering into a contract. The same reasoning applies to purchasing shares. There is no legal justification for thinking a shareholder is entrusting her money to the corporation's directors when purchasing shares.

Second, once a shareholder purchases shares, the money is no longer hers. It now belongs to the corporation, as explained later in this chapter. The corporation holds legal title to and becomes the sole legal owner of all assets, including the financial capital it receives from issuing the shares (Berle & Means, 1992). The purchase of shares does not magically transform a shareholder into an owner of the corporation, whether actual, beneficial, or residual. She is only an owner of the shares, not of the corporation.

The fiduciary duty said to be owed by directors to shareholders rests on two separate but mutually exclusive legal theories – directors are agents of shareholders, or directors are trustees of shareholders. There can be no fiduciary duty unless one of the legal theories applies to the exclusion of the other. However, since directors are neither agents nor trustees, then they do not and cannot owe a fiduciary duty to shareholders.

> The first theory is that directors are agents of shareholders. A multitude of judicial opinions have ruled that directors are agents of corporations. If directors are agents of shareholders than a fiduciary duty naturally attaches to directors based on common law principles as discussed in Chapter 0 and 2. Yet, if directors are agents of shareholders, shareholders are the principals of directors which would make shareholders liable for the acts of the directors as their agents as explained in Chapter 2.
>
> But while the fiduciary and principal-agent are powerful metaphors, they misrepresent the realities of the shareholder-director relationship since shareholders are not owners of corporations, principals to directors, or individuals dependent on fiduciaries (Green, 1993).

The second theory which is said to create a fiduciary duty owed by directors to shareholders is found in trust law, as several judicial opinions have ruled. As seen in Chapter 3, in a trust relationship, the trustee takes legal title (legal ownership) to administer the trust for the benefit of the beneficial owner (the beneficiary). Directors are said to be the trustees, and shareholders are said to be beneficial owners. Yet there is no trustor. Furthermore, the directors do not take legal title to any property. It is the corporation that takes title to the property – the cash received from purchasers of shares in an IPO.

Shepherd (1981) emphasizes the fact that "The whole purpose of a trustee's existence is to administer property on behalf of another," which is precisely the reason why directors cannot be trustees. In order to administer property on behalf of another, the trustee must hold legal title to the property, an absolute requirement. Since directors do not have legal title to the corporation or the corporation's property, directors cannot be trustees of either the corporation or the shareholders.

Creation and termination of a corporation

Creation of a corporation

First and foremost, corporations can only be created by statute. Unlike partnerships, corporations cannot be implied by law or created by simple agreement, whether oral or written. If the creation of corporations is governed by statutory law, operations must likewise be governed by statutory law, which will override common law unless statutory law is silent or ambiguous. Corporate statutory law controls both the creation and the operations of corporations and takes precedence over common law if there is a conflict between statutory law and common law. Common law only enters into an interpretation of corporate statutory law if corporate statutory law is ambiguous or silent.

Each state has its own particular statute governing the creation of a corporation, a consequence of the Tenth Amendment to the U.S. Constitution.[13] Delaware is the most popular state in which Fortune 500 corporations are incorporated.[14] Therefore, the Delaware General Corporation Law will be used as a reference point, with comparisons to the New York Business Corporation Law and the Model Business Corporation Act to highlight both similarities and differences, with occasional comparison to corporate law of other states, particularly California. However, even with differences, state corporation laws have many similarities.

The Delaware General Corporation Law sets forth the requirements for creating a corporation.

> Any person, partnership, association or corporation, singly or jointly with others, and without regard to such person's or entity's residence, domicile or state of incorporation, may incorporate or organize a corporation under this chapter by filing with the Division of Corporations in the Department of State a certificate of incorporation which shall be executed, acknowledged and filed in accordance with § 103 of this title.[15]

The New York Business Corporation Law, on the other hand, limits the formation of a corporation to natural, not artificial, legal, or fictitious persons.

> Incorporators. One or more natural persons of the age of eighteen years or over may act as incorporators of a corporation to be formed under this chapter.[16]

One would think at first that the Model Business Corporation Act is similar to the New York statute because it states,

> One or more persons may act as the incorporator or incorporators of a corporation by delivering articles of incorporation to the secretary of state for filing.[17]

However, unlike the New York statute, which limits the formation of corporations to natural persons, the Model Business Corporation Act defines "person" to include "entities,"[18] which in turn include "domestic and foreign business corporation; domestic and foreign nonprofit corporation; estate; trust; domestic and foreign unincorporated entity; and state, United States, and foreign government."[19]

Termination of a corporation

Unlike a partnership, which can be terminated by simple agreement of the partners (or even if there is no agreement, such as when a partner unilaterally disassociates herself from the partnership), a corporation cannot be terminated by simple agreement of the shareholders. While, as will be seen, shareholders can vote to voluntarily dissolve the corporation, they cannot just quit and walk away. Once a shareholder, always a shareholder unless the shares are sold or transferred to another person. Since corporations can only be created according to statutes, they can only be terminated according to statutes, which means formalities must be followed.

When a corporation is terminated (dissolved), the assets are liquidated, the liabilities paid, and the net assets distributed to the shareholders according to law. The shareholders may voluntarily agree to dissolve the corporation. The corporation may be declared bankrupt and liquidated either voluntarily or involuntarily. The corporation may be dissolved by judicial decree, either by the attorney general, who may petition the court to dissolve the corporation, or by a petition by one or more shareholders.

Voluntarily agreeing to dissolve the corporation

The Delaware General Corporation Law provides that "Every corporation created under this chapter shall have power to. . . . Wind up and dissolve itself."[20] Voluntarily dissolution requires a majority vote of stockholders permitted to vote.[21]

Similarly, a New York corporation can be dissolved by a majority vote of voting shares.[22] The Model Business Corporation Act also authorizes a corporation to be dissolved by a majority vote of voting shares.[23]

When a majority of shareholders vote to dissolve the corporation, a certificate of dissolution must be filed with the state, just as articles of incorporation must be filed with the state to create the corporation.

Bankruptcy and liquidation

A corporation may be terminated and liquidated by order of a bankruptcy court in a bankruptcy proceeding, whether the proceeding is initiated voluntarily or involuntarily. All liabilities are settled, and net proceeds are distributed to the shareholders according to the articles of incorporation and the class of stock.

Judicial dissolution

Under the Delaware General Corporation Law,[24] the New York Business Corporation Law,[25] and the Model Business Corporation Act,[26] the attorney general may petition the court for the judicial dissolution of a corporation.

Shareholders may also petition the court for dissolution. Under the Delaware General Corporation Law, for example, a stockholder may petition the court to appoint a custodian when the stockholders have failed to elect successors to directors whose terms have expired; the business of the corporation is suffering or is threatened with irreparable injury because the directors are so divided respecting the management of the affairs of the corporation that the required vote for action by the board of directors cannot be obtained; or the corporation has abandoned its business and has failed within a reasonable time to take steps to dissolve, liquidate or distribute its assets. The custodian may dissolve the corporation by order of the court.[27]

The New York Business Corporation Law and the Model Business Corporation Act have similar provisions.

Corporate existence, governance, and operations

Corporate existence

In all jurisdictions, corporations begin their existence and operation when the articles of incorporation are filed with the secretary (or department) of state, not when shares are issued or assets transferred to the corporation.

In Delaware, once the certificate of incorporation is filed in accordance with the Delaware General Corporation Law, the corporation begins its existence.

> Upon the filing with the Secretary of State of the certificate of incorporation, executed and acknowledged in accordance with § 103 of this title, the incorporator or incorporators who signed the certificate, and such incorporator's or incorporators' successors and assigns, shall, from the date of such filing, be and constitute a body corporate, by the name set forth in the certificate, subject to § 103(d) of this title and subject to dissolution or other termination of its existence as provided in this chapter.[28]

The New York Business Corporation Law is more emphatic. Upon the filing of the certificate of incorporation by the department of state, the corporate existence shall begin.[29]

The Model Business Corporation Act is similar to the New York statute: "The corporate existence begins when the articles of incorporation are filed."[30]

It is important to note that the corporation at this time exists without assets, without shares, and without shareholders. Significantly, the corporation begins its existence and the governance structure is in place prior to the election of the directors by the shareholders. There are in fact no shares outstanding at this time, so there are no shareholders to elect the directors.[31] The duties of directors to the corporation begin at the time the directors are named in the articles of incorporation and filed or when they are appointed by the incorporators.

In Delaware, unless otherwise stated in the certificate of incorporation, the corporation has a perpetual existence.[32] Likewise, in New York, a corporation has perpetual existence unless otherwise stated in the articles of incorporation.[33] Similarly, the Model Business Corporation Act also gives corporations a perpetual existence.[34]

Corporate governance

Corporate governance must first be in accordance with corporate statutory law. Common law only enters into the interpretation of corporate governance when statutory law is ambiguous or silent.

Corporate governance is the foundation of the economic "theory of the firm" since corporate governance addresses the theory of "separation of ownership and control" and "agency theory," discussed in Chapter 11 and in *Economics, Capitalism, and Corporations: Contradictions of Corporate Law, Economics, and the Theory of the Firm*. As a prelude to the corporate governance and theory of the firm, the statutory and common law requirements of corporate governance must be examined.

The debate over shareholder primacy versus director primacy, i.e., who does or should have primacy in corporate control, is zealous, if not outright fanatical, and is mostly limited to legal scholarship rather than judicial opinions. When judicial opinions are issued, they rarely use the terms "shareholder primacy" and "director primacy," even though they may espouse one or the other. As with many other things in corporate law, the debate over shareholder versus director primacy is the result of misinterpretation of property laws and agency laws with respect to corporations.

Shareholder primacy

Theories of shareholder primacy assume that shareholders control (or at least should control) the corporation and are the beneficiaries of director fiduciary duties (Bainbridge, 2003). Velasco (2010) argues that, "if shareholders are owners, then the purpose of the corporation must be to pursue their interests. . . . In other words, shareholder primacy becomes the fundamental value of corporate governance, in terms of both end and means" (p. 902).

Director primacy

The director primacy theory maintains that directors have "a contractual obligation to maximize the value of the shareholders' residual claim. In other words, the director primacy theory embraces the shareholder wealth maximization norm even as it rejects the theory of shareholder primacy" (Bainbridge, 2003, p. 547). Yet any argument regarding shareholders having residual claims is meaningless because shareholders have no claim at all, as I explain here.

Corporate governance in statutory law

The Delaware General Corporation Law provides "The business and affairs of every corporation organized under this chapter shall be managed by or under the direction of a board of directors."[35] "Managed by or under the direction of a board of directors" necessarily includes decisions on how to allocate corporate resources.

In New York, "the business of a corporation shall be managed under the direction of its board of directors."[36]

Under the Model Business Corporation Act,

> each corporation shall have a board of directors . . . all corporate powers shall be exercised by or under the authority of the board of directors, and the business and affairs of the corporation shall be managed by or under the direction, and subject to the oversight, of the board of directors.[37]

Shareholders usually have the right to elect the board of directors, but that right may be denied by the articles of incorporation or class of stock.

In Delaware, if shareholders' voting rights are not denied, after incorporation and either the naming of directors in the articles of incorporation or their election by the incorporators, "Directors shall be elected by a plurality of the votes" present at an annual meeting.[38]2

In New York, initial directors are not named in the certificate of incorporation. If shareholders' voting rights are not denied, after the articles of incorporation are filed, "an organization meeting of the incorporator or incorporators shall be held within or without this state, for the purpose of . . . electing directors to hold office until the first annual meeting of shareholders."[39]

In the Model Business Corporation Act, the incorporators have the option of naming the initial directors in the certificate of incorporation: "The articles of incorporation *may* set forth: (1) the names and addresses of the individuals who are to serve as the initial directors" (emphasis added),[40] after which shareholders elect directors unless voting is disallowed by the articles of incorporation or the class of stock.

Note that under the Delaware General Corporation Law,[41] the New York Business Corporation Law,[42] and the Model Business Corporation Act,[43] after the certificate of incorporation is filed, if directors are not named in the certificate of incorporation, the incorporators must hold an organizational meeting to elect directors until the first annual meeting of shareholders is held, at which time the shareholders elect directors. Either way, the corporation has begun its existence and operations, and it is important to understand at this point that whether the directors are named in the articles of incorporation or are appointed by the incorporators, it is the unelected directors who are in control of, govern, and manage the corporation, prior to the existence of shareholders. For example, in Delaware,

> If the persons who are to serve as directors until the first annual meeting of stockholders have not been named in the certificate of incorporation, the incorporator or incorporators, until the directors are elected, shall manage the affairs of the corporation and may do whatever is necessary and proper to perfect the organization of the corporation, including the adoption of the original bylaws of the corporation and the election of directors.[44]

That undeniably demonstrates the fact that the corporation is operational and corporate governance is in place prior to shareholders owning shares, and therefore directors are not agents of shareholders since there are no shareholders.

Corporate operations

As noted earlier, the Delaware General Corporation Law, the New York Business Corporation Law, and the Model Business Corporation Act all provide that the corporation is to be managed by or under the direction of a board of directors, whether or not the directors of the corporation have been elected by the shareholders.

In order for there to be shareholders, the initial directors must issue shares. Shareholders must pay for the shares the price determined by the directors in an arm's-length transaction. When shareholders purchase shares, they are not purchasing $x \div n\%$ of the corporation or $x \div n\%$ of the assets of the corporation. They are purchasing $x \div n\%$ of the shares issued by the corporation where x is the number of shares they purchase, and n is the total number of shares issued. They are purchasing a set of rights and expectations as determined by the articles of incorporation and the terms of the class of stock they are purchasing.

Recall from Chapter 0 that in addition to property (cash in the case of purchasing shares issued in an IPO), consideration can include a surrender of rights. That is, of course, what happens when shareholders purchase shares. In addition to the cash paid, shareholders surrender their rights to decide how to allocate their assets (cash) in exchange for obtaining other rights (e.g., the right to vote as discussed later) and a set of expectations.

In all jurisdictions, as with corporate existence, corporate operations begin when the articles of incorporation are filed with the secretary (or department) of state, not when assets are transferred to the corporation. Indeed, the corporation cannot issue shares and assets cannot be transferred to the corporation unless there are directors and it has begun operations. (See Huber, 2017, for a novel argument that a not-for-profit corporation never began operations even though there were directors because no assets were transferred to the corporation.)

The initial directors must issue shares. While shares and shareholders are not necessary to begin operations, issuing shares is necessary in order to receive financial capital, which shareholders provide when they purchase stock in an IPO. Prior to stock being issued, the corporation could borrow money or at least arrange to borrow money once shares are issued. It can also sign contracts.

Only the directors may issue stock on behalf of the corporation. Under the Delaware General Corporation Law, the initial board of directors, who have not been elected by shareholders, "may authorize capital stock to be issued for consideration consisting of cash, any tangible or intangible property or any benefit to the corporation, or any combination thereof."[45] The shares issued by the corporation need not be evidenced by a certificate (i.e., a piece of paper).[46]

> Every corporation may issue 1 or more classes of stock or 1 or more series of stock within any class thereof, any or all of which classes may be of stock with par value or stock without par value and which classes or series may have such voting powers, full or limited, or no voting powers, and such designations, preferences and relative, participating, optional or other special rights, and qualifications, limitations or restrictions thereof, as shall be stated and

expressed in the certificate of incorporation or of any amendment thereto, or in the resolution or resolutions providing for the issue of such stock adopted by the board of directors pursuant to authority expressly vested in it by the provisions of its certificate of incorporation.[47]

The consideration, as determined pursuant to § 153(a) and (b) of this title, for subscriptions to, or the purchase of, the capital stock to be issued by a corporation shall be paid in such form and in such manner as the board of directors shall determine. . . . The board of directors may determine the amount of consideration for which shares may be issued by setting a minimum amount of consideration.[48]

The New York Business Corporation Law contains similar provisions:

Consideration for the issue of shares shall consist of money or other property, tangible or intangible; labor or services actually received by or performed for the corporation or for its benefit or in its formation or reorganization; a binding obligation to pay the purchase price or the subscription price in cash or other property.[49]

In the Model Business Corporation Act:

(b) The board of directors may authorize shares to be issued for consideration consisting of any tangible or intangible property or benefit to the corporation, including cash, promissory notes, services performed, contracts for services to be performed, or other securities of the corporation. (c) Before the corporation issues shares, the board of directors shall determine that the consideration received or to be received for shares to be issued is adequate.[50]

In all jurisdictions, shareholders may subscribe to shares prior to the shares being issued to the shareholders. Subscribing to shares forms a contract. As such, the subscriber may be sued if she does not pay for the shares. Subscriptions need not be paid in full prior to the issuance of the shares to the shareholders, an important point in considering the application of contract law and trust law to corporations, discussed next.

Corporations and agency and trust law

Judges and legal scholars ignore the fact that if shareholders are beneficial owners, then trust laws must be applied. If directors are agents of shareholders, then agency laws must be applied. Judges cannot impose or create an agency or trust relationship between shareholders and directors if to do so violates or contradicts agency law or trust law. Yet that is what they do on a routine basis.

State corporation statues do not make directors either agents or trustees of shareholders. A trust relationship or agency relationship between directors and shareholders is actually precluded by property law, agency law, trust law, and corporate statutory law. Courts that rule that directors are agents or trustees of shareholders are engaging in making laws, conflicting laws at that, rather than interpreting laws.

Recall from Chapter 3 first, that a person who has the capacity to hold legal title to trust property can be a beneficial owner of the trust property.[51] A shareholder does not have legal capacity to have legal title to the corporation's property. As a matter of statutory law, the corporation owns its property exclusive of any other claims to it. Therefore, there is no trust; therefore, directors are not trustees, and therefore, they have no fiduciary duty to shareholders.

Second, a trust cannot exist when the legal and beneficial interests are in the same person. Thus, if a person has a legal interest in property, he cannot have a beneficial interest in the property. Therefore, again, no trust relationship exists; therefore, directors cannot be trustees, and therefore, they have no fiduciary duty to shareholders.

Corporations and agency law

As discussed in Chapter 2, the parties required in order to create an agency relationship are the principal and the agent. In order to create the agency relationship, the principal appoints or hires the agent to act on his or her behalf. An agent does not appoint a principal.

This presents a conundrum that those who promote the theory that directors are agents of shareholders, upon which the entire economic "theory of the firm" is built, cannot resolve. First, corporate directors exist before shareholders exist. If directors are agents of shareholders, they are agents of non-existent principals, which is not allowed under agency law. Second, only directors can issue shares. When a corporation is formed, there are no shareholders, only directors. Directors then issue the shares, creating shareholders. Thus, agents are creating the principals! This is, of course, contrary to agency law and nullifies the theory that directors are agents of shareholders, which undermines the economic theory of the firm. Furthermore, if directors are agents of shareholders, directors would have rights against the shareholders.

Corporations and trust law

The second theory that is said to create a fiduciary duty owed by directors to shareholders is found in trust law, as several judicial opinions have ruled. As seen in Chapter 3, in the case of a trust, the trustee takes legal title (legal ownership) to administer the trust for the benefit of the beneficial owner (the beneficiary). Shareholders are said to be beneficial owners. As a matter of trust law, as seen in Chapter 3, one cannot be both an owner of property (shares) with legal title to the property (shares) and a beneficial owner of the same property (shares) with no legal title to the property (shares). In a trust, the beneficiary/beneficial owner is not a party to the contract between the trustor and the trustee the way that a shareholder is a party to the purchase of shares. The shareholder is not a beneficial owner of a *trust corpus* since the shareholder owns the shares as a party to a contract.

Directors are not and cannot be trustees of shareholders. As discussed in Chapter 3, creating a trust relationship requires the trustor to deliver the trust *corpus* (trust *res*), either money or property, to the trustee. If directors were trustees, shareholders would deliver the property (money) to the directors. They don't. They deliver the money to the corporation and receive shares in return.

Purchasing shares in an IPO ("initial public offering," discussed later in this chapter) is a contract, but not a contract of principal and agent relationship, or trustor-trustee-beneficiary relationship. As Easterbrook and Fischel (1989) state, it is a contract of adhesion. The articles of incorporation set forth the terms of shareholders' and directors' respective rights and duties, which bind both shareholders and directors and which shareholders explicitly agree to by purchasing the shares in a take-it-or-leave-it transaction. There is no negotiation.

When you purchase shares in an IPO, the corporation offers to sell you shares and the rights accompanying the shares for consideration as determined by the articles of incorporation and the class of stock. You accept the offer by delivering the consideration (cash) to the corporation and surrendering your rights to decide what to do with the cash paid to the corporation. Such a transaction simply does not fulfill the requirements for a trust relationship as discussed in Chapter 3.

The mistake is to assume the money paid for shares in an IPO is the shareholders' money after they purchase the shares. It is not. The corporation gives consideration to shareholders during the IPO process in the form of a promise, which is legal consideration. The corporation promises potential shareholders that, in exchange for cash and a surrender of rights, the corporation will give them the right to vote for directors and that the shareholders might receive a share of the corporate profits in the form of a dividend (an expectation). The shareholders relinquish all title to ownership of the money, just as when a person buys a car, he relinquishes title to ownership of the money.

Statutory corporate law does not impose on directors a fiduciary duty as agents of shareholders, which even Berle and Means acknowledged ("The directors of the corporation . . . are not agents of the stockholders" p. xxi)[52] but which is almost universally ignored. Indeed, the entire theory of the firm is built on the theory that directors are agents of shareholders. Robé (2011) explains (although without evidence):

> In fulfilling their duties, the directors are required to act under the high standards imposed on fiduciaries. The directors of the corporation have to make their decisions in the best interests of the *corporation*, with a duty of loyalty and a duty of care . . . the duty of care requires that . . . directors act in the honest belief that the action taken was in the best interest of the *company* (not the shareholders).
>
> (p. 34, emphasis added.)

To see how judges and legal scholars confound corporate law, consider first that many legal scholars in particular disparage corporate governance for separating ownership and control, arguing for greater shareholder rights. This criticism is echoed by judges. Courts have ruled that shareholder owners are beneficial owners and directors are trustees. But a beneficial owner of a trust does not control the trust; the trustee does. So if, according to popular theory, shareholders are beneficial owners and directors are their trustees, shareholders cannot by definition have rights of control.

Another way that judges and legal scholars confuse corporate law is that a trustee receives nothing in return for accepting the trust *corpus*. There is no promise in exchange for a promise, a requirement for an enforceable contract. There is no consideration (although the compensation paid to the trustee for the administration of the trust is consideration). The trustor transfers the trust property to the trustee for the benefit of the beneficiary, who also gave no promise and gave no consideration to the trustee.

According to the law of trusts, a trust cannot be created by the purchase of shares. The purchase of shares is a simple matter of contract. The shareholders receive shares with their concomitant rights in exchange for consideration (cash) and a surrender by the shareholders of their rights. (Stout, 2012).

Even Berle and Means knew that purchasing shares was a contract and not a trust. In exchange for the shares and the rights conferred by the shares, purchasers agree to surrender certain of their rights – the right to decide which corporate resources to purchase or sell, the right to decide how to allocate corporate resources. They understood that a shareholder of large corporation "so far surrenders his wealth to those in control of the Corporation that he had exchanged the position of independent owner for one in which he may become merely a recipient of wage capital" (Berle & Means, 1992).

Berle and Means go on to explain, "In place of actual physical properties over which the owner could exercise direction and for which he was responsible, the owner now holds a piece of paper representing a set of rights and expectations with respect to an enterprise" (p. 64). They continue, "It follows from all the foregoing that the shareholder in the modern corporate situation has surrendered a set of definite rights for certain indefinite expectations" (p. 244).

Corporation rights and duties

Corporation rights

General rights

Corporate rights are extremely broad. First, a corporation has the right to sue and be sued as a corporation; i.e., as an entity in the name of the corporation.

The Delaware General Corporation Law provides that

> Every corporation created under this chapter shall have power to . . . Sue and be sued in all courts and participate, as a party or otherwise, in any judicial, administrative, arbitrative or other proceeding, in its corporate name.[53]

Thus, e.g., if a corporation sustains economic damages, it is the corporation that must bring the action to recover damages, not the shareholders. If the corporation causes injury, the injured party must sue the corporation, not the shareholders. (See shareholders' protection later in this chapter.)

Furthermore, if a director causes the injury, the plaintiff must sue the corporation as the principal, not the shareholders as principals, which would be the case if directors were agents of the shareholders since principals are responsible for the acts of their agents.

New York grants similar rights.

> Each corporation, subject to any limitations provided in this chapter or any other statute of this state or its certificate of incorporation, shall have power in furtherance of its corporate purposes. . . . (2) To sue and be sued in all courts and to participate in actions and proceedings, whether judicial, administrative, arbitrative or otherwise, in like cases *as natural persons.*
>
> (Emphasis added.)[54]

Likewise, the Model Business Corporation Act provides that

> Unless its articles of incorporation provide otherwise, every corporation has perpetual duration and succession in its corporate name and has *the same powers as an individual* to do all things necessary or convenient to carry out its business and affairs, including power: (a) to sue and be sued, complain and defend in its corporate name.
>
> (Emphasis added.)[55]

In addition to the right to sue and be sued, corporations have very expansive powers. The Delaware General Corporation Law grants

> In addition to the powers enumerated in § 122 of this title, every corporation, its officers, directors and stockholders shall possess and may exercise all the powers and privileges granted by this chapter or by any other law or by its certificate of incorporation, together with any powers incidental thereto, so far as such powers and privileges are necessary or convenient to the conduct, promotion or attainment of the business or purposes set forth in its certificate of incorporation.[56]

The powers of a corporation are not unlimited, however. In Delaware, for example, "Every corporation shall be governed by the provisions and be subject to the restrictions and liabilities contained in this chapter."[57]

In New York, corporations shall "have and exercise all powers necessary or convenient to effect any or all of the purposes for which the corporation is formed."[58]

The Model Business Corporation Act provides "Unless its articles of incorporation provide otherwise, every corporation has perpetual duration and succession in its corporate name and has the same powers as an individual to do all things necessary or convenient to carry out its business and affairs."[59]

Property rights

Corporate property rights will be discussed in greater detail next. The Delaware General Corporation Law is very explicit in explaining the rights of a corporation in relationship to property.

> Every corporation created under this chapter shall have power to. . . . *Purchase*, receive, take by grant, gift, devise, bequest or otherwise, lease, or otherwise acquire, *own*, hold, improve, employ, use and otherwise deal in and with real or personal property, or any interest therein, wherever situated, and to *sell*, convey, lease, exchange, transfer or otherwise dispose of, or mortgage or pledge, *all or any of its property and ass*ets, or any interest therein, wherever situated.
> (Emphasis added.)[60]

The New York Business Corporation Law provides that

> Each corporation . . . shall have power in furtherance of its corporate purposes . . . (4) To *purchase*, receive, take by grant, gift, devise, bequest or otherwise, lease, or otherwise acquire, *own*, hold, improve, employ, use and otherwise deal in and with, real or personal property, or any interest therein, wherever situated; (5) To *sell*, convey, lease, exchange, transfer or otherwise dispose of, or mortgage or pledge, or create a security interest in, all or any of its property, or any interest therein, wherever situated; (6) To *purchase*, take, receive, subscribe for, or otherwise acquire, own, hold, vote, employ, sell, lend, lease, exchange, transfer, or otherwise dispose of, mortgage, pledge, use and otherwise deal in and with, bonds and other obligations, shares, or other securities or interests issued by others, whether engaged in similar or different business, governmental, or other activities; (7)To *make contracts*, give guarantees and incur liabilities, borrow money at such rates of interest as the corporation may determine, issue its notes, bonds and other obligations, and secure any of its obligations by mortgage or pledge of all or any of its property or any interest therein, wherever situated. (8) To lend money, invest and reinvest its funds, and take and hold real and personal property as security for the payment of funds so loaned or invested.
> (Emphasis added.)[61]

The Model Business Corporation Act is as explicit and exhaustive as the New York Business Corporation Law.

> Unless its articles of incorporation provide otherwise, every corporation . . . has the same powers as an individual to do all things necessary or convenient

to carry out its business and affairs, including power . . . (d) to *purchase*, receive, lease, or otherwise acquire, and *own*, hold, improve, use, and otherwise deal with, real or personal property, or any legal or equitable interest in property, wherever located; (e) to *sell*, convey, mortgage, pledge, lease, exchange, and otherwise dispose of all or any part of its property; (f) to purchase, receive, subscribe for, or otherwise acquire, own, hold, vote, use, sell, mortgage, lend, pledge, or otherwise dispose of, and deal in and with shares or other interests in, or obligations of, any other entity; (g) to *make contracts* and guarantees, incur liabilities, borrow money, issue its notes, bonds, and other securities and obligations (which may be convertible into or include the option to purchase other securities of the corporation), and secure any of its obligations by mortgage or pledge of any of its property, franchises, or income.

(Emphasis added.)[62]

Corporation duties

The powers of a Delaware corporation are not unlimited. The Delaware General Corporation Law states, "Every corporation shall be governed by the provisions and be subject to the restrictions and liabilities contained in this chapter."[63]

Obviously, a corporation has a duty to obey and comply with all laws and regulations. The statutory duties of a corporation include paying taxes to state and federal governments. In *Schenley Distillers Corp. v. United States* the United States Supreme Court said, "The fact that several corporations are used in carrying on one business does not relieve them of their several statutory obligations more than it relieves them of the taxes severally laid upon them." A publicly traded corporation also has duties under the federal securities laws.

To the extent that responsibility is synonymous with duty, Friedman (1970) taught that "The Social Responsibility [i.e., duty] of Business Is to Increase Its Profits." That is certainly not a statutory, nor even a common law, duty. So on what basis did Friedman promote the concept that corporations had a duty to increase its profits? He based his philosophy on the legally erroneous belief that shareholders own the corporation and that directors are agents of the shareholders.

In a free-enterprise, private-property system, a corporate executive is an employee of the owners of the business. He has direct responsibility to his employers. That responsibility is to conduct the business in accordance with their desires . . . the key point is that, in his capacity as a corporate executive, the manager is the agent of the individuals who own the corporation . . . and his primary responsibility is to them.

If shareholders do not own the corporation and directors are not agents of shareholders, Friedman's thesis, like the economic theory of the firm, disintegrates into nothing more than dust in the wind.

Directors' rights and duties

Directors' rights

Like those of the corporation itself, directors' rights are quite broad, especially when compared to shareholders' rights, as discussed later in this chapter.

In all jurisdictions, the first right of directors is to issue shares, both initially and subsequently, and to set the amount of consideration for the shares. Incorporators have no power to issue shares.

The second right of directors is to manage the corporation. In Delaware, "The business and affairs of every corporation organized under this chapter shall be managed by or under the direction of a board of directors."[64] Thus, the directors have the right to manage (control) the corporation without interference from stockholders.

In New York, "Subject to any provision in the certificate of incorporation . . . the business of a corporation shall be managed under the direction of its board of directors."[65] Again, the directors have the right to manage (control) the corporation without interference from stockholders.

The Model Business Corporation Act is similar to the New York statute. The Model Business Corporation Act sets forth the requirement for and functions of the board of directors:

> [E]ach corporation shall have a board of directors . . . all corporate powers shall be exercised by or under the authority of the board of directors, and the business and affairs of the corporation shall be managed by or under the direction, and subject to the oversight, of the board of directors.[66]

Directors' duties

The primary duty, as well as right, of directors (at least he initial directors) is to issue shares in accordance with the articles of incorporation. While issuing shares is not a duty imposed on directors by the Delaware General Corporation Law, the New York Business Corporation Law, or the Model Business Corporation Act, and the corporation can operate prior to shares being issued (which, in fact, the Delaware General Corporation Law specifically requires), the corporation must issue shares in order to receive financial capital, which is necessary for the corporation to fulfill its purpose as stated in the articles of incorporation. Thus, the directors have an implicit duty to issue shares.

Fiduciary duty

Directors' duties begin at the time initial directors are named, whether in the articles of incorporation, as in Delaware, or by the incorporators in an organization meeting, as in New York.

Directors have a fiduciary duty to the corporation. On that there is no disagreement. Whether a director has a fiduciary duty to shareholders, however, is one of the most hotly contested arguments in corporate law.[67] Furthermore, there are conflicting laws regarding what constitutes fiduciary duty.

Many courts have ruled that directors have a fiduciary duty to shareholders because they are agents of shareholders. But making directors agents of shareholders is contrary to the laws of agency.

Several court rulings have held that directors have a fiduciary duty to shareholders because they are trustees of shareholders. But if directors have a fiduciary duty to shareholders because they are trustees of shareholders, then they cannot at the same time have a fiduciary duty to the corporation, for which they are not trustees. Such a conflict of interest in a fiduciary duty is expressly prohibited in agency and trust law.

Some courts have held that directors' fiduciary duty includes the duty of loyalty, but statutory law contradicts this.

The duty of loyalty in the Delaware General Corporation Law is absolute. The certificate of incorporation may contain a

> provision eliminating or limiting the personal liability of a director to the corporation or its stockholders for monetary damages for breach of fiduciary duty as a director, provided that such provision shall not eliminate or limit the liability of a director: (i) For any breach of the director's duty of loyalty to the corporation or its stockholders. (Emphasis added.)[68]

Two things are important to note here. First, it is of the utmost importance to understand that the fiduciary duty here is merely implied. It is not imposed.

Second, contrary to what several courts have ruled, the duty of loyalty and fiduciary duties are not identical or synonymous. This is seen in the Delaware General Corporation Law's provision permitting the articles of incorporation to eliminate or limit the personal liability of directors for breach of fiduciary duty, but personal liability of directors for breach of a duty of loyalty may not be eliminated or limited.

Neither fiduciary duty nor duty of loyalty is defined by the Delaware General Corporation Law, and thus the interpretation of such duties is a matter of common law.[69] ("The common understanding is that corporate officers and directors owe fiduciary duties to the firm and its shareholders" Alces, 2009, p. 243.)[70] However, a court's interpretation of fiduciary duty may not conflict with explicit statutory provisions, something that many courts ignore.

Managing the corporation is a duty as well as a right. But how must the corporation be managed? One of the key issues in the intense debate over shareholders as owners and directors as agents of shareholders centers around the duties of directors and to whom the duties are owed. As noted, a widely held belief is that directors are agents of shareholders and therefore have a fiduciary duty to shareholders. But the Delaware General Corporation Law, the New York Business Corporation Law, and the Model Business Corporation Act do not impose on directors a fiduciary duty to stockholders.

That directors have a fiduciary duty to shareholders is a function of common law (Berle & Means, 1992), a belief started decades, if not centuries, ago, which has merely been repeated and reinforced in dozens of authoritative court rulings, a classic example of when something is repeated often enough people will believe it even if it is not true. The courts' rulings that directors have a fiduciary duty to shareholders were not the result of a rigorous analysis of corporate statutes, laws of property, or laws of agency. They were, and continue to be, unjustified and unjustifiable assumptions. (But see the Delaware General Corporation Law later in this chapter.)

For example, the controlling case in Delaware is *Loft v. Guth*,[71] a 1938 case decided by the Delaware Court of Chancery.[72] In *Loft v. Guth*, the Delaware Court of Chancery stated,

> It has frequently been said by this court and clearly enunciated by the Supreme Court of this State in *Lofland et al. v. Cahall, Rec'r.*,[73] that the directors of a corporation stand in a fiduciary relation to the corporation and its stockholders.

Turning to the 1922 case of *Lofland et al. v. Cahall, Rec'r*, we see that the Supreme Court of Delaware held that

> [it] would be violative of well settled principles of equity applicable to trustees and . . . inconsistent with the fiduciary relation existing between directors and stockholders, to hold that there was an implied agreement on the part of the company to pay the six appellants for the services they claim to have rendered in the organization of the company and in the sale of its capital stock.

The idea that a fiduciary relation exists between directors and stockholders was basically created by judicial fiat. There was never any attempt by either the Delaware Supreme Court or the Delaware Court of Chancery to analyze the relationship of shareholders, corporations, directors, and corporate property or how a fiduciary duty to shareholders is or could be implemented, as explained later in this chapter.

One problem with the *Loft* ruling, therefore, and one that the court should have known, is that directors cannot be trustees of shareholders under "well settled principles of equity applicable to trustees" because that would be contrary to the laws of trusts. A careful analysis of well-settled principles of trust law would have revealed that such a duty cannot exist given the laws of trust, property, and agency.[74] The reasoning of the court was nothing more than smoke and mirrors. The Delaware General Corporation Law does not make directors trustees of shareholders.

The Delaware Supreme Court revisited the issue in 1998. In *Malone v. Brincat*,[75] the Court ruled

> An underlying premise for the imposition of fiduciary duties is a separation of legal control from beneficial ownership. Equitable principles act in those

circumstances to protect the beneficiaries who are not in a position to protect themselves. One of the fundamental tenets of Delaware corporate law provides for a separation of control and ownership. The board of directors has the legal responsibility to manage the business of a corporation *for the benefit of its shareholder owners.* Accordingly, fiduciary duties are imposed on the directors of Delaware corporations to regulate their conduct when they discharge that function.

The directors of Delaware corporations stand in a fiduciary relationship not only to the stockholders but also to the corporations upon whose boards they serve. The director's *fiduciary duty to both* the corporation and its shareholders has been characterized by this Court as a triad: due care, good faith, and loyalty.

(Emphasis added.)

Note that the court erroneously interpreted fiduciary duty as characterized by the duty of loyalty even though they are not the same under the Delaware General Corporation Law.

By "beneficial owners," the Delaware Supreme Court meant that shareholders are owners of the corporation, which is made explicit by its statement that

One of the fundamental tenets of Delaware corporate law provides for a separation of control and ownership. The board of directors has the legal responsibility to manage the business of a corporation for the *benefit of its shareholder owners.* Accordingly, fiduciary duties are *imposed* on the directors of Delaware corporations.

The court did not say how fiduciary duties are imposed on the directors of Delaware corporations. It is certainly not imposed by the Delaware General Corporation Law, which must mean it is imposed by the court. But the court is not empowered to impose such a duty contrary to unambiguous statutory law. The Delaware Supreme Court was, simply, wrong.

Another problem with the *Malone* ruling is that Delaware corporate law does not make shareholders the owners of the corporation. It is simply not true that "Delaware corporate law provides for a separation of control and ownership," and nowhere in Delaware General Corporation Law is there any section or paragraph that "provides for a separation of control and ownership." It does not exist. It is an unjustifiable construct created with smoke and mirrors.

In *NACEPF, Inc v. Rob Gheewalla, et al.*,[76] the Delaware Supreme Court ruled, "the *creditors* of a Delaware corporation . . . *have no right, as a matter of law*, to assert direct claims for breach of fiduciary duty against the corporation's directors." (Emphasis added.)

Therefore, consider that normally, as a matter of law, creditors have no right to vote for directors of a corporation (although sometimes they can). Shareholders do have a right to vote for directors of a corporation (although that right may be denied in the articles of incorporation). Creditors are not referred to as "owners" or "beneficial owners," even though bondholders may be entitled to vote. Thus, the *NACEPF* ruling can mean nothing other than that the distinction between creditors, who normally have no right to vote for directors of a corporation and are not considered "beneficial owners," and shareholders, who normally have the right to vote for directors of a corporation and who are referred to as "beneficial owners," is simply the right to vote. But nothing in the Delaware General Corporation Law confers on shareholders the ownership of the corporation, with or without voting rights.

Delaware Supreme Court decisions that hold Delaware corporate law makes shareholders the owners of a corporation, that Delaware corporate law provides for the separation of ownership and control, or that Delaware corporate law makes directors agents or trustees of shareholders have no foundation in the Delaware General Corporation law. If, as Robé (2011, 2019) and others have concluded, shareholders do not own the corporation, the Delaware Supreme Court was wrong. The Delaware Supreme Court expanded and interpreted Delaware corporate law well beyond the plain language of the statute. Can there be any question why corporate law is in such a state of confusion when courts cannot make up their minds, and their rulings conflict with statutory law?

Several things must be noted here. First and foremost, this section of the Delaware General Corporation Law does not impose on directors a fiduciary duty to stockholders. Contrary to the court's ruling, nowhere in the entire statute is a fiduciary duty to stockholders imposed on directors. Therefore, we must turn to shareholders' rights, discussed later in this chapter, to see the meaning of directors' fiduciary duty to stockholders.

The second thing that must be noted here is that the statutes of other states do not impose on directors a fiduciary duty to stockholders. When legal scholars refer to the fiduciary duty of directors to stockholders, they use the term "generically," as if a director's fiduciary duty to stockholders can be applied to all directors in all corporations in all jurisdictions.

The duties of directors as defined by the New York Business Corporation Law does not include a fiduciary duty to stockholders or a duty of loyalty *per se*. Instead, the duties of directors seem to incorporate some sense of "corporate social responsibility" (which is beyond the scope of this book). The New York Business Corporation Law is very explicit and comprehensive in defining the duties of directors:

> (a) A director shall perform his duties as a director . . . *in good faith* and with that degree of care which an ordinarily prudent person in a like position would use under similar circumstances. . . . (b) In taking action, including, without limitation, action which may involve or relate to a change or potential change in the control of the corporation, a director shall be entitled to consider, without limitation, (1) both the long-term and the short-term interests of the corporation and its shareholders and (2) the effects that the corporations [sic] actions may have in the short-term or in the long-term upon any of the following: (i) the prospects for potential growth, development, productivity and profitability of

the corporation; (ii) the corporations [sic] current employees; (iii) the corporations [sic] retired employees and other beneficiaries receiving or entitled to receive retirement, welfare or similar benefits from or pursuant to any plan sponsored, or agreement entered into, by the corporation; (iv) the corporations [sic] customers and creditors; and (v) the ability of the corporation to provide, as a going concern, goods, services, employment opportunities and employment benefits and otherwise to contribute to the communities in which it does business. *Nothing in this paragraph shall* create any duties owed by any director to any person or entity to consider or afford any particular weight to any of the foregoing or abrogate any duty of the directors, either statutory or recognized by common law or court decisions. For purposes of this paragraph, *"control" shall mean the possession, directly or indirectly, of the power to direct or cause the direction of the management and policies of the corporation*, whether through the ownership of voting stock, by contract, or otherwise.[77]

Note first that nothing in the paragraph either creates or abrogates any duty of the directors, whether statutory or recognized by common law or court decisions. Thus, no fiduciary duty between directors and shareholders is created by the statute. Furthermore, if there is a duty created by common law, such as a fiduciary duty, it is not abrogated. Thus, it is up to the courts to interpret fiduciary duty.

Nor does the Model Business Corporation Act impose on directors a fiduciary duty to stockholders.

Each member of the board of directors, when discharging the duties of a director, shall act: (i) in good faith, and (ii) in a manner the director reasonably believes to be in the *best interests of the corporation*. (b) The members of the board of directors . . . shall discharge their duties with the care that a person in a like position would reasonably believe appropriate under similar circumstances.

(Emphasis added.)[78]

The astute reader can immediately see the problem, a direct result of the director-as-agent-of-shareholders theory. The problem is whether the initial directors are named in the certificate of incorporation or are elected by the incorporators at the organization meeting, there are directors prior to shares being issued and prior to there being any shareholders. One might ask, therefore, how can directors be agents of shareholders when shareholders do not exist? How can directors owe a fiduciary duty to shareholders or a duty of loyalty to shareholders when shareholders do not exist? How is a fiduciary duty to shareholders implemented when there are no shareholders? This problem will resurface in subsequent chapters.

There are other questions that cannot be easily answered by imposing a fiduciary duty on directors. If directors owe a fiduciary duty to shareholders, what duty is owed to day traders or flash traders?

The average purchaser of stock trading on an exchange holds a share of stock for only 200 days (Economist, 2016), while high-frequency traders hold shares for seconds up to a few hours and account for 55% of the trading volume in the U.S. markets (Miller & Shorter, 2016). Day traders hold stocks from seconds up to five days (Weston & Ciccotello, 2018; Sincere & Wagner, 2000). High-frequency traders and day traders make their buy/sell decisions using technical analysis – moving averages, trading volume, price momentum, etc. (Weston & Ciccotello, 2018).[79] The objectives of the two types of shareholders are in conflict, which leads to the next question.

How is the fiduciary duty owed by directors to shareholders fulfilled when there are conflicting interests not just between the corporation and the shareholders, but between shareholders? Agency law does not allow a fiduciary to serve conflicts of interest. To paraphrase an old saying, you cannot serve hundreds or thousands of masters. Even if maximizing profits is in the interest of all shareholders, the way in which profits are maximized may not be agreed upon. And here we witness a contradiction.

A director who owes a fiduciary duty to shareholders, either as an agent or trustee, must fulfill that duty according to the fiduciary duties imposed by agency or trust law. Upon the establishment of a principal-agent relationship, a fiduciary duty of the agent to the principal arises as a matter of law.[80] That is, "an agent has a fiduciary duty to act loyally for the principal's benefit in all matters connected with the agency relationship."[81] This is, of course, the duty the director owes to the corporation. (The Delaware Supreme Court considers directors' fiduciary duty to consist of a "triad" of duties – good faith, loyalty, and due care.)[82] But in a trust relationship, "the fiduciary nature of the relationship between the trustee and the beneficiary demands an unusually high standard of ethical or moral conduct." The Supreme Court of Utah has emphasized that "trustees are charged as fiduciaries with one of the *highest duties of care and loyalty known in the law*." (Emphasis added.)[83]

At the same time, directors need only exercise "business judgment." The business judgment rule, as it is known, is a common law rule that has existed for at least 150 years (Hinsey, 1985). *Am Jur 2d* described the rationale for the business judgment rule as a policy of judicial noninterference with business decisions "designed to limit judicial involvement in business decision-making so long as a *minimum level of care* is exercised in arriving at the decision." (Emphasis added.)[84] As explained by the Delaware Supreme Court, the business judgment rule

> creates a [rebuttable] presumption that in making a business decision, the directors of a corporation acted on an informed basis (i.e., with due care), in *good faith and in the honest belief* that the action taken was in the best interest of the company.
>
> (Emphasis added.)[85]

This is a different standard than that imposed under agency law or trust law. To see this, consider another Delaware Supreme Court ruling:

> This Court has traditionally and consistently defined the duty of loyalty of officers and directors to their corporation and its shareholders in broad and

unyielding terms. . . . A public policy, existing through the years, and derived from a profound knowledge of human characteristics and motives, has established *a rule that demands of a corporate officer or director, peremptorily and inexorably, the most scrupulous observance of his duty*. . . . The [business judgment] rule that requires an undivided and unselfish loyalty to the corporation demands that there be *no conflict between duty and self-interest*.

(Emphasis added.)[86]

There is another perplexing problem, however. A corporation has perpetual existence. Shareholders own the shares for a limited time (not to exceed the life of the shareholder). Directors owe a fiduciary duty to the corporation by statute, while owing a fiduciary duty to shareholders is based on common law. But directors' actions must be in the corporation's best interest, which means directors must manage the corporation in order to sustain and maintain the perpetual life of the corporation. This is in direct conflict with shareholders' interests, which have a limited time horizon. Neither statutory duties nor common law fiduciary duties of directors to the corporation can be reconciled with either the statutory duties or the common law fiduciary duties of directors to shareholders. The problem is generated by courts imposing on directors fiduciary duties to shareholders contrary to agency law and trust law.

While the Delaware General Corporation Law does refer to a fiduciary duty of directors, the Delaware General Corporation Law does not impose a fiduciary duty on directors, and neither fiduciary duty nor duty of loyalty is even mentioned in the duties of directors in the New York Business Corporation Law or the Model Business Corporation Act.

A fiduciary duty of directors to shareholders that has been imposed on directors by courts simply cannot be implemented the way the Delaware Supreme Court interprets it without violating trust law and agency law. There is a time when directors do owe a fiduciary duty to shareholders, but it has nothing to do with operations or management. It has to do with shareholders' rights in dissolution and liquidation, which are discussed later in this chapter.

Duty of loyalty

Directors' duty of loyalty is absolute in the Delaware General Corporation Law. In the Delaware General Corporation Law, a corporation "*may* contain a provision eliminating or limiting the personal liability of a director to the corporation or its stockholders for monetary damages for breach of fiduciary duty as a director, provided that such provision shall not eliminate or limit the liability of a director: (i) For any breach of the director's duty of loyalty to the corporation or its stockholders." (Emphasis added.)[87]

It is important to understand that no matter what the courts say, a duty of loyalty is not the same as a fiduciary duty. If it were, then the Delaware General Corporation Law could not say that the articles of incorporation may eliminate a director's personal liability for a breach of fiduciary duty, but not of a duty of loyalty.

Duties in dissolution and liquidation

As previously discussed, a corporation can be dissolved voluntarily; voluntarily or involuntarily in a bankruptcy proceeding; or involuntarily by petition of shareholders, creditors, or directors. Directors' duties in a corporate dissolution highlight the trustee relationship of directors to the corporation and to shareholders.

Dissolution procedures and directors' duties in the dissolution of a Delaware corporation are extensive, and therefore the statutory provisions must be examined *in toto* as they relate to fiduciary duties. The dissolution and subsequent liquidation shed light on the fiduciary duties of directors.

> All corporations, whether they expire by their own limitation or are otherwise dissolved, shall nevertheless be continued, for the term of 3 years . . . for the purpose of prosecuting and defending suits . . . and of enabling them gradually to settle and close their business, to *dispose of and convey their property, to discharge their liabilities and to distribute to their stockholders any remaining assets.*
>
> (Emphasis added.)[88]

> When any corporation organized under this chapter shall be dissolved *in any manner* whatever [i.e., voluntarily or involuntarily], the Court of Chancery, *on application of* any creditor, *stockholder* or director of the corporation, or any other person who shows good cause therefor, at any time, *may either appoint 1 or more of the directors of the corporation to be trustees*, or appoint 1 or more persons to be receivers, of and for the corporation, *to take charge of the corporation's property.*
>
> (Emphasis added.)[89]

> Trustees . . . appointed by the Court of Chancery . . . shall, upon their appointment and qualification . . . be vested *by operation of law* and without any act or deed, *with the title of the corporation to all of its property,* real, personal or mixed of whatsoever nature, kind, class or description, and wheresoever situate, except real estate situate outside this State.
>
> (Emphasis added.)[90]

Whereas prior to dissolution, the corporation owned its property, it is now the trustee who takes title to the corporation and its property.

The trustee does not take title to or own the shares. The trustee only takes title to the corporation and to corporate property. Shareholders still own their shares, so owning shares does not give shareholders title (ownership) to the corporation. If owning shares meant that shareholders own either the corporation or corporate property, then the trustee taking title to the property would be taking shareholders' property to pay creditors of the corporation. Yet shareholders are protected from liability to pay creditors.

The Delaware General Corporation Law does not say when or under what circumstances directors owe a fiduciary duty to shareholders, but a fiduciary duty can only be owed to shareholders in liquidation in spite of what the courts say, or else the directors encounter the conflicts of interest identified earlier. The law makes the trustees owners of the corporation and corporate property in order first to pay creditors and second to distribute net assets to the shareholders which are now, by operation of law, owed to (not owned by) the shareholders.

Similar to a Delaware corporation, a New York corporation may be voluntarily dissolved by a majority vote of shareholders entitled to vote.[91] Creditors must be paid, and the net assets must be distributed to the shareholders. Therefore, a fiduciary duty arises because the net assets are owed to the shareholders.

As in Delaware and New York, the Model Business Corporation Act provides that the corporation may be voluntarily dissolved by a majority vote of shareholders entitled to vote.[92] Creditors must be paid, and the net assets must be distributed to the shareholders. Therefore, a fiduciary duty arises because the net assets are owed to, not owned by, the shareholders.

Corporations and corporate property

Shareholders do not have an economic interest in the property of the corporation in which they own shares the way partners have an economic interest in partnership property, where the equity (net assets) of the partnership is owned by the partners in proportion to their partnership interest. That is, partners own the partnership, and thus partners have an economic interest in the partnership property. Shareholders, on the other hand, do not own either the corporation or corporate property and have no economic interest in either. Their interest is in the shares as a financial asset. Partners can sell their interest in the partnership property to others (subject to the agreement of the other partners). Shareholders only own shares, which are not an economic interest in the corporate property. When shareholders sell their shares, they are not selling an interest in the corporate property.

The Delaware and New York corporation laws and the Model Business Corporation Act regarding corporations and property were discussed earlier in the section on corporation property rights. Nevertheless, they bear repeating here not just for emphasis, but for convenience. However, reviewing the laws of Delaware and New York, consider the Model Business Corporation Act, which contains a bold provision.

> A *shareholder of the corporation does not have a vested property right* resulting from any provision in the articles of incorporation, including provisions relating to management, control, capital structure, dividend entitlement, or purpose or duration of the corporation.
>
> (Emphasis added.)[93]

Such a provision negates any suggestion of a proprietary or economic interest in the corporation. One may ponder why shareholders complain about not having control when it is stated at the outset that shareholders have no vested property rights in or control of the corporation. Shareholders' attempts to gain more control of the corporation are attempts to assert rights over the corporation to which they are not entitled.

While the Model Business Corporation Act is not law (unless a state has adopted it), it is a stark revelation of what some have argued, but few have acknowledged. A shareholder has no ownership rights in the corporation. On its face, it is also inconsistent with California General Corporation Law § 184, which defines "shares" as "the units into which the *proprietary* interests in a corporation are divided in the articles [of incorporation]." But as discussed later in this chapter, a proprietary interest in a corporation is not an ownership right in the corporation.

The Delaware General Corporation Law is very explicit in explaining the relationship of a corporation to corporate property.

> Every corporation created under this chapter shall have power to. . . . *Purchase*, receive, take by grant, gift, devise, bequest or otherwise, lease, or otherwise acquire, *own*, hold, improve, employ, use and otherwise deal in and with real or personal property, or any interest therein, wherever situated, and to *sell*, convey, lease, exchange, transfer or otherwise dispose of, or mortgage or pledge, *all or any of its property and ass*ets, or any interest therein, wherever situated.
>
> (Emphasis added.)[94]

The New York Business Corporation Law is more exhaustive.

> (a) Each corporation . . . shall have power in furtherance of its corporate purposes. . . . (4) To *purchase*, receive, take by grant, gift, devise, bequest or otherwise, lease, or otherwise acquire, *own*, hold, improve, employ, use and otherwise deal in and with, real or personal property, or any interest therein, wherever situated; (5) To *sell*, convey, lease, exchange, transfer or otherwise dispose of, or mortgage or pledge, or create a security interest in, all or any of its property, or any interest therein, wherever situated; (6) To *purchase*, take, receive, subscribe for, or otherwise acquire, own, hold, vote, employ, sell, lend, lease, exchange, transfer, or otherwise dispose of, mortgage, pledge, use and otherwise deal in and with, bonds and other obligations, shares, or other securities or interests issued by others, whether engaged in similar or different business, governmental, or other activities; (7) To *make contracts*, give guarantees and incur liabilities, borrow money at such rates of interest as the corporation may determine, issue its notes, bonds and other obligations, and secure any of its obligations by mortgage or pledge of all or any of its property or any interest therein, wherever situated. (8) To lend money, invest and reinvest its funds, and take and hold real and personal property as security for the payment of funds so loaned or invested.
>
> (Emphasis added.)[95]

The Model Business Corporation Act is as exhaustive as the New York Business Corporation Law.

> Unless its articles of incorporation provide otherwise, every corporation . . . has the same powers as an individual to do all things necessary or convenient to carry out its business and affairs, including power . . . (d) to *purchase*, receive, lease, or otherwise acquire, and *own*, hold, improve, use, and otherwise deal with, real or personal property, or any legal or equitable interest in property, wherever located; (e) to *sell*, convey, mortgage, pledge, lease, exchange, and otherwise dispose of all or any part of its property; (f) to purchase, receive, subscribe for, or otherwise acquire, own, hold, vote, use, sell, mortgage, lend, pledge, or otherwise dispose of, and deal in and with shares or other interests in, or obligations of, any other entity; (g) to *make contracts* and guarantees, incur liabilities, borrow money, issue its notes, bonds, and other securities and obligations (which may be convertible into or include the option to purchase other securities of the corporation), and secure any of its obligations by mortgage or pledge of any of its property, franchises, or income.
>
> (Emphasis added.)[96]

Furthermore, the Delaware General Corporation Law classifies ownership of shares of stock as personal property. "The shares of stock in every corporation shall be deemed *personal property* and transferable as provided in Article 8 of subtitle I of Title 6." (Emphasis added.)[97] Article 8 of Subtitle I of Title 6 is the Uniform Commercial Code which deals with investment securities.[98] The UCC defines a security as a financial asset[99] that includes "a share or similar equity interest issued by a corporation." "Investment security" explicitly excludes an interest in a partnership, which is an "economic interest."

In order to understand "equity interest," we need to understand "equity." The equity of a corporation is the net assets of the corporation (assets – liabilities = equity, discussed more fully in *Economics, Capitalism, and Corporations: Contradictions of Corporate Law, Economics, and the Theory of the Firm*), which arises in the first instance when the corporation issues shares and subsequently increased (or decreased) by changes in retained earnings. But the equity does not belong to the shareholder. The equity belongs to the corporation.

In order to see this, consider the fact that shareholders do not own the corporation's assets, i.e., its property. The corporation owns the assets, i.e., its property. Therefore, assuming the corporation has no liabilities, the assets equal the equity (the net assets). That is, assets – liabilities (which are zero) = equity (i.e., net assets).

Therefore, we may ask, if the corporation owns the assets, how are the net assets, i.e., the equity, magically transformed into *shareholders'* equity? Assets are owned by the corporation. Liabilities are owed by the corporation. If there are liabilities, then assets – liabilities = net assets, which of course equals equity. If shareholders do not own the assets or owe the liabilities, how can shareholders own the net assets, i.e. the equity? How is the *corporation's* equity magically transformed into *shareholders'* equity? Transforming the net assets that are owned by the corporation into net assets owned by shareholders is worthy of anything coming out of the Wizarding World!

California General Corporation Law §§ 184 and 185 present an interesting perspective not seen in the New York or Delaware corporation statutes, or the Model Business Corporation Act.

Section 185 of the California General Corporation Law defines "shareholder" as "one who is a *holder of record of shares*" while § 184 defines "shares" as "the units into which the *proprietary interests* in a corporation are divided in the articles [of incorporation]." (Emphases added.) Thus, a shareholder is the holder of record of units of proprietary interest in the corporation.

The California General Corporation Law does not define "proprietary interest." There has been no California Supreme Court ruling on the meaning of § 184 "proprietary interest." So, assuming for the sake of argument that § 184 "proprietary interest" actually means "ownership interest," what is it exactly that shareholders own? To say that shareholders hold units into which the proprietary interests in a corporation are divided in the articles of incorporation is meaningless with regards to ownership of either a corporation or corporate property.

To understand why it is meaningless, consider the definition of "proprietary interest." A proprietary interest is defined as "the interest of an owner of property together with all rights appurtenant thereto such as the right to vote shares of stock and *right to participate in managing* if the person has a proprietary interest in the shares."[100] (Emphasis added.) Elsewhere, proprietary interest is defined as a "legally enforceable right to possess or use property in accordance with an official recognition of that right."[101]

First, a *corporation* does not have "rights appurtenant thereto such as the right to vote shares of stock and right to participate in managing if the person has a proprietary interest in the shares." It is the *shares* owned by shareholders that have "rights appurtenant thereto such as the right to vote shares of stock and right to participate in managing if the person has a proprietary interest in the shares."

Second, the implication of § 184 is that a shareholder has the right to participate in managing the corporation. But that is not permitted by the California General Corporation Law itself. As in Delaware, New York, and the Model Business Corporation Act, California General Corporation Law prohibits shareholders from participating in managing the corporation because it places management of the corporation in the board of directors, thus negating any legitimate interpretation that the "propriety interest" of shares provides a right to participate in managing the corporation:

> Subject to the provisions of this division and any limitations in the articles relating to action required to be approved by the shareholders (Section 153) or by the outstanding shares (Section 152), or by a less than majority vote of a class or series of preferred shares (Section 402.5), the business and affairs of the corporation shall be managed and all corporate powers shall be exercised by or under the direction of the board. The board may delegate the

management of the day-to-day operation of the business of the corporation to a management company or other person provided that the business and affairs of the corporation shall be managed and all corporate powers shall be exercised under the ultimate direction of the board.[102]

Note that while the board of directors may delegate the management of the corporation to others, shareholders do not delegate management to the board of directors. Directors are created by law, not by shareholders, and shareholders have no choice whether or not the board of directors manages or controls the corporation.

Third, a corporation does not correspond to any classification of property, as seen in Chapter 1. A corporation is obviously not tangible, but neither is it intangible. Recall that intangible property consists of legal rights. A corporation is neither a legal right nor a bundle of legal rights. The rights are in the shares. Indeed, the California Supreme Court acknowledged in *Miller v. McColgan* that it is the ownership of shares that is the legally recognized property interest. "The property of the shareholders in their respective *shares* is distinct from the corporate property" (emphasis added),[103] thus negating any proprietary interest in the corporation itself.

But the California Supreme Court went further.

[L]et us first consider the nature of this property – corporate stock – and the status of corporations and shareholders. [1] It is fundamental, of course, that the corporation has a personality distinct from that of its *shareholders, and that the latter neither own the corporate property nor the corporate earnings*. The shareholder simply has an expectancy in each, and he becomes the owner of a portion of each only when the corporation is liquidated by action of the directors or when a portion of the corporation's earnings is segregated and set aside for dividend payments on action of the directors in declaring a dividend. This well-settled proposition was amplified in Rhode Island Hospital Trust Co. v. Doughton, 270 U.S. 69, 81 [46 S. Ct. 256, 70 L. Ed. 475], wherein appears the following cogent language: "The owner of the shares of stock in a company is not the owner of the corporation's property. He has a right to his share in the earnings of the corporation, as they may be declared in dividends arising from the use of all its property. In the dissolution of the corporation he may take his proportionate share in what is left, after all the debts of the corporation have been paid and the assets are divided in accordance with the law of its creation. But he does not own the corporate property."
(Emphasis added.)

Therefore, a shareholder does not earn a profit from the corporation. He earns a profit from the shares. And if the shareholder does not earn a profit from the corporation, the shareholder has no proprietary interest in the corporation.

Fourth, a corporation is not a financial asset. The corporation cannot be a financial asset. It is the shares that are financial assets.[104]

Fifth, since it is firmly established that shareholders do not own the total assets (property) of the corporation, it is impossible for shareholders to own the net assets (equity) of the corporation. If shareholders do not own the corporate assets, net assets, or its earnings, there can be no proprietary interest in the corporation.

Sixth, §§ 184 and 185 do not distinguish between common shares with voting rights and preferred shares with voting rights. Therefore, if a shareholder is one who is a holder of record of shares which are the units into which the proprietary interests in a corporation are divided in the articles of incorporation, then those shares necessarily include both preferred shares with voting rights and common shares with voting rights. Yet preferred shareholders are never referred to as owners of a corporation or having a proprietary interest in the corporation.

Finally, property law does not confer on shareholders the right to possess or use the corporation or corporate property. Nor does property law or corporate law give shareholders an ownership right in the earnings of the corporation, as the California Supreme Court ruled in *Miller v. McColgan*. Thus, California General Corporation Law § 184 is a nullity pursuant to the California Supreme Court's ruling in *Miller v. McColgan*.

The California Supreme Court in 1941 in *Miller v. McColgan* relied on the United States Supreme Court ruling in *Rhode Island Hospital Trust Co. v. Doughton*[105] which held

> The owner of the shares of stock in a company is not the owner of the corporation's property. He has a right to his share in the earnings of the corporation, as they may be declared in dividends arising from the use of all *its* property. In the dissolution of the corporation he may take his proportionate share in what is left, after all the debts of the corporation have been paid and the assets are divided in accordance with the law of its creation. But he does not own the corporate property. . . . The interest of the shareholder entitles him to participate in the net profits earned by the bank in the employment of *its* capital, during the existence of its charter, in proportion to the number of his shares; and, upon its dissolution or termination, to his proportion of the property that may remain of the corporation after the payment of its debts. This a distinct independent interest or property, held by the shareholder like any other property that may belong to him.
>
> (Emphasis added.)

Miller must be compared to the Model Business Corporation Act, which states,

> A *shareholder of the corporation does not have a vested property right* resulting from any provision in the articles of incorporation, including provisions relating to management, control, capital structure, dividend entitlement, or purpose or duration of the corporation.
>
> (Emphasis added.)[106]

As noted, the California statute that declares shareholders have a proprietary interest in a corporation is meaningless. If proprietary interest in a corporation is equivalent to ownership interest in a corporation, a shareholder would have the right to use corporate property the way partners have a right to use partnership property. Nevertheless, even if, for the sake of argument, proprietary interest could be interpreted as ownership interest, it is only one jurisdiction and cannot thus be attributed to corporations in general as the economic theory of the firm is wont to do.

Residual claimants

One of the more egregious examples of the distorted doctrines advanced by the theory of the firm is the idea of shareholders as "residual claimants," subsequently assimilated into judicial rulings.

Perhaps the earliest reference to shareholders as residual claimants dates back to Schwartz (1936). Coming during the Great Depression, and on the heels of Berle and Means (although it is unknown how much, if at all, he was influenced by their work since he did not refer to it), Schwartz had this to say:

> The theory of capitalist enterprise is simple. A special class acts as intermediaries between the ultimate consumers of goods and services and the persons whose labour and property is used to produce the goods and services. This special class assumes the responsible direction of economic life and all the risks associated with that function. In return it is entitled to any profits which may result from the operations it directs; profits made up by the margin between the costs incurred and the ultimate receipts. The claim of this specialised class is a residual claim. . . . The *residual claimants* who draw on the profit margin are, in our complicated modern organisation, a diverse group made up chiefly of minority shareholders.
>
> (p. 70, emphasis added.)

The doctrine of shareholders as residual claimants infiltrated judicial reasoning. For example, in *Applebaum v. Avaya, Inc.*, the Delaware Supreme Court held that "Shares of stock are issued to provide a verifiable property interest for the *residual claimants* of the corporation." (Emphasis added.)[107]

Thus it is said that shareholders are residual claimants because it is assumed they have a "residual claim" on the equity (net assets) of the corporation, meaning they have a claim on the equity after corporate debts are paid. Alces (2009) states unequivocally that "the distinction between creditors and shareholders is well reasoned. Shareholders are the residual claimants, the 'owners' of the corporation." But when we examine the law and logic of the assumption, we find that shareholders are not claimants, residual or otherwise.

We begin with Roberts (1955), who describes the balance sheet equation (assets – liabilities = equity) as demonstrating that the corporation is owned by the stockholders and that their claims are residual in nature. But that is incorrect on at least two counts. First, the balance sheet does not show who owns the corporation. It does not even show who owns the equity (net assets). It only shows the value of net assets of the corporation, i.e., the equity, with no regard to ownership.

Second, it does not show that shareholders are residual claimants, or any other type of claimants. That shareholders are residual claimants is an assumption not supported by law. In order to be a claimant, a person must have a legally valid, enforceable right. As seen in Chapter 1, a claim is an enforceable right referred to as a "chose in action."

Shareholders have no enforceable rights against the corporation, the corporation's assets (whether total or net), or its directors. The rights of shareholders are limited to the rights discussed later in this chapter. None of those rights encompasses a valid, enforceable claim against either the corporation, the income of the corporation, or the property of the corporation. Without a valid, enforceable claim against either the corporation, the income of the corporation, or the property of the corporation, shareholders are not claimants, let alone residual claimants.

Shareholders have no greater claim on the net assets than they do on the total assets. The corporation owns the assets, and shareholders have no claim against the total assets. The corporation owns the equity; thus, the shareholders have no claim against the equity.

Roberts (1955) does correctly note that the dividends are a distribution of the corporation's profits that are residual in nature, i.e., distributed out of net income or retained earnings after all expenses have been paid, whereas the interest paid to the creditors represents a direct claim against the corporation. If the corporation does not pay the interest due to creditors, the creditors may enforce their claims in a court of law.

However, the fact that dividends are residual in nature does not translate into a residual claim by shareholders against the corporation or its net income since shareholders have no claim to dividends. As Berle and Means note, shareholders trade their property rights with respect to the resources of production for a mere expectation of dividends, which Roberts does acknowledge ("The corporation has an obligation to pay the interest due bondholders but there is no obligation on the corporate enterprise to pay dividends"), but he then misses the connection between the corporation having no obligation to pay dividends and shareholders having no claim for dividends. There can be no claim by one person (a shareholder) against another person (the corporation) if the second person (the corporation) has no obligation (duty) to the first person (a shareholder).

Creditors have a claim against the corporation for both interest and principal if neither is paid. Shareholders have no claim against the corporation for dividends or "principal," which Roberts also acknowledges. ("The bondholders have a claim for a specific amount to be paid within a certain time period whereas the stockholders have no such claim.") But Roberts, like all the others, nevertheless continues to assert that stockholders are residual claimants, which, as a matter of property law and contract law, they cannot be.

Roberts also errs in stating that "The stockholder owns the capital stock which represents a residual interest in the assets of the corporation. The stockholder is the last recipient of distributed corporate assets." Stockholders have no legal interest in the total assets of the corporation. If they have no interest in the total assets of the corporation, they have no legal interest in the net assets of the corporation.

Indeed, Roberts states, "The bondholder can demand payment when the debt is due but the stockholder cannot demand payment." Therefore, if stockholders cannot demand payment, they are not claimants.

To see this point in perspective, consider the following cases from Delaware. In *Production Resources v. NCT Group*.[108] the court ruled

> By definition, the fact of insolvency places the creditors in the shoes normally occupied by the shareholders – that of residual risk-bearers . . . creditors become the residual claimants of a corporation when the equity of the corporation has no value . . . when a firm is insolvent, creditors do not become residual claimants with interests entirely identical to stockholders, they simply become the class of constituents with the key claim to the firm's remaining assets.

And in *In re Trados Incorporated Shareholder Litigation*,[109] the court stated,

> Even when a corporation is insolvent, creditors lack standing to assert a direct claim for breach of fiduciary duty; they merely gain standing to sue derivatively because they have joined the ranks of the residual claimants.

Obviously, as a matter of contract, creditors must first be paid in the event of insolvency. But that is not the point. The point is that in a bankruptcy proceeding, all creditors and all shareholders become residual claimants, so to categorize shareholders as residual claimants since they are paid after creditors are paid in a bankruptcy proceeding creates a false impression, particularly since creditors must actually file claims in the bankruptcy court in order to be paid, and shareholders need not file claims.

In *Applebaum v. Avaya, Inc.*,[110] the court stated, "Shares of stock are issued to provide a *verifiable property interest for the residual claimants* of the corporation." (Emphasis added.) Two points must be made here. One, the court is equating owners of shares with residual claimants, but as discussed earlier, shareholders are not claimants of any type.

Two, when the court states that shares of stock provide a verifiable property interest, the court is not saying that shares of stock provide an ownership interest in the corporation. Delaware General Corporation Law makes a share of stock an item of personal property, and therefore it cannot be a property interest in the corporation. However, corporations are not actually required to issue certificated shares. Owning shares may be uncertificated. The certificated share of stock merely verifies the property interest in the shares.

To see that a share is a verifiable property interest in the shares and not a property interest in the corporation, compare a share of stock to a deed or title to an automobile. A deed to real property is not a financial asset and is obviously not the real property itself. It is the verifiable property interest in the real property – namely, that of the owner. The title to an automobile is not a financial asset and is obviously not the personal property, which is the automobile. "*Corporate securities* are a species of *property right* that represent not only a firm's fundamental source for raising capital, but also now a publicly traded commodity." (Emphasis added.)[111] A share of stock is a financial asset as defined by the Uniform Commercial Code and a publicly traded commodity. Furthermore, shares are personal property according to the Delaware General Corporation Law.

Since the Delaware General Corporation Law, as well as the corporation laws of every other jurisdiction, grants to corporations the right to acquire and own assets, but explicitly makes shares of stock personal property as an investment security, shareholders are prohibited by statute from owning either the corporation or the assets of the corporation.

Furthermore, by making shares of stock personal property transferable only in accordance with the Uniform Commercial Code's provision for investment securities, shareholders cannot both own the shares as investment securities and own the corporation itself. Since they own shares as investment securities, they cannot own the corporation itself. There is no type of property by which a corporation can be classified. Since a corporation is not property or a property right, it cannot be owned.

At first glance, the UCC's definition of a security as "a share or similar equity interest issued by a corporation" suggests an ownership interest in the corporation, but that is not the case. First, the definition does not state that a share *is* an equity interest, only that a share may be *similar* to an equity interest. But that distinction is not controlling.

The Delaware General Corporation Law "shall not be construed as repealing, modifying or restricting the applicable provisions of law relating to incorporations [or] sales of securities . . . except insofar as such laws conflict with this chapter."[112] To the extent that the UCC's definition of a security conflicts with the Delaware General Corporation Law, the Delaware General Corporation Law prevails. Thus, while the Delaware General Corporation Law provides that shares of stock shall be sold in accordance with the UCC, the UCC cannot make a share of stock an equity interest in the corporation.

The equity of a corporation is the net assets of the corporation (assets – liabilities = equity, discussed more fully in *Economics, Capitalism, and Corporations: Contradictions of Corporate Law, Economics, and the Theory of the Firm*), which arises in the first instance when the corporation issues shares in an IPO and subsequently by retained earnings. But the equity is not owned by the shareholder. It is owned by the corporation. The shareholder only has a right to receive net assets when the corporation is liquidated, and the net assets are required by law to be distributed to the shareholder.

An equity interest issued by a corporation is not the same as the "economic interest" partners have in a partnership. The economic interest a partner has in a partnership is defined as "a partner's share of the profits and losses of a partnership and the partner's right to receive distributions."[113] Shareholders are never defined as having an "economic interest" in the corporation or its profits and losses, and indeed, shareholders cannot have an economic interest in the corporation if they do not have an ownership interest in the corporation or its assets. Shareholders have no right as a matter of law to share in the profits and losses of a corporation and no right to receive distributions, other than in a liquidation.

The Delaware General Corporation Law provides that "The directors of every corporation, subject to any restrictions contained in its certificate of incorporation, *may* declare and pay dividends upon the shares of its capital stock."[114] Thus, not only do directors have no duty to declare dividends, shareholders have no right to receive a dividend until it is declared by the directors. Thus, receiving a dividend is no more than a mere expectation – a hope, really – as acknowledged by Berle and Means.

When a partnership suffers a loss, the loss is distributed among the partners' capital accounts in proportion to their capital contributions. However, when a corporation suffers a loss, the loss is not distributed among the shareholders' capital accounts in proportion to their capital contributions (which arise in an IPO) because they have no capital accounts. They merely have a ledger identifying the number of shares they own.

That shareholders cannot own the corporation is further confirmed by Delaware General Corporation Law § 292(a), which states,

> Trustees or receivers appointed by the Court of Chancery of and for any corporation, and their respective survivors and successors, shall, upon their appointment and qualification or upon the death, resignation or discharge of any co-trustee or co-receiver, be vested by operation of law and without any act or deed, with the title of the corporation to all of its property, real, personal or mixed of whatsoever nature, kind, class or description, and wheresoever situate, except real estate situate outside this State.

If shareholders owned either the corporation or corporate property, then the trustee would be seizing someone else's assets without compensation to pay the creditors of the corporation, which is anathema to property law, agency law, and corporate law. Furthermore, a trustee appointed by a court is acting under the auspices of the court (government). Thus, to take title to the corporation and the corporation's assets would also mean seizing the "equity interest" of the shareholders, i.e., the property, without compensation and without due process of law, which is prohibited by the Constitution. Thus, "equity interest" cannot mean ownership of the corporation, its assets, its net assets, or its earnings.

So what can "equity interest" mean if it cannot mean ownership of the corporation, its assets, or its earnings? As discussed more fully later, shareholders have a right in the equity of the corporation, i.e., its net assets (assets remaining after liabilities are paid), but only upon liquidation and dissolution of the corporation. Shareholders otherwise have no legal rights to the corporation's assets, its net assets, or its equity.

Shareholders' rights and duties

Shareholders' rights

Shareholders have rights, but not all rights are absolute. Some rights may be denied in the articles of incorporation or in the class of stock issued by the corporation. It is not the corporation that gives the rights to shareholders; it is the shares.

The rights are attached to the shares, and it is the owner of the shares who may exercise those rights.

Shareholders' right to vote

Shareholders normally have a right to vote, but shareholders' right to vote in Delaware and other jurisdictions may be denied.

> *Unless otherwise provided* in the certificate of incorporation and subject to § 213 of this title, each stockholder shall be entitled to 1 vote for each share of capital stock held by such stockholder.
>
> (Emphasis added.)[115]

Preferred shareholders may have the right to vote, and even bondholders may have the right to vote.

> Every corporation *may* in its certificate of incorporation *confer upon the holders of any bonds*, debentures or other obligations issued or to be issued by the corporation *the power to vote* in respect to the corporate affairs and management of the corporation to the extent and in the manner provided in the certificate of incorporation.
>
> (Emphasis added.)[116]

Yet neither preferred shareholders nor bondholders are considered owners of a corporation, even with a right to vote, while common shareholders are considered owners even if they have no right to vote.

In New York,

> Every corporation shall have power to create and issue the number of shares stated in its certificate of incorporation. Such shares may be all of one class or may be divided into two or more classes. . . . *The certificate of incorporation may deny*, limit or otherwise define the *voting rights* and may limit or otherwise define the dividend or liquidation rights of shares of any class, *but no such denial*, limitation or definition *of voting rights shall be effective unless at the time one or more classes of outstanding shares or bonds, singly or in the aggregate, are entitled to full voting rights*, and no such limitation or definition of dividend or liquidation rights shall be effective unless at the time one or more classes of outstanding shares, singly or in the aggregate, are entitled to unlimited dividend and liquidation rights.
>
> (Emphasis added.)[117]

In the Model Business Corporation Act,

> unless the articles of incorporation provide otherwise, each outstanding share, regardless of class or series, is entitled to one vote on each matter voted on at a shareholders' meeting. Only shares are entitled to vote.[118]

This is contrary to the Delaware provision that allows the articles of incorporation to entitle bondholders to vote.

None of these rights to vote confer on shareholders ownership of the corporation or of corporate property.

Right to vote on amending articles of incorporation

In Delaware, unless stated otherwise in the articles of incorporation, amending the articles of incorporation must be approved by a majority vote of the shareholders.[119] Similarly, in New York, unless stated otherwise in the articles of incorporation, amending the articles of incorporation must be approved by a majority vote of the shareholders.[120] In the Model Business Corporation Act, unless stated otherwise in the articles of incorporation, amendment must be approved by a majority vote of the shareholders.[121] Thus, the right to vote on amending the articles of incorporation may be denied.

Right to vote for directors

Shareholders' right to vote for directors is assumed to be absolute. But while shareholders' right to vote for directors is common, it is not absolute or guaranteed. In Delaware, shareholders' right to vote for directors is not absolute. In Delaware,

> The certificate of incorporation shall set forth . . . a statement of the designations and the powers, preferences and rights, and the qualifications, limitations or restrictions thereof, which are permitted by § 151 of this title in respect of any class or classes of stock.[122]

Section 151 of the Delaware General Corporation Law states,

> Every corporation may issue 1 or more classes of stock or 1 or more series of stock within any class thereof, any or all of which classes may be of stock with par value or stock without par value and which classes or series may have such voting powers, full or limited, or no voting powers.[123]

The New York Business Corporation Law is similar to Delaware's General Corporation Law:

> The certificate of incorporation may set forth any provision, not inconsistent with this chapter or any other statute of this state, relating to the business of the corporation, its affairs, its rights or powers, or the rights or powers of its shareholders, directors or officers including any provision relating to matters which under this chapter are required or permitted to be set forth in the by-laws. It is not necessary to set forth in the certificate of incorporation any of the powers enumerated in this chapter.[124]

The New York Business Corporation Law continues to explain limitations on shareholders' right to vote:

> Every shareholder of record shall be entitled at every meeting of shareholders to one vote for every share standing in his name on the record of shareholders, unless otherwise provided in the certificate of incorporation.[125]

In New York,

> At each annual meeting of shareholders, directors shall be elected to hold office until the next annual meeting. . . . The certificate of incorporation may provide for the election of one or more directors by the holders of the shares of any class or series, or by the holders of bonds entitled to vote in the election of directors.[126]

In the Model Business Corporation Act,

> unless the articles of incorporation provide otherwise, each outstanding share, regardless of class or series, is entitled to one vote on each matter voted on at a shareholders' meeting. Only shares are entitled to vote.[127]

And

> Unless otherwise provided in the articles of incorporation, directors are elected by a plurality of the votes cast by the shares entitled to vote in the election at a meeting at which a quorum is present.[128]

Note that, unlike the Delaware General Corporation Law and the New York Business Corporation Law, in the Model Business Corporation Act, only shares, not bonds, are entitled to vote.

Right to vote on mergers

Mergers inevitably affect the shares of both corporations. Therefore, shareholders have a right to vote on anything that affects their shares. In Delaware,

> Any 2 or more corporations of this State may merge into a single surviving corporation . . . pursuant to an agreement of merger or consolidation. . . . The agreement required by subsection (b) of this section shall be submitted to the stockholders of each constituent corporation . . . the agreement shall be considered and a vote taken for its adoption or rejection.[129]

Both the New York Business Corporation Law[130] and the Model Business Corporation Act[131] have similar provisions.

Right to vote on voluntary dissolution

As noted earlier, all jurisdictions allow a majority of voting shares to vote for a voluntary dissolution of the corporation.

Right to protection from creditors

What is referred to as "limited liability" is perhaps the right most well known by the public and is one of the major attractions for people to invest in shares. Yet this is a common misconception. Shareholders have no liability, limited or otherwise. What is really meant by the phrase "limited liability" is "limited risk." Even Posner (2014) had it wrong when he said, "shareholders' liability for corporate debt is limited to the value of his shares" (p. 536). While shareholders may lose the entire value of their shares when the market price falls to zero, they are not liable for any corporate debts. Their risk of loss is limited to the market value of their shares.

When a partner is bankrupt, creditors can satisfy their claims against his partnership in the partnership because the partners own the partnership. (See Chapter 4.) When a shareholder is bankrupt, the shareholder's creditors cannot satisfy their claims against the corporation because the shareholder does not own the corporation. Creditors can only satisfy their claims against the shareholder against the shares of the shareholder because the shares are personal property that can be sold to satisfy the shareholder's creditors' claims.

Most important, if directors are agents of shareholders, "limited liability" of shareholders is contrary to the laws of agency, in which third parties have recourse against principals for acts of the agents as discussed in Chapter 2, thus again negating the applicability of agency law to shareholders and directors. Note also that the corporation, not the shareholders, is liable as a principal for the acts of its directors.

For the most part, shareholders are protected from creditors' claims against the corporation. The exception is for unpaid subscriptions to stock. Stockholders are protected from creditors in two situations. One situation is in a dissolved corporation, and the other is for normal operations.

In Delaware,

> In any event "The aggregate liability of any stockholder of a dissolved corporation for claims against the dissolved corporation shall not exceed the amount distributed to such stockholder in dissolution."[132]

In New York, shareholder limited liability is more implied than express.[133]
The Model Business Corporation Act has similar provisions.

> A shareholder of a corporation is not personally liable for any liabilities of the corporation (including liabilities arising from acts of the corporation) except (i) to the extent provided in a provision of the articles of incorporation permitted by section 2.02(b)(2)(v), and (ii) that a shareholder may become personally liable by reason of the shareholder's own acts or conduct.[134]

It is important to note that stockholders in all jurisdictions are liable for the purchase of the stock or subscriptions that are not paid in full if the assets of the corporation are otherwise insufficient to satisfy creditors' claims. This is more proof that the purchase of shares is a matter of contract, not of creating a trust. The shareholder of an unpaid balance is liable for payment as a breach of contract, not as a principal of an agent and certainly not as either a trustor or a beneficial owner. A shareholder is never described as a principal of a corporation, and a corporation is never described as an agent of a shareholder.

Furthermore, when the power of a corporation to purchase, own, or sell property is combined with (1) agency law, which makes principals liable for the acts of their agents as discussed in Chapter 2, and (2) the rights of corporations to sue and be sued, then if directors were agents of shareholders, shareholders would be liable as principals in a lawsuit for the contracts made by directors.

Right to dividends and distributions

In an IPO, everyone pays the same price for a share of stock. If another IPO is issued, the price of a share of stock will most likely be different than in the first IPO. Sharing profits by way of dividends is based on the number of shares owned, not on the consideration paid to the corporation in an IPO and certainly not on the consideration paid in acquiring the shares on an exchange, as in a partnership. In a partnership, shared profit is normally based on the amount paid into the partnership (assuming no agreement to the contrary), which constitutes the economic interest a partner has in the partnership.

While shareholders have a right to dividends, that right is not absolute. Under Delaware General Corporation Law, "The directors of every corporation, subject to any restrictions contained in its certificate of incorporation, may declare and pay dividends upon the shares of its capital stock."[135] Thus, receiving dividends is merely an expectation.

In New York, "a corporation may declare and pay dividends or make other distributions in cash or its bonds or its property, including the shares or bonds of other corporations, on its outstanding shares."[136]

The Model Business Corporation Act is even shorter than New York. "A board of directors may authorize and the corporation may make distributions to its shareholders."[137] Elsewhere, a distribution is defined as

> a direct or indirect transfer of cash or other property (except a corporation's own shares) or incurrence of indebtedness by a corporation to or for the benefit of its shareholders in respect of any of its shares. A distribution may be in the form of a payment of a dividend; a purchase, redemption, or other acquisition of shares; a distribution of indebtedness; a distribution in liquidation; or otherwise.[138]

Right to liquidation proceeds

Shareholders have a right to net liquidation proceeds regardless of when they purchased the shares (i.e., in an IPO or in the market). But the net liquidation proceeds are based on the number of shares, not on the purchase price of the shares and not on equity interest. Therefore, each shareholder receives an amount calculated as (net liquidation proceeds ÷ number of shares), which means each shareholder receives a different amount of proceeds based on the proportion of the number of shares they own to total shares, not on the price paid for the shares or their capital contribution as is the case for partnerships.

Shareholders have been referred to as "residual claimants." The term "residual claimant" refers to the theory that shareholders have a claim on net assets after all liabilities are satisfied. While shareholders have a right to receive a distribution of the net assets, they have no claim on either the total assets or the net assets (equity) of the corporation.

In Delaware, for example, upon dissolution, "any assets remaining after payment of claims and liabilities, shall be distributed to the stockholders."[139] In New York, after paying all liabilities,

> The corporation, if authorized at a meeting of shareholders by a majority of the votes of all outstanding shares entitled to vote thereon may sell its remaining assets . . . and distribute the same among the shareholders according to their respective rights.[140]

The Model Business Corporation Act contains substantial provisions.

> A corporation that has dissolved continues its corporate existence but the dissolved corporation may not carry on any business except that appropriate to wind up and liquidate its business and affairs, including . . . making distributions of its remaining assets among its shareholders according to their interests.[141]

Shareholders can assert no claim against the corporation. Thus, by law, shareholders are not claimants residual or otherwise.

It is easily seen that not one of these rights confers an ownership interest in the corporation. Not one of these rights is a right associated with rights of ownership of the corporation as property of the shareholder the way the rights of partners are associated with the ownership of the partnership as property of the partners.

Shareholders' duties

One does not usually think of shareholders having duties, but they do. Their duty, created by purchasing or subscribing to shares, is to pay for the shares. If directors were the agents of shareholders, shareholders would owe duties to the directors. They do not.

Corporate law and control of corporations

Berle and Means defined the control of a corporation as the power to select a majority of the board of directors. Stigler and Friedland (1983) maintain that "The majority of the voting stock is the ultimate control over a corporation even if that stock is diffused among many owners."

The Delaware General Corporation Law distinguishes between management and control. According to Delaware General Corporation Law, a corporation's business and affairs are to be managed and all corporate powers shall be exercised by or under the direction of the board, and all corporate powers are to be exercised under the ultimate direction of the board.[142] Yet control

> means the possession, directly or indirectly, of the power to direct or cause the direction of the management . . . through the ownership of voting stock . . . [a] person who is the owner of 20% or more of the outstanding voting stock of any corporation . . . shall be presumed to have control of such entity, in the absence of proof by a preponderance of the evidence to the contrary.[143]

Note first that this is a rebuttable presumption, but at the same time, it does not preclude a less than 20% shareholder from exercising what the statute defines as control. While it is true that not many shareholders of publicly traded corporations own 20% or more of the outstanding stock,[144] the point is, if they do own 20% or more of the outstanding stock, and if shareholders own the corporation as the theory of separation and control asserts, the theories of the firm and of separation and control are largely invalidated.

The California General Corporation Law does not use a number. It merely defines control as "the possession, direct or indirect, of the power to direct or cause the direction of the management and policies of a corporation."[145]

Another problem presents itself in such a situation. If there are two (or up to five) shareholders each owning 20% of the outstanding voting shares, and directors have a fiduciary duty to shareholders, to whom do the directors owe the fiduciary duty if the shareholders are in conflict with one another? This is another argument against directors owing a fiduciary duty to shareholders *and* the corporation and for directors owing a fiduciary duty to the corporation only.

But the more egregious fact that shouts at economists and legal scholars holding to the theory of separation and control is the inversion of the separation of ownership and control. The theory of the firm rests on the proposition that shareholders own the corporation yet do not control it. In a bit of twisted legal logic, we are confronted here with the situation of a shareholder controlling a corporation she does not own!

Finally, it must be noted that shareholders do control corporations. They just do not own them. When speaking of control of corporations, the question simply becomes, which shareholders control the corporation?

Chapter summary

This chapter has provided evidence in the form of a rigorous and comprehensive analysis of corporate law, property law, and agency law sufficient to prove that shareholders are not legal owners, beneficial owners, or residual owners of corporations; directors are not agents of shareholders; directors, except in very limited circumstances, do not owe a fiduciary duty to shareholders; and directors are not trustees of shareholders. To impose on directors a fiduciary duty to shareholders is contrary to explicit statutory and common laws of property and agency.

Although common shareholders provide financial capital to a corporation in an IPO and bear risk, residual or otherwise, this does not make them owners of the corporation. Bond holders and preferred stockholders also provide financial capital to corporations in an IPO, bear risk, and may even be entitled to vote, yet they are not referred to as owners of a corporation.

Common stockholders are frequently referred to as residual claimants or risk bearers, suggesting that those with the highest risk of loss are owners of the corporation. But the relative risks can be inverted such that those with lower risk (bond holders and preferred stockholders) have voting rights while those with higher risk have no voting rights, so neither risk of loss nor voting rights confers ownership.

Directors are often referred to as agents of shareholders, but if directors were agents of shareholders, shareholders would be liable as principals. Since shareholders are not liable as principals, they cannot be principals and, therefore, directors cannot be their agents.

Directors are often referred to as trustees of shareholders, but that would require shareholders to transfer property to directors to own in trust. Shareholders do not transfer property to directors. Shareholders transfer property to corporations.

Making shareholders "beneficial owners" of the corporation is not consistent with the definition of "beneficial owner" in trust law. Furthermore, one cannot be both an owner and a beneficial owner at the same time. They are mutually exclusive. A shareholder cannot own shares as personal property and, at the same time, be a beneficial owner of the corporation.

Purchasing shares is a contract for the sale and purchase of the shares. It is not creating a trust. Shareholders are purchasing rights and expectations. There is offer and acceptance; there is consideration (cash and a surrender of rights for an indefinite expectation of sharing profits and different rights); there is legal capacity. Shareholders are purchasing rights and expectations.

Unlike partners in a partnership, who have a *right* to share in the profits of the partnership, shareholders have *no* right to share in the profits of the corporation. Shareholders only have an expectation (really just a hope) to share in the profits of the corporation in the form of dividends. Unlike partners in a partnership, shareholders do not share in the losses of the corporation, at least not directly, the way partners share in losses. If there is a loss, it might result in a decrease in the value of the share in the market. The reason shareholders have no right to share in the profits of a corporation the way partners share in partnership profits is, as Robé (2011) explains, owning shares in a corporation is not co-owning a corporation. Shareholders do not share ownership in the corporation as joint tenants or tenants in common.

As a final note, consider that audit reports of publicly traded corporations are addressed "To the Board of Directors and Shareholders of [Corporation]," not "To the Board of Directors and Owners of [Corporation]."

Notes

1　That the legal structure of the corporation necessarily determines the economic theory of the firm is seen in the fact that the theory of the firm is built on the separation of ownership and control, which is part of the legal structure of the corporation. See Chapter 11 and *Economics, Capitalism, and Corporations: Contradictions of Corporate Law, Economics, and the Theory of the Firm.*
2　"By 2000. . . the standard shareholder oriented model of the Corporation had achieved 'ideological hegemony'" (Stout, 2012).
3　Veblen (1923) commented on "absentee ownership" more than once. "[T]his particular form of words – 'Absentee Ownership' – has not been commonly employed to describe this peculiar institution which now engrosses public policy and about which controversy is beginning to gather. But that only marks a deficiency of speech. It is only within the last few decades, and only by degrees, that the facts in the case have been changing in such a way as to call for the habitual use of such a phrase as 'absentee ownership.' It is only within the last few decades, and only by degrees, that absentee ownership has visibly come to be the main controlling factor in the established order of things" (p. 4). These "time-worn principles of ownership and control, which are now coming to a head in a system of absentee ownership and control, are beginning to come in for an uneasy and reluctant reconsideration" (p. 5). Yet the separation of ownership and control did not catch on in the legal or economic literature until Berle and Means.
4　*The Modern Corporation and Private Property* was first published in 1932 when sexist language was the norm.
5　Issues concerning ownership of stock and control of a corporation do arise in the context of non–publicly traded, closely held corporations. However, since they are closely held, ownership of stock and control of a corporation are not the result of the wider dispersion of stock and therefore not associated with agency theory.
6　The New York Court of Appeals is the highest court in New York, the equivalent of the "supreme court."
7　Mason v. Curtis, 223 N. Y. 313 (NY, 1918).
8　The court went on to state "The relation of the directors to the stockholders is essentially that of trustee and *cestui que trust*," and stockholders "are the complete owners of the corporation," which, although not supported by law, is not unusual for either that time period or this.
9　Both preferred stock and bonds may have voting rights, and common stock might not have voting rights, as spelled out in the articles of incorporation or the particular class of stock. This is discussed in more detail in the following sections.
10　Bonds also mature, while preferred stock does not, but that is not a distinction since bonds can have voting rights while preferred stock may not have voting rights.
11　Shareholders do not invest in corporations. They invest in the shares of the corporation.
12　George Gershwin, *Porgy and Bess*, 1935.
13　"The powers not delegated to the United States by the Constitution, nor prohibited by it to the States, are reserved to the States respectively, or to the people." U.S. Constitution, Amendment X. The Constitution does not delegate to the United States the authority to create corporations.
14　Sixty-two percent of Fortune 500 companies are incorporated in Delaware. Delaware Division of Corporations. Annual Report Statistics.
15　Delaware General Corporation Law, § 101.
16　New York Business Corporation Law, Sec. 401.
17　Model Business Corporation Act, § 2.02.
18　Model Business Corporation Act, § 1.40.
19　Model Business Corporation Act, § 1.40.
20　Delaware General Corporation Law, § 122.
21　Delaware General Corporation Law, § 275.

22 New York Business Corporation Law, Sec. 1001.
23 Model Business Corporation Act, § 14.02.
24 Delaware General Corporation Law, § 284.
25 New York Business Corporation Law, Sec. 1101.
26 Model Business Corporation Act, § 14.30.
27 Delaware General Corporation Law, § 226.
28 Delaware General Corporation Law, § 106.
29 New York Business Corporation Law, Sec. 403.
30 Model Business Corporation Act, § 2.03(a).
31 Delaware General Corporation Law, § 106. "Commencement of corporate existence. Upon the filing with the Secretary of State of the certificate of incorporation, executed and acknowledged in accordance with § 103 of this title, the incorporator or incorporators who signed the certificate, and such incorporator's or incorporators' successors and assigns, shall, from the date of such filing, be and constitute a body corporate, by the name set forth in the certificate, subject to § 103(d) of this title and subject to dissolution or other termination of its existence as provided in this chapter."
32 Delaware General Corporation Law, § 102(b)(5).
33 New York Business Corporation Law, Sec. 402(a)(9).
34 Model Business Corporation Act, § 3.02.
35 Delaware General Corporation Law, § 141(a).
36 New York Business Corporation Law, Sec. 701.
37 Model Business Corporation Act, § 8.01.
38 Delaware General Corporation Law, § 216.
39 New York Business Corporation Law, Sec. 404(a).
40 Model Business Corporation Act, § 2.02(b)(1).
41 Delaware General Corporation Law, § 108, "Organization meeting of incorporators or directors named in certificate of incorporation. (a) After the filing of the certificate of incorporation an organization meeting of the incorporator or incorporators, or of the board of directors if the initial directors were named in the certificate of incorporation, shall be held, either within or without this State, at the call of a majority of the incorporators or directors, as the case may be, for the purposes of adopting bylaws, electing directors (if the meeting is of the incorporators) to serve or hold office until the first annual meeting of stockholders or until their successors are elected and qualify, electing officers if the meeting is of the directors, doing any other or further acts to perfect the organization of the corporation, and transacting such other business as may come before the meeting."
42 New York Business Corporation Law, Sec. 404(a). "After the corporate existence has begun, an organization meeting of the incorporator or incorporators shall be held . . . for the purpose of adopting by-laws, electing directors to hold office until the first annual meeting of shareholders."
43 Model Business Corporation Act, § 2.05(a)(2). "After incorporation . . . if initial directors are not named in the articles of incorporation, the incorporator or incorporators shall hold an organizational meeting at the call of a majority of the incorporators: (i) to elect initial directors and complete the organization of the corporation."
44 Delaware General Corporation Law, § 107.
45 Delaware General Corporation Law, § 152. Shares issued in an IPO are issued for cash. See Chapter 6.
46 Delaware General Corporation Law, § 158. Stock certificates; uncertificated shares. "The shares of a corporation shall be represented by certificates, provided that the board of directors of the corporation may provide by resolution or resolutions that some or all of any or all classes or series of its stock shall be uncertificated shares."
47 Delaware General Corporation Law, § 151.
48 Delaware General Corporation Law, § 152.
49 New York Business Corporation Law, Sec. 504(a).

50 Model Business Corporation Act, § 6.21.
51 Am Jur 2d, Trusts, § 241.
52 It must be noted that even Berle and Means acknowledged that directors are not agents of the stockholders. Yet agency theory, which dominates the theory of the firm, is built on the concept that directors are agents of stockholders.
53 Delaware General Corporation Law, § 122(i)(2).
54 New York Business Corporation Law, Sec. 202(a)(2).
55 Model Business Corporation Act, § 3.02(a).
56 Delaware General Corporation Law, § 121(a).
57 Delaware General Corporation Law, § 121(b).
58 New York Business Corporation Law, Sec. 202(a()16).
59 Delaware General Corporation Law, § 302.
60 Delaware General Corporation Law, § 122(4).
61 New York Business Corporation Law, Sec. 202.
62 Model Business Corporation Act, § 3.02.
63 Delaware General Corporation Law, § 121(b).
64 Delaware General Corporation Law, § 141(a).
65 New York Business Corporation Law, Sec. 701.
66 Model Business Corporation Act, § 8.01.
67 Federal securities laws impose fiduciary duties on publicly traded corporations. See Chapter 8.
68 Delaware General Corporation Law, § 102(b)(7).
69 There is a fundamental problem with imposing a duty to both the corporation and its stockholders since the interests of the corporation, which has a (theoretical) perpetual existence, may conflict with the interests of the stockholders, especially day traders and flash traders. This conflict is discussed in greater detail later in this chapter.
70 Alces believes that the Delaware common law doctrine that directors owe a fiduciary duty to shareholders has narrowed and become irrelevant and obsolete. That is far from agreed upon, however.
71 Loft v. Guth, 2 A.2d 225 (Del. Ch. 1938).
72 "The Delaware Court of Chancery is widely recognized as the nation's preeminent forum for the determination of disputes involving the internal affairs of Delaware corporations." https://courts.delaware.gov/chancery/.
73 Lofland et al. v. Cahall, Rec'r., 13 Del. Ch. 384 (Del. 1922).
74 Recognizing that there is no fiduciary relation existing between directors and stockholders does not imply that the final judgment in the case would have been different, only that the reason for the final judgment may have been different.
75 Malone v. Brincat, 722 A.2d 5, 8 (Del. 1998).
76 North American Catholic Educational Programming Foundation, Inc v. Rob Gheewalla, Gerry Cardinale and Jack Daly, 930 A.2d 92 (2007).
77 New York Business Corporation Law, Sec. 717.
78 Model Business Corporation Act, § 8.30(a).
79 Adapted from Huber (2020b) with permission.
80 Am Jur 2d, Agency, § 192.
81 Am Jur 2d, Agency, § 192.
82 Cede & Co., v. Technicolor, Inc., 634 A.2d at 361 (DE, 1993).
83 Pepper v. Zions First Nat'l Bank, N.A., 801 P. 2d 144, 151, 1990 (UT, 1990).
84 Am Jur 2d, Corporations, § 1451.
85 Citron v. Fairchild Camera & Instrument Corp., 569 A.2d 53 (DE, 1989).
86 Cede & Co., v. Technicolor, Inc., 634 A.2d at 361 (DE, 1993).
87 Delaware General Corporation Law, § 102(b)(7).
88 Delaware General Corporation Law, § 278.
89 Delaware General Corporation Law, § 279.
90 Delaware General Corporation Law, § 292(a).

91 New York Business Corporation Law, Sec. 1001.
92 Model Business Corporation Act, § 14.02.
93 Model Business Corporation Act, § 10.01(b).
94 Delaware General Corporation Law, § 122(4).
95 New York Business Corporation Law, Sec. 202.
96 Model Business Corporation Act, § 3.02.
97 Model Business Corporation Act, § 159.
98 Delaware Code. https://delcode.delaware.gov/title6/c008/sc01/index.shtml.
99 Delaware General Corporation Law, §§ 8–102(a), (9)(i).
100 Black's Law Dictionary.
101 What Is a Proprietary Interest? https://lawpath.com.au/blog/what-is-a-proprietary-interest-an-explainer.
102 California General Corporation Law, § 300(a).
103 Miller v. McColgan, 17 Cal.2d 432, 436 (CA, 1941).
104 Uniform Commercial Code, § 8–102: "(9) 'Financial asset' . . . means: (i) a security." Uniform Commercial Code, § 8–103: "(15) 'Security' . . . means . . . a share, participation, or other interest in an issuer or in property or an enterprise of an issuer . . . (iii) which: (A) is, or is of a type, dealt in or traded on securities exchanges or securities markets."
105 Rhode Island Hospital Trust Co. v. Doughton, 270 U.S. 69, 81, 46 S.Ct. 256 70, L.Ed. 475 (1926).
106 Model Business Corporation Act, § 10.01(b).
107 Applebaum v. Avaya, Inc., 812 A.2d 880 (2002).
108 Production Resources v. NCT Group, 863 A.2d 772 (DE, 2004).
109 In re Trados Incorporated Shareholder Litigation, 73 A.3d 17 (DE, 2013).
110 Applebaum v. Avaya, Inc., 812 A.2d 880 (2002).
111 Kalageorgi v. Victor Kamkin, Inc., 750 A.2d 531, 538 (DE, 1999).
112 Delaware General Corporation Law, § 619.
113 Delaware Revised Uniform Partnership Act, § (17).
114 Delaware General Corporation Law, § 170.
115 Delaware General Corporation Law, § 212.
116 Delaware General Corporation Law, § 22.
117 New York Business Corporation Law, Sec. 501.
118 Model Business Corporation Act, § 7.21.
119 Delaware General Corporation Law, § 242.
120 New York Business Corporation Law, Sec. 803.
121 Model Business Corporation Act, § 10.04
122 Delaware General Corporation Law, § 102(a).
123 Delaware General Corporation Law, § 151(a).
124 New York Business Corporation Law, Sec. 402(c).
125 New York Business Corporation Law, Sec. 612(a).
126 New York Business Corporation Law, Sec. 703(a).
127 Model Business Corporation Act, § 7.21(a).
128 Model Business Corporation Act, § 7.28.
129 Delaware General Corporation Law, § 251.
130 New York Business Corporation Law, Sec. 903.
131 Model Business Corporation Act, § 11.02.
132 Delaware General Corporation Law, § 282.
133 New York Business Corporation Law, Sec. 628, 630.
134 Model Business Corporation Act, § 6.22.
135 Delaware General Corporation Law, § 170(a).
136 New York Business Corporation Law, Sec. 510.
137 Model Business Corporation Act, § 6.40.

138 Model Business Corporation Act, § 1.40.
139 Delaware General Corporation Law, § 281(b).
140 New York Business Corporation Law, Sec. 1005(d).
141 Model Business Corporation Act, § 14.05(a).
142 California General Corporation Law, § 300(a).
143 Delaware General Corporation Law, § 203(c)(4).
144 It is rare for an individual to own 20% of the voting stock of a publicly traded corporation. A publicly traded corporation can own 20% or more of another publicly
traded corporation, in which case it would be reported as a subsidiary according to
Generally Accepted Accounting Principles. There can be several tiers of subsidiary
corporations, but eventually, the shares of the parent of all subsidiary tiers would be
owned by individuals.
145 California General Corporation Law, § 160.

Bibliography

Cases

Applebaum v. Avaya, Inc., 812 A.2d 880 (2002).
Cede & Co., v. Technicolor, Inc., 634 A.2d at 361 (DE, 1993).
In re Trados Incorporated Shareholder Litigation, 73 A.3d 17 (DE, 2013).
Kalageorgi v. Victor Kamkin, Inc., 750 A.2d 531, 538 (DE, 1999).
Lofland et al. v. Cahall, Rec'r., 13 Del.Ch. 384, 118 A. 1 (DE, 1922).
Loft v. Guth, 2 A.2d 225 (DE, 1938).
Malone v. Brincat, 722 A.2d 5 (DE,1998).
Mason v. Curtis, 223 N. Y. 313 (NY, 1918).
Miller v. McColgan, 17 Cal.2d 432 (CA, 1941).
North American Catholic Educational Programming Foundation, Inc v. Rob Gheewalla,
Gerry Cardinale and Jack Daly, 930 A.2d 92 (DE, 2007).
Production Resources v. NCT Group, 863 A.2d 772 (DE, 2004).
Rhode Island Hospital Trust Co. v. Doughton, 270 U.S. 69, 81, 46 S.Ct. 256 70, L.Ed. 475
(1926).
Schenley Distillers Corp. v. United States, 326 U.S. 432 (1946).

Authors, publications, and statutes

Alces, K.A. (2009). Debunking the corporate fiduciary myth. *Iowa Journal of Corporation
Law*, 35(2), 239–282. Retrieved from https://ssrn.com/abstract=1352595.
Bainbridge, S.M. (2003). Director primacy: The means and ends of corporate governance.
Northwestern University Law Review, 97(2), 547–606. Retrieved from http://heinonline.
org/HOL/Page?handle=hein.journals/illlr97&div=19.
Banner, S. (2011). *American property: A history of how, why, and what we own*. Boston:
Harvard University Press.
Berle, A.A., & Means, G.C. (1992). *The modern corporation and private property*
(2nd ed.). New York: Routledge.
Black's law dictionary. (1979). St. Paul, MN: West Publishing Co.
Booth, R.A. (2001). Who owns a corporation and who cares? *Chicago-Kent Law Review*,
77(1), 147–178. Retrieved from https://scholarship.kentlaw.iit.edu/cklawreview/vol77/
iss1/8.

Delaware General Corporation Law. Retrieved from https://delcode.delaware.gov/title8/title8.pdf.

Easterbrook, F.H., & Fischel, D.R. (1983). Voting in corporate law. *Journal of Law & Economics*, 26, 395. Retrieved from www.jstor.org/stable/725110.

Easterbrook, F.H., & Fischel, D.R. (1989). The corporate contract. *Columbia Law Review*, 89, 1416–1448. Retrieved from https://chicagounbound.uchicago.edu/cgi/viewcontent.cgi?article=2163&context=journal_articles.

Economist. (Oct. 6, 2016). *Quick and Dirty*. Retrieved from www.economist.com/news/business/21708287-are-companies-too-short-termist-quick-and-dirty [https://perma.cc/TCF6-84NK].

Friedman, M. (1970, Sept. 13). The social responsibility of business is to increase its profits. *New York Times Magazine*, p. 2.

Green, R.M. (1993). Shareholders as stakeholders: Changing metaphors of corporate governance. *Washington and Lee Law Review*, 50(4), 1409–1421. Retrieved from https://scholarlycommons.law.wlu.edu/wlulr/vol50/iss4/4.

Hinsey IV, J. (1985). American law institute's corporate governance project: Duty of care: Business judgment and the American law institute's corporate governance project: The rule, the doctrine, and the reality. *The George Washington Law Review*, 52, 609–623.

Huber, W.D. (2017). The saga of Huber vs. the American accounting association: Forensic accounting and the law. *Journal of Forensic & Investigative Accounting*, 9(2), 870–879. Retrieved from https://papers.ssrn.com/sol3/papers.cfm?abstract_id=2970636.

Huber, W.D. (2020a) *Economics, capitalism, and corporations: Contradictions of corporate law, economics, and the theory of the firm*. London: Routledge.

Huber, W.D. (2020b). The FASB conceptual framework – a case of the Emperor's new clothes. Forthcoming.

Iwai, K. (1999). Persons, things and corporations: The corporate personality controversy and comparative corporate governance. *American Journal of Comparative Law*, 47(4), 583–632. Retrieved from www.jstor.org/stable/841070.

Jensen, M.C., & Meckling, W.H. (1976). Theory of the firm: Managerial behavior, agency costs and ownership structure. *Journal of Financial Economics*, 3, 305–360. doi: 10.1016/0304-405X(76)90026-X.

Levitt Jr., A. (2008, July 1). How to boost shareholder democracy. *Wall Street Journal*, p. A17.

Masten, S.E. (1993). A legal basis for the firm. In Oliver E. Williamson and Sidney G. Winter (Eds). *The nature of the firm: Origins, evolution, and development*. London: Oxford University Press.

Miller, R.S., & Shorter, G. (2016). High frequency trading: Overview of recent developments. *Congressional Research Service*. Retrieved from https://fas.org/sgp/crs/misc/r44443.pdf [https://perma.cc/kvm7-g7pz].

Mizruchi, M.S., & Fein, L.C. (1999). The social construction of organizational knowledge: A study of the uses of coercive, mimetic, and normative isomorphism. *Administrative Science Quarterly*, 44(4), 653–683. Retrieved from www.jstor.org/stable/2667051.

Mizruchi, M.S., & Hirschman, D. (2010). The modern corporation as social construction. *Seattle University Law Review*, 33(4), 1065–1108. Retrieved from https://digitalcommons.law.seattleu.edu/cgi/viewcontent.cgi?article=1011&context=sulr.

Model Business Corporation Act. Retrieved from www.americanbar.org/content/dam/aba/administrative/business_law/corplaws/2016_Model Business Corporation Act. authcheckdam.pdf.

New York Business Corporation Law. Retrieved from https://newyork.public.law/laws/
n.y._business_corporation_law.

Orts, E.W. (2013). *Business persons: A legal theory of the firm*. London: Oxford University
Press.

Posner, R.A. (2014). *Economic analysis of law* (9th ed.). New York: Wolters Kluwer.

Putterman, L. (1993). Ownership and the nature of the firm. *Journal of Comparative Economics*, 17, 243–263. Retrieved from https://econpapers.repec.org/repec:eee:jcecon:v:
17:y:1993:i:2.

Reich-Graefe, R. (2011). Deconstructing corporate governance: Director primacy without
principle? *Fordham Journal of Corporate and Financial Law*, 16, 465–506. Retrieved
from https://ssrn.com/abstract=1971300.

Robé, J-P. (2011). The legal structure of the firm. *Accounting, Economics, and Law –
A Convivium*, 1(1), 1–85. doi: 10.2202/2152-2820.1001.

Robé, J-P. (2019). The shareholder value mess (and how to clean it up). *Accounting, Economics, and Law—A convivium*, 9(3), 1–27. doi 10.1515/ael-2019-0039.

Roberts, A.T. (1955). *The proprietary theory and the entity theory of corporate enterprise*
(Doctoral Dissertation). Louisiana State University and Agricultural & Mechanical College, Retrieved from https://digitalcommons.lsu.edu/gradschool_disstheses/132/.

Schwartz, G.L. (1936). Capitalism on the dole. *Political Quarterly*, 7(1), 70–83. doi: 10.
1111/j.1467-923X.1936.tb01290.x.

Shepherd, J.C. (1981). *The law of fiduciaries*. London: The Carswell Company Ltd.

Sincere, M., & Wagner, D. (2000). *The long-term day trader: Short-term strategies to
boost your long-term profits*. Wayne, NJ: Career Press.

Stigler, G.J., & Friedland, C. (1983). The literature of economics: The case of Berle and
Means. *The Journal of Law & Economics*, 26(2), 237–268. doi: 10.1086/467032.

Stout, L. (2003). Shareholder as Ulysses: Some empirical evidence on why investors in
public corporations tolerate board governance. *University of Pennsylvania Law Review*,
152(2), 1–47. doi: 10.2139/ssrn.452700.

Stout, L. (2012). *The shareholder value myth: How putting shareholders first harms investors, corporations, and the public*. Oakland, CA: Berrett-Koehler Publishers.

Suojanen, W.W. (1954). Accounting theory and the large corporation. *The Accounting
Review*, 29(3), 391–398. Retrieved from www.jstor.org/stable/241556?seq=1#metadata_
info_tab_contents.

Veblen, T. (1923). *Absentee ownership and business enterprise in recent times: The case of
America*. New York: B.W. Huebsch.

Velasco, J. (2010). Shareholder ownership and primacy. *University of Illinois Law Review*
(3), 897–956. doi: 0.2139/ssrn.1274244.

Walker, P. (2016). *The theory of the firm: An overview of the economic mainstream*. London: Routledge.

Weston, H., & Ciccotello, C. (2018). Flash traders (milliseconds) to indexed institutions (centuries): The challenges of an agency theory approach to governance in the
era of diverse investor time horizons. *Seattle University Law Review*, 41(2), 613–653.
Retrieved from https://digitalcommons.law.seattleu.edu/sulr/vol41/iss2/51/.

6 The contradictions of corporate law

Introduction

Corporate law is rife with contradictions.[1] The contradictions of corporate law are evident in state supreme court rulings up to the United States Supreme Court in a kind of "trickle up" manner since federal courts, including the United States Supreme Court, must follow state law and state supreme court interpretations of state common and statutory law in matters reserved to states under the United States Constitution. Then, once the United States Supreme Court has ruled, state courts follow the United States Supreme Court's ruling. The contradictions were then woven into the theory of the firm, which was then incorporated into subsequent judicial decisions, a cycle that has endured for decades and has, to this point, been impervious to the few weak attempts to rectify them.

Some of the contradictions in corporate law were expressly alluded to in Chapter 5, but readers may not have realized the breadth, depth, and scope of how pervasive the contradictions are. Other contradictions, which some readers may not have identified, were implicit. Both the explicit and implicit contradictions are brought together and organized in this chapter to provide perspective and demonstrate the chaotic, confused, and contradictory state of corporate law.

As seen in Chapter 1, with some exceptions that are not relevant here, property laws are mostly functions of common law. Similarly, as discussed in Chapters 2 and 3, agency law and trust law are mostly functions of common law. The contradictions that exist between property law and corporate law, between agency law and corporate law, and between trust law and corporate law are the result of attempts to apply the common law of property, the common law of agency, and the common law of trusts to corporations, which are governed mostly by corporate statutory law but are interpreted according to principles of common law. It is like mixing oil and water.

The contradictions in corporate law are even more prominent in the literature of the economic theory of the firm, which is examined in Chapter 11 and in more detail in *Economics, Capitalism, and Corporations: Contradictions of Corporate Law, Economics, and the Theory of the Firm.*

We begin by examining the contradictions between property law and corporate law, followed by an examination of the contradictions between agency law and corporate law, which is followed by a discussion of the contradictions between trust law and corporate law. Finally, the contradictions within corporate law itself will be discussed.

The contradictions of property law and corporate law

Contradiction 1: Shareholders are owners of corporations

Shareholders have been cast in judicial decisions as owners of the corporation. For example, in *Malone v. Brincat*,[2] the Delaware Supreme Court ruled

> One of the fundamental tenets of Delaware corporate law provides for a separation of control and ownership. The board of directors has the legal responsibility to manage the business of a corporation *for the benefit of its shareholder owners.*

Rulings such as these thus transform corporations into property that can be owned. But corporations fit no definition of property, as discussed in Chapter 1.

Judicial rulings that shareholders are owners of corporations are contradicted by corporate statutory law. First, no corporate statutory law makes shareholders owners of corporations the way statutory property law makes a real property owner the owner of real property by virtue of and evidenced by a deed, the owner of an automobile the owner of the automobile by virtue of and evidenced by the title, or a patent holder the owner of the patent by virtue of and evidenced by the awarding of the patent.

The owner of real property does not own the deed; she owns the real property described in the deed. The owner of an automobile does not own the title to the automobile; he owns the automobile described in the title. It is the automobile that is the personal property of the owner. The owner of a patent does not own the patent as a piece of paper but owns the rights to the object described in the patent. However, the owner of a share of stock owns the share of stock, whether certificated or not. The share itself is the property.

Even California General Corporation Law §§ 184 and 185 (see Chapter 5) do not make shareholders owners of corporations.

But what corporate statutory laws do not do is overshadowed by what corporate statutory laws actually do. The Delaware General Corporation Law explicitly makes shares the personal property of the shareholder subject to the provisions of the Uniform Commercial Code. A shareholder cannot both own shares and own the corporation. Shareholders as owners of shares excludes shareholders as owners of the corporation. The corporation is not the shares. The corporation exists independent of the shares, just as real property exists independent of the deed. (As seen in Chapter 5, the corporation exists prior to shares being issued.) To invest in the corporation would mean investing directly in the corporation, not purchasing the shares of the corporation, like partners invest in a partnership, each with a capital account.

Recall from Chapter 1 that one of the fundamental rights of private property is the right of exclusion. If shareholders owned the corporation, they would be able to exclude anyone else from entering or using the corporate property, including directors. Obviously, they do not have that right.

Chassagnon and Hollandts (2014) are to be lauded for their valiant "attemp[t] to prove that shareholders cannot legally be considered owners [of corporations]." Chassagnon and Hollandts regard the argument that "shares are considered to be the title deeds of a corporation and individuals who possess shares are consequently 'owners' of the subject of these title deeds, i.e., the corporation itself" as incorrect. (Unfortunately, they fall short in that attempt in that although they correctly state "a thorough analysis of [the] question shows that the firm – or more precisely the corporation – cannot be a subject of property," they do not actually provide a "thorough analysis" based on property law and corporate law to support their conclusion.

Contradiction 2: Shareholders are beneficial owners

State courts have ruled that shareholders are beneficial owners of corporations, although it is not clear exactly what they are beneficial owners of. (See discussion later in this chapter.) If shareholders are beneficial owners, then trust law must be applied. Shareholders being beneficial owners of corporate property is related to the contradictions of trust law and corporate law, discussed later. This section views the contradictions from the shareholders' side.

In *Malone v. Brincat*,[3] the Delaware Supreme Court ruled

> The board of directors has the legal responsibility to manage the business of a corporation *for the benefit of its shareholder owners*.

As seen in Chapter 3, beneficial owners of property have an absolute right to receive the income earned from the property (assuming there is an income). Beneficial owners have no control, rights, or influence over the trustee of the property, who invests the property solely for the benefit of the beneficial owner, not for the benefit of the trust. Yet, directors' primary duty is to the corporation:

> the fact of insolvency does not change *the primary object of the director's duties, which is the firm itself.* . . . Put simply, when a director of an insolvent corporation, through a breach of fiduciary duty, injures the firm itself, the claim against the director is still one belonging to the corporation. (Emphasis added.)[4]

The corporation-shareholder relationship is formed by contract when the corporation makes an offer to the public to sell the shares (a promise to deliver shares) and the public accepts the offer by purchasing shares. The purchase of shares from the corporation cannot and does not make the shareholder a beneficial owner of the corporation or the corporation's property.

The Delaware General Corporation Law is very explicit in explaining the rights of a corporation in relationship to property.

> Every corporation created under this chapter shall have power to. . . . *Purchase . . . own . . .* and to *sell . . .* or otherwise dispose of, . . . *all or any of its property and ass*ets, or any interest therein, wherever situated.
>
> (Emphasis added.)[5]

The New York Business Corporation Law provides that

> Each corporation . . . shall have power in furtherance of its corporate purposes. . . . (4) To *purchase . . . own . . .* [and] *sell . . .* all or any of its property [and] . . . To *make contracts*, give guarantees and incur liabilities."
>
> (Emphasis added.)[6]

According to the law of trusts, in order to create a beneficial owner, property must be delivered to the trustee by the trustor. In the case of corporations, property is delivered to the corporation when shares are purchased in an IPO. That makes the corporation the trustee by the law of trusts. Yet the corporation has never been ruled to be the trustee of shareholders' property. It is the directors who are referred to as trustees. Since shareholders do not deliver property to the directors, directors cannot be trustees.

Shareholders cannot be both owners of shares as personal property and beneficial owners of the corporation or corporate property. Having shareholders as beneficial owners and as owners of personal property is contradictory. The two are mutually exclusive.

If shareholders were beneficial owners, neither the corporation nor the directors would be permitted by law to sell or dispose of all the corporate property, thereby depriving the "beneficial owners," i.e., shareholders, of the benefit of the income derived from the property.

Recall from Chapter 3 that a beneficial owner has the right to the income produced from the trust property. Shareholders have no right to the income produced from the property of the corporation, thus negating any legal basis for considering shareholders as beneficial owners.

Contradiction 3: Shareholders are residual claimants

Shareholders have been ruled to be residual claimants, although no court has ever definitively ruled on what shareholders are residual claimants of. The corporation's property (assets)? Its earnings? Its equity (net assets)? The corporation itself? But putting that ambiguity aside for the moment, consider what it actually means to be a residual claimant.

In *Prod. Res. Group, L.L.C. v. NCT Group, Inc.*,[7] the Delaware Supreme Court ruled

> The reality that *creditors become the residual claimants* of a corporation when the equity of the corporation has no value does not justify expanding

the types of claims that the corporation itself has against its directors. . . .
In insolvency, creditors, as *residual claimants* to a definitionally-inadequate
pool of assets, become exposed to substantial risk as the entity goes for-
ward . . . the transformation of a creditor into a *residual owner* does not
change the nature of the harm in a typical claim for breach of fiduciary duty
by corporate directors.

(Emphasis added.)

If creditors "become the residual claimants" and, at the same time, a creditor is
"transform[ed] . . . into a residual owner," the logic is undeniable and inescapable.
By the transitive property of equality, residual claimants are residual owners. Yet
creditors are not owners of the corporation, residual or otherwise.

It matters not whether the residual claimant/residual owner is a creditor or a
shareholder. Residual claimants are residual owners. If only creditors became
residual owners, and shareholders remained beneficial owners, then creditors
rights would be subordinated to shareholder's rights.

So if shareholders are residual claimants, that means they are residual owners
(of something), and if they are residual owners, they cannot be beneficial owners.
Rulings by state courts that shareholders are beneficial owners and at the same
time (but in other cases) that shareholders are residual claimants are contradictory
and mutually exclusive.

Contradiction 4: Shareholders are investors in the corporation

State courts have ruled that shareholders are investors in corporations. In *Malone
v. Brincat*,[8] the court ruled "The board of directors has the legal responsibility to
manage the business of a corporation *for the benefit of its shareholder owners*.
Accordingly, fiduciary duties are imposed on the directors of Delaware corporations to regulate their conduct when they discharge that function."

An investment is something you expect to receive a return from. But to be an
investor requires an ownership interest in that which you invest in. Beneficial
owners cannot be investors. An investor can only invest in property to which
property rights are attached.

> An investment is an asset or item acquired with the goal of generating income
> or appreciation . . . an investment is a monetary asset purchased with the idea
> that the asset will provide income in the future or will later be sold at a higher
> price for a profit.[9]

If a shareholder is an investor in the corporation, she cannot be a beneficial owner,
thus negating any ruling that holds shareholders are beneficial owners. If a shareholder is a beneficial owner, she cannot be an investor, thus negating any ruling
that holds shareholders are investors. The two rulings are contradictory. They are
not only mutually exclusive; they actually cancel each other out so that neither
one is true, much like a collision of matter and anti-matter.

Corporate statutory law is emphatic that corporations own the assets (property) as seen, e.g., in the Delaware General Corporation Law and the New York Business Corporation Law. It is also quite clear that corporations can incur liabilities. Finally, the most well-known characteristic of corporations is what is known as shareholders' "limited liability," which means shareholders are not liable for the liabilities (debt) of the corporation, as discussed in Chapter 5.

The corporation owns the assets and owes the liabilities. Therefore, the corporation owns the net assets (assets – liabilities = net assets). Since the net assets are the equity, the corporation also owns the equity, not shareholders and not investors. If the corporation owns the equity, the shareholders cannot own the equity. Thus, the shareholders have no ownership interest in the corporation or its equity and are not investors in the corporation.

The contradictions of agency law and corporate law

State courts have ruled that there is an agency relationship between shareholders and directors, which need not be repeated here. Whenever an agency relationship exists, that automatically requires the application of agency law.

Recall from Chapter 2 that in order to create an agency relationship, the parties must exist – the principal and the agent. In order to create the agency relationship, the principal hires or appoints the agent to act on his or her behalf. An agent does not hire a principal. Furthermore, the principal does not transfer legal title of property to the agent. If any one of the requirements is absent, there can be no principal-agent relationship.

Corporate statutory law does not make directors agents of shareholders.

Contradiction 5: Shareholders are principals, and directors are agents of shareholders

State courts have ruled that shareholders are principals of directors by virtue of the fact that the courts have ruled that directors the agents of shareholders. Agents cannot exist without principals.

In order for there to be a principal-agent relationship, there must actually be principals and agents, and in order for there to be principals and agents, agency law must be complied with.

Recall from Chapter 5 the creation of shareholders and directors. In Delaware, once the certificate of incorporation is filed in accordance with the Delaware General Corporation Law, the corporation begins its existence.

> Upon the filing with the Secretary of State of the certificate of incorporation, executed and acknowledged in accordance with § 103 of this title, the incorporator or incorporators who signed the certificate, and such incorporator's or incorporators' successors and assigns, shall, from the date of such filing, be and constitute a body corporate, by the name set forth in the certificate, subject to § 103(d) of this title and subject to dissolution or other termination of its existence as provided in this chapter.[10]

The New York Business Corporation Law is more emphatic.

> Upon the filing of the certificate of incorporation by the department of state, the corporate existence shall begin.[11]

The corporation begins its existence and the governance structure is in place prior to the election of the directors by the shareholders. There are, in fact, no shares outstanding at this time, so there are no shareholders to elect the directors.[12] The duties of directors to the corporation begin when the certificate of incorporation is filed, if the directors are named in the certificate of incorporation, or when the incorporators meet and name the directors. Either way, directors exist prior to shareholders existing, and thus, directors cannot be agents of shareholders. This presents a conundrum that judges and those who promote the theory that directors are agents of shareholders, upon which the entire economic "theory of the firm" is built, cannot resolve.

First, corporate directors exist before shareholders exist. If directors are agents of shareholders, they are agents of non-existent principals, which is not allowed under agency law. Second, only directors can issue shares. When a corporation is formed, there are no shareholders, only directors. Directors then issue the shares, creating shareholders. Thus, agents are creating the principals! This is, of course, contrary to agency law and nullifies the theory that directors are agents of shareholders, which also undermines the economic theory of the firm.

For example, in Delaware,

> If the persons who are to serve as directors until the first annual meeting of stockholders have not been named in the certificate of incorporation, the incorporator or incorporators, until the directors are elected, shall manage the affairs of the corporation and may do whatever is necessary and proper to perfect the organization of the corporation, including the adoption of the original bylaws of the corporation and the election of directors.[13]

Rulings that shareholders are investors in the corporation contradict rulings that there is a principal-agent relationship between shareholders and directors. If shareholders are investors in the corporation, then they cannot be principals. Being an investor requires transferring property (cash) to the object the investor is investing in and acquiring an ownership interest in the object the investor is investing in. If shareholders are principals of directors, they cannot be investors in the corporation. These rulings contradict each other and cancel each other out.

Contradiction 6: Directors owe a fiduciary duty to shareholders

State courts have ruled that directors owe a fiduciary duty to shareholders because directors are agents of shareholders.

For example, in *Loft v. Guth*,[14] the Delaware Court of Chancery stated,

> It has frequently been said by this court and clearly enunciated by the Supreme Court of this State in *Lofland et al. v. Cahall, Rec'r.*,[15] that the directors of a

corporation stand in a fiduciary relation to the corporation *and its stockholders*. (Emphasis added.)

In *Lofland et al. v. Cahall, Rec'r*, the Supreme Court of Delaware held that there are "well settled *principles of equity applicable to trustees* and . . . the *fiduciary relation existing between directors and stockholders*." (Emphasis added.)

Directors cannot be trustees of shareholders under "well settled principles of equity applicable to trustees" because that would be contrary to the laws of trusts. Trust law requires that the property be delivered to the trustee. Shareholders do not deliver property to the directors. They "deliver" property to the corporation when they purchase the shares in an IPO.

The Delaware Supreme Court revisited the issue in 1998. In *Malone v. Brincat*,[16] the court ruled

> An underlying premise for the imposition of fiduciary duties is a separation of legal control from beneficial ownership. Equitable principles act in those circumstances to protect the beneficiaries who are not in a position to protect themselves. One of the fundamental tenets of Delaware corporate law provides for a separation of control and ownership. The board of directors has the legal responsibility to manage the business of a corporation *for the benefit of its shareholder owners. Accordingly*, fiduciary duties are imposed on the directors of Delaware corporations to regulate their conduct when they discharge that function.
>
> The directors of Delaware corporations stand in a fiduciary relationship not only to the stockholders but also to the corporations upon whose boards they serve. The director's *fiduciary duty to both* the corporation and its shareholders has been characterized by this Court as a triad: due care, good faith, and loyalty.
>
> (Emphasis added.)

But the court erroneously interpreted fiduciary duty as characterized by the duty of loyalty, even though they are not the same under the Delaware General Corporation Law, as seen in Chapter 5, since corporations have the option of eliminating the fiduciary duty but not the duty of loyalty.[17] Note also that fiduciary duties to shareholders are imposed on directors by the courts because shareholders are owners of the corporation: "The board of directors has the legal responsibility to manage the business of a corporation *for the benefit of its shareholder owners. Accordingly*, fiduciary duties are imposed on the directors."

By "beneficial owners," the Delaware Supreme Court meant that shareholders are owners of the corporation, which is made explicit by its statement that

> One of the fundamental tenets of Delaware corporate law provides for a separation of control and ownership. The board of directors has the legal responsibility to manage the business of a corporation for the *benefit of its shareholder owners*. Accordingly, fiduciary duties are *imposed* on the directors of Delaware corporations.

The court did not say how fiduciary duties are imposed on the directors of Delaware corporations. It is certainly not by the Delaware General Corporation Law, which must mean they are imposed by the court. But the court is not empowered to create such duties contrary to unambiguous statutory law. The Delaware Supreme Court was, simply, wrong.

Another problem with the *Malone* ruling is that Delaware corporate law does not make shareholders the owners of the corporation. It is simply not true that "Delaware corporate law provides for a separation of control and ownership," and nowhere in Delaware General Corporation Law is there any section or paragraph that "provides for a separation of control and ownership." Ownership of the corporation does not even exist in the Delaware General Corporation Law. It is an unjustifiable construct created with smoke and mirrors.

Delaware Supreme Court decisions that hold Delaware corporate law makes shareholders the owners of a corporation, that Delaware corporate law provides for the separation of ownership and control, or that Delaware corporate law makes directors trustees, or agents, of shareholders have no foundation in the Delaware General Corporation law and are contradicted by property law and agency law. If, as Robé (2011, 2019) and others have concluded, shareholders do not own the corporation, the Delaware Supreme Court was wrong. The Delaware Supreme Court expanded and interpreted Delaware corporate law well beyond the plain language of the statute. Can there be any question why corporate law is in such a state of confusion when courts cannot make up their minds, and their rulings conflict with statutory law?

Several things must be noted here. First and foremost, this section of the Delaware General Corporation Law does not impose on directors a fiduciary duty to stockholders. Contrary to the court's ruling, nowhere in the entire statute is a fiduciary duty to stockholders imposed on directors.

The astute reader can no doubt immediately see the problem, a direct result of the director-as-agent-of-shareholders theory. The problem is that, whether the initial directors are named in the certificate of incorporation or are elected by the incorporators at the organization meeting, there are directors prior to shares being issued and prior to there being any shareholders. One might ask, therefore, how directors can be agents of shareholders when shareholders do not exist. How can directors owe a fiduciary duty to shareholders or a duty of loyalty to shareholders when shareholders do not exist? How is a fiduciary duty to shareholders implemented when there are no shareholders?

Directors as trustees and directors as agents are contradictory and mutually exclusive. As with the others, they, in fact, cancel each other out.

The contradictions of trust law and corporate law

Contradiction 7: Directors are trustees of shareholders

State courts have ruled that directors are trustees of shareholders. That automatically requires the application of trust law.

Recall from Chapter 3 first that in order to create a trust relationship, three separate parties must exist – the trustor, the trustee, and the beneficial owner. Creating a trust requires the transfer of property (cash) from the trustor to the trustee. Second, recall that if any one of the required elements is missing, there cannot be a trust, meaning no trustor, no trustee, and no beneficial owner.

If shareholders are investors in the corporation, directors cannot be trustees. Thus, these rulings are contradictory and cancel each other out.

If shareholders are owners of the corporation, directors cannot be trustees. Thus, these rulings are contradictory and cancel each other out.

The contradictions of duties of directors

Contradiction 8: Directors must exercise business judgment vs. fiduciary duties of directors

A director who owes a fiduciary duty to a shareholder, either as an agent or a trustee, must fulfill that duty according to the fiduciary duties imposed by agency law or trust law. Upon the establishment of a principal-agent relationship, a fiduciary duty of the agent to the principal arises as a matter of law.[18] That is, "an agent has a fiduciary duty to act loyally for the principal's benefit in all matters connected with the agency relationship."[19] This is, of course, the duty the director owes to the corporation. But in a trust relationship, "the fiduciary nature of the relationship between the trustee and the beneficiary demands an unusually high standard of ethical or moral conduct." The Supreme Court of Utah has emphasized that "trustees are charged as fiduciaries with one of the highest duties of care and loyalty known in the law."[20]

However, directors of a corporation need only exercise "business judgment" in order to "maximize profits" or "maximize shareholder wealth." The business judgment rule, as it is known, requires directors to exercise "business judgment," which merely requires directors to exercise "a *minimum level of care* . . . in arriving at the decision"[21] and "in *good faith and in the honest belief* that the action taken was in the best interest of the company." (Emphasis added.)[22] And here we witness a contradiction in the duties directors owe and the standards by which directors are judged in complying with those duties. Directors cannot owe a fiduciary duty while at the same time being required only to exercise "business judgment."

Chapter summary

This chapter summarized and organized the contradictions between property law and corporate law, between agency law and corporate law, between trust law and corporate law, and within corporate law.

Shareholders have been ruled to be owners of the corporation. Yet they have been ruled to be beneficial owners.

Shareholders have been ruled to be investors in the corporation. Yet they have been ruled to be beneficial owners.

Shareholders have been ruled to be residual claimants. Yet they have been ruled to be beneficial owners.

Shareholders have been ruled to be residual owners. Yet they have been ruled to be beneficial owners.

Shareholders have been ruled to be principals. Yet they have been ruled to be beneficial owners.

Directors have been ruled to be agents of shareholders. Yet they have been ruled to be trustees of shareholders.

Directors owe a fiduciary duty but need only exercise business judgment.

All these rulings are contradictory.

- Shareholders cannot be investors in the corporation and at the same time be beneficial owners.
- Shareholders cannot be residual claimants and at the same time be beneficial owners.
- Trustees cannot be agents and at the same time be trustees.
- Agency law cannot be applied to the shareholder-director relationship because directors exist as a matter of statutory law, independent of shareholders.
- Trust law cannot be applied to directors because directors do not take legal title to the property. The corporation has legal title to the property.
- Directors cannot be trustees since property is not delivered to them but to the corporation.
- The law of agency and the law of trusts cannot apply at the same time.
- Shareholders cannot be beneficial owners if they are principals.

All these contradictions have been built into the social construction and cultural power of corporations and shareholders, examined in the next chapter.

Notes

1 "Corporate law" encompasses both corporate statutory law and corporate common law, as well as judicial rulings interpreting corporate law and the rights and duties of corporations, directors, shareholders, and investors.
2 Malone v. Brincat, 722 A.2d 5, 8 (DE, 1998).
3 Malone v. Brincat, 722 A.2d 5, 8 (DE, 1998).
4 Prod. Res. Group, L.L.C. v. NCT Group, Inc., 863 A.2d 772 (DE, 2004).
5 Delaware General Corporation Law, § 122(4).
6 New York Business Corporation Law, Sec. 202.
7 Prod. Res. Group, L.L.C. v. NCT Group, Inc., 863 A.2d 772 (DE, 2004).
8 Malone v. Brincat, 722 A.2d 5, 8 (DE, 1998).
9 Investment. *Investopedia*. www.investopedia.com/terms/i/investment.as.
10 Delaware General Corporation Law, § 106.
11 New York Business Corporation Law, Sec. 403.
12 Delaware General Corporation Law, § 106. "Commencement of corporate existence. Upon the filing with the Secretary of State of the certificate of incorporation, executed and acknowledged in accordance with § 103 of this title, the incorporator or incorporators who signed the certificate, and such incorporator's or incorporators' successors and assigns, shall, from the date of such filing, be and constitute a body corporate, by

the name set forth in the certificate, subject to § 103(d) of this title and subject to dissolution or other termination of its existence as provided in this chapter."

13 Delaware General Corporation Law, § 107.
14 Loft v. Guth, 2 A.2d 225 (Del. Ch. 1938).
15 Lofland et al. v. Cahall, Rec'r., 13 Del. Ch. 384 (DE, 1922).
16 Malone v. Brincat, 722 A.2d 5, 8 (DE, 1998).
17 Delaware General Corporation Law, § 102(b)(7).
18 Am Jur 2d, Agency, § 192.
19 Am Jur 2d, Agency, § 192.
20 Pepper v. Zions First Nat'l Bank, N.A., 801 P. 2d 144, 151, 1990 (UT, 1990).
21 Am Jur 2d, Corporations, § 1451.
22 Citron v. Fairchild Camera & Instrument Corp., 569 A.2d 53 (DE, 1989).

Bibliography

Cases

Citron v. Fairchild Camera & Instrument Corp., 569 A.2d 53 (DE, 1989).
Lofland et al. v. Cahall, Rec'r., 13 Del.Ch. 384, 118 A. 1 (Del. Ch. 1922).
Loft v. Guth, 2 A.2d 225 (Del. Ch. 1938).
Malone v. Brincat, 722 A.2d 5 (Del. 1998).
Pepper v. Zions First Nat'l Bank, N.A., 801 P. 2d 144, 151, 1990 (UT, 1990).
Prod. Res. Group, L.L.C. v. NCT Group, Inc., 863 A.2d 772 (DE, 2004).

Authors and publications

Chassagnon, V., & Hollandts, X. (2014). Who are the owners of the firm: Shareholders, employees or no one? *Journal of Institutional Economics*, 10(1), 47–69. doi: 10.1017/S1744137413000301.
Robé, J-P. (2011). The legal structure of the firm. *Accounting, Economics, and Law – A Convivium*, 1(1), 1–85. doi: 10.2202/2152-2820.1001.
Robé, J-P. (2019). The shareholder value mess (and how to clean it up). *Accounting, Economics, and Law—A convivium*, 9(3), 1–27. doi: 10.1515/ael-2019-0039.

Part III

Sociology, culture, and corporations

Sociology and culture are inseparably intertwined with corporations, directors, owners of shares, investors in shares, and the contradictions of their relationships with each other. Our understanding of corporations, directors, owners of shares, and investors in shares has been twisted by their social construction and cultural reproduction. This section first discusses the social construction of corporations, directors, owners of shares, and investors in shares, then proceeds to a discussion of the cultural reproduction of corporations, directors, owners of shares, and investors in shares. It then proposes a reconstruction of corporations, directors, owners of shares, and investors in shares. This will set the stage for an examination of the corporation as a legal person and the theory of the firm in Part IV.

7   The social construction of the social reality of directors, owners of shares, and investors in shares

Introduction

In the previous chapters, I presented a rigorous analysis of property law, agency law, and trust law; their application to corporate law; and the relationship between corporations, directors, owners of shares, and investors in shares. What the analysis shows is that, as a matter of law, shareholders do not and cannot own corporations, directors are not and cannot be agents or trustees of shareholders, and owners of shares are not and cannot be investors in the corporation. But state and federal judges, legal scholars, and economists have hijacked the discourse concerning corporations and the relationship between corporations, directors, owners of shares, and investors in shares and constructed a reality of the roles and relationships between corporations, directors, owners of shares, and investors in shares inconsistent with property law, agency law, trust law, and corporate law.

In this chapter, I examine the social construction of the social reality of the roles and relationships between corporations, directors, owners of shares, and investors in shares as constructed by economists, legal scholars, and state and federal judges and the consequences of that construction. In Chapter 9, I present a reconstruction of the relationship between corporations, directors, owners of shares, and investors in shares that is more consistent with principles of common law, property law, agency law, and corporate law.

In the following sections, I first consider the social construction of the social reality and symbolic power of corporations, investors, and directors. I then discuss how corporations and the relationship between corporations, directors, owners of shares, and investors in shares are socially constructed contrary to law and the relevance of such social construction to symbolic power.

The social construction of social reality

Subjective social reality must be juxtaposed against "objective" reality. Subjective social reality vs. objective reality is the subject of multitudinous books and papers in philosophy and sociology. However, an in-depth discussion of social reality vs. objective reality is beyond the scope of this book. Sufficient for purposes of this book is merely to identify and distinguish objective reality from social reality in simplest terms before moving on to an investigation of the social construction of corporations, directors, owners of shares, and investors in shares.

Objective reality is, e.g., gravity or the speed of light, which exists outside of human (*homo sapiens*) existence. Gravity and the speed of light existed prior to the existence of humans. Gravity and the speed of light do not change as a consequence of human intervention or existence. Gravity and the speed of light will continue to exist when humans cease to exist.

Social reality, on the other hand, exists only because humans exist.[1] Social reality is what humans have constructed and determined to exist. Social reality did not exist prior to human existence and will cease to exist when humans cease to exist. Human institutions such as government, nations, empires, prisons, political parties, private property, and the church (this is not to invite a theological or religious debate) were constructed by humans for purposes that are not relevant here. Social reality is constructed, evolves, and is transformed over time. Our perception and understanding of reality are thus socially constructed.

While there are others, the three major works expounding on the social construction of social reality are Berger and Luckmann's *The Social Construction of Reality* (1966) and Searle's *The Construction of Social Reality* (1995) and *Making the Social World: The Structure of Human Civilization* (2010).

Although the three titles sound similar, i.e., merely rearranging the word order, they are not identical. The difference between a

> "construction of something social" and a "social construction of something" is subtle: in the first case the emphasis is on the *social*, the reality of which is being constructed . . . in the second case the stress is on *reality* . . . that is being constructed – hence, subjectively by the human mind.
> (Mattessich, 2013, p. 98)

Berger and Luckmann and Searle approach the subject from different perspectives; i.e., one focuses on the thing that is constructed and the other on how it is constructed. Naturally, there are significant overlaps and the following sections focus on the similarities.

Social constructs are inseparable from power. Consider, e.g., the power of the government or the church, both of which are social constructs. Yet within those constructs, there is inherent power that finds expression in every aspect of society. Thus, the social construction of reality inevitably and unavoidably introduces the concept of power, in particular symbolic power (discussed in greater detail in Chapter 8), which is exercised when the dominant power is capable of imposing meaning as legitimate while concealing the relations that are the basis of its power (Bourdieu & Passeron, 1990; Bourdieu, 1993).

The social construction of reality

According to Berger and Luckmann (1966), our perceptions of institutions such as government, religion, family, economics, law, and corporations are determined by how the institutions have been constructed by society in the past and how they continue to be formed and reformed in the present. Institutions are experienced as reality because they predate individual existence, but not human existence in totality. While institutions may appear objective, they are, nevertheless, a human constructed objectivity (p. 60) and thus subject to alteration. That is, institutions form our perceptions of the institutions.

Berger and Luckmann (1966) also maintain that what is known about human society and institutions includes the processes by which that knowledge comes to be socially established as reality. More than just forming our perceptions of society and institutions, however, institutions imply history and, more important, control. "Institutions, also, by the very fact of their existence control human conduct by setting up predefined patterns of conduct which channel it in one direction as against the many other directions that would theoretically be possible" (Berger & Luckmann, 1966, p. 55). The transmission of institutional meanings implies control and is attached to the institutions themselves and administered by the transmitting personnel (p. 71). The mere act of transmitting a message within a relationship of a pedagogic communication such as in law schools and schools of economics imposes a social definition of the institutions and relationships.

There are various methods by which institutional meanings can be transmitted. One method is through pedagogy, a method in which Bourdieu figures prominently and is discussed in the following chapter. Another method by which institutional meanings can be transmitted is through authoritative court rulings. A third method by which institutional meanings can be transmitted is through legislation. A fourth method is through legal scholarship. In the case of corporations, directors, owners of shares, and investors in shares, all four methods are evident.

The construction of social reality

Searle (1995, 2010) emphasizes language and the role of language in shaping our understanding of the social world and institutions. That is, language creates institutional reality such as money, government, and corporations. Institutional facts are created by performative utterances. Performative utterances are declaratory speech acts (although they can be written) in which the state of affairs represented by the utterance is brought into existence by the utterance and becomes an institutional fact (p. 34), a characteristic not unlike something out of the Wizarding World.[2]

Searle uses money as an example. Money is an institutional reality because it is declared to be money by an institution with the power to determine what constitutes money. The United States paper currency states, "This [Federal Reserve] note is legal tender for all debts, public and private." Bitcoin, on the other hand, is not legal tender. It is useless to ask, "How do you know this note is legal tender?" The answer is, because the U.S. Treasury says it is legal tender, it is declaring it to be legal tender rather than announcing it as an empirical, objective fact. However, if everyone stops believing money is money, it ceases to function as money and eventually ceases to be money. The meaning and function of a Federal Reserve note is thus socially constructed by a declarative act.

Another example Searle uses is that of private property rights. The moment that all or most of the members of society refuse to acknowledge private property rights, he states, private property rights, and therefore private property, cease to exist. Recall, for example, the 1917 Bolshevik Revolution and the 1959 Cuban Revolution, in which private property was prohibited.

The creation of institutional facts is a matter of imposing a status with those facts and, with that status, a function and a power. "[I]n general the creation of a status-function is a matter of conferring some new power" (Searle, 1995, p. 95).

This, of course, leads to a consideration of corporations, directors, owners of shares, and investors in shares and their relationships, and the status function and the power conferred upon them by their social construction. Although the relationships between corporations, directors, owners of shares, and investors in shares do not exist in isolation, they are considered separately in the following sections for analytical purposes.

Social construction of social reality and symbolic power

Symbolic power is created, well, symbolically. That is, symbolic power is not directly created by the use of, e.g., military force or police power or by law, although symbolic power may be enforced by military force, police power, or law. Symbolic power is created by the establishment of institutions, symbols, relationships, and status.

The social construction of corporations

The social construction of corporations is considered briefly here merely to provide context for the analysis of the social construction of directors, owners of shares, and investors in shares.

Corporations unquestionably fall into the category of a social construct. There was a time when corporations did not exist, and now, because of human actions, they do exist. Corporations are a social construct, but the social construction of corporations does not concern us here other than to provide context. A corporation is "a creature of the law, known to it under a given name, whose essence is in that name, and *the social identity it implies*" (Bratton, 1989). (Emphasis added.)

As discussed in Chapter 5, corporations are created by statute. But in addition to being created by statute, they have also been socially constructed by the courts to be legal persons. Corporations are not legally created as legal persons; i.e., corporate statutes do not declare corporations to be legal persons. The concept of corporations as legal persons is a creature of judicial decisions. The extent to which corporations as legal persons have legal significance in addition to social significance and how the significance contributes to the contradictions of property law, agency law, and corporate law will be discussed in Chapter 10.

Corporations have economic, political, and social power, but that power is a result of the social construction of corporations. The legal, economic, political, and social power of corporations is a closed system. The power of corporations is a consequence of the legal construction of corporations, and the social construction of the corporation is a consequence of the legal construction of corporations. Both the legal power and the social construction of corporations are consequences of the institutionalization of the contradictions of property law, agency law, and corporate law, discussed in the previous chapters. It is a closed system between judicial rulings and academia.

The creation of a corporation is accomplished by a speech (written) act – filing articles of incorporation. Corporations are thus created *ex nihilo* (Searle, 2010; Huber, 2018). A corporation is an institutional fact even though the articles of incorporation are written because they are declaratory speech (Searle, 1995, 2010). Subsequent to their legal creation, corporations have been socially constructed by judicial declarations to be "legal persons," "fictitious persons," or "artificial persons."

For Searle, the corporation is a social entity constructed, defined, and instantiated through social practice, which developed as a social institution in history and through the interactions of law, economics, and politics. Humans invented the corporation. It is, therefore, an artificially created fictional institution with "real" social effects and consequences.

For example (although not the first, it is the most well known), the United States Supreme Court ruled in *County of Santa Clara v. Southern Pac. R. Co. People of The State of California*[3] that corporations are persons.

> The court does not wish to hear argument on the question whether the provision in the Fourteenth Amendment to the Constitution, which forbids a State to deny to any person within its jurisdiction the equal protection of the laws, applies to these corporations. We are all of opinion that it does.

Thus, with no analysis, the Supreme Court unquestionably established corporations as legal persons, i.e., a judicial construction thereafter incorporated into their social construction.

The social construction of directors, owners of shares, and investors in shares

The social construction of owners of shares

There are legal relationships between directors, owners of shares, and investors in shares, but the legal relationships are not created directly by law. The legal relationships are derivative of the creation of corporations. In other words, directors, owners of shares, and investors in shares and their relationships are not created directly by corporate statutory law, as is the corporation, but are created as a result of the corporation first being created with its directors, and subsequently created by the corporation issuing shares, thus creating owners of shares and investors in shares. There can be no directors, owners of shares, or investors in shares without there first existing a corporation. (Note, however, that the legal creation of a corporation is itself a social construct.)

Likewise, there are socially constructed relationships between directors, owners of shares, and investors in shares, but those relationships are not socially constructed directly. Shareholders and directors must first exist legally before they can be constructed socially. While there is a legal relationship between corporations and shareholders, between corporations and directors, and between shareholders and directors, the relationships between shareholders, directors, owners of shares, and investors in shares have subsequently and consequently been transformed and socially constructed contrary to property law, agency law, and trust law.

Social constructs encompass political constructs. Even Berle and Means (1991) considered corporations to be political constructs. Power is inherent in political constructs. The definition of primacy, whether director or shareholder, is "the state of being first (as in importance, order, or rank)."[4] Substitute the word "power" for "primacy" and you have a different perspective of director primacy vs. shareholder primacy – directors' powers vs. shareholders' powers. Status is inherently related to power and primacy.

The creation of a corporation automatically creates legal, social, and political relationships of people to the corporation and to each other – shareholders (both as owners of shares of the corporations and as investors in the shares) and directors – without whom corporations, while existing, cannot operate except minimally to appoint directors and issue shares as discussed in Chapter 5. The automatic creation of shareholders and directors occurs when incorporators appoint directors and directors issue shares to the public. Creating shareholders and directors by issuing shares does not require a separate legal procedure. It is a matter of contract[5] between private parties, one real (shareholders) and one fictitious (the corporation). Once the shares are issued and the relationships established, the power struggle begins.

However, it is how those relationships have been socially constructed after the legal creation of the corporation, shareholders, and directors to which we must now turn our attention since the social construction of those relationships has unleashed a barrage of theories – all wrong – on the economic theory of the firm discussed in Chapter 11 and in *Economics, Capitalism, and Corporations: Contradictions of Corporate Law, Economics, and the Theory of the Firm.*

Shareholders as principals and directors as agents are inseparable, being two sides of the same coin, so to speak. According to the laws of agency, there cannot be one without the other. Yet that is what courts have done by declaring directors to be agents of shareholders although it is impossible for shareholders to be principals, and shareholders have not been directly declared to be principals. However, shareholders as principals and directors as agents are considered separately here to emphasize their respective social constructions.

Social construction of shareholders as owners of corporations

Owners of shares have been judicially and socially constructed to be owners, beneficial owners, and residual owners of the corporation, contrary to the property laws, agency laws, and trust laws. Shares are the personal property of the shareholders, subject to all laws pertaining to personal property. While the concept of shareholders as owners of the corporation was discussed in detail in Chapter 5, the diverse theories of shareholders as owners of the corporation are collected here for convenience.

Shareholders as Owners of the Corporation

The common view is that shareholders are the owners of the corporation (Robé, 2011, 2019). In 1998, for example, the Delaware Supreme Court ruled

> One of the fundamental tenets of Delaware corporate law provides for a separation of control and ownership. The board of directors has the legal responsibility to manage the business of a corporation for the benefit of its *shareholder owners*.
>
> (Emphasis added.)[6]

But, of course, as seen in Chapter 5, Delaware corporate *statutory* law does not provide for the separation of control and ownership because it does not provide for the ownership of the corporation by shareholders. It is only the court's common law interpretation that shareholders own corporations.

Shareholders as Beneficial Owners of the Corporation

To see shareholders as beneficial owners of a corporation, we turn again to the Delaware Supreme Court. The Delaware Supreme Court ruled on the issue in 1998 in *Malone v. Brincat*:[7] "An underlying premise for the imposition of fiduciary duties is a separation of legal control from *beneficial ownership*."

Shareholders as Residual Owners of the Corporation

Shareholders have been judicially ruled to be residual owners by virtue of their being ruled residual claimants since the only way to have a claim is to have an ownership interest in the claim. But the concept of shareholders as residual owners and residual claimants originated in economic literature and is a favorite of the theory of the firm, as discussed in Chapter 11. The proponents of the theory of the firm are adamant that shareholders are residual owners and residual claimants.

The doctrine of shareholders as residual claimants infiltrated judicial reasoning. To see shareholders as residual owners of a corporation, we once more turn to the Delaware Supreme Court. In *Applebaum v. Avaya, Inc.*,[8] the court stated, "Shares of stock are issued to provide a verifiable property interest for the *residual claimants* of the corporation." (Emphasis added.)

When we examine property law and trust law and their relationship to corporate law, it is quite easy to ascertain that a shareholder as the owner of a corporation is contradictory to the shareholder as a residual owner, which is contradictory to the shareholder as a beneficial owner. Shareholders are never described as owners of corporations in corporate statutory law. Therefore, shareholders are only judicially and socially constructed to be owners of corporations: first, in terms of authority by judicial declaration and subsequently reinforced by pedagogical communications of the university and researchers.

This social construction of shareholders as owners of corporations, whether actual, beneficial, or residual, creates a class distinction and a shared false consciousness of power in the class of shareholders that has no basis in law.

Social construction of shareholders as principals

Owners of shares have been judicially and socially constructed as principals of directors of the corporation as a result of directors being judicially and socially constructed as agents of shareholders, contrary to agency laws and again reinforced by the pedagogical communications of economists and legal scholars. Judicial decisions do not actually declare shareholders to be principals, and corporate statutory laws certainly do not. It is judicial decisions that declare directors to be agents. Thus, the concept of shareholders as principals is implicit in judicial decisions. Judicial decisions are then again reinforced by academic research that socially constructs shareholders to be principals.

The arguments concerning shareholders as principals of directors need not be repeated here. But we must remain cognizant of the fact that none of the requirements of agency law exist in the shareholder-director relationship. As a matter of law and logic, before there can be agents of shareholders, there must be shareholders. Directors exist before shareholders exist.

The idea that shareholders are principals of directors is a judicial and social construction that has no basis in law. Like shareholders as owners of corporations, shareholders as principals of directors is a social construction that imbues shareholders with a shared false consciousness of power that has no basis in law.

Social construction of shareholders as investors in the corporation

Shareholders have been judicially and socially constructed as investors in the corporation. Arguments surrounding shareholders as investors in the corporation need not be repeated here.

That shareholders are considered to be investors in corporations permeates legal, economic, and finance literature as well as judicial opinions in state and federal courts. But the concept of shareholders as investors in the corporation has, for reasons unknown, never been examined or even questioned. This section questions the validity of the assumption that shareholders are investors in corporations. It will be examined in greater depth in *Economics, Capitalism, and Corporations: Contradictions of Corporate Law, Economics, and the Theory of the Firm.*

It is not possible that shareholders are investors in the corporation. To see this, consider the following definition of "investment":

> An investment is an asset or item acquired with the goal of generating income or appreciation . . . an investment is a monetary asset purchased with the idea that the asset will provide income in the future or will later be sold at a higher price for a profit.[9]

The problem, of course, is that you do not put money into a corporation when you purchase shares, even in an IPO. You put money into the shares when you purchase the shares from the corporation or in the market. Purchasing shares in an IPO is like purchasing an automobile. You do not put money into the dealership. You put it into the automobile and acquire rights in the form of warranties. If you later sell the automobile, then the money paid by the purchaser goes to you, not the dealership. Similarly, if you put money into a corporation when you purchase shares in the market, where most of the trading in shares takes place, the money would go to the corporation. It does not. It goes to the previous owner of the shares.

Furthermore, you do not even earn a profit from the corporation. You earn a profit from the shares, as confirmed by the California Supreme Court in 1941 in *Miller v. McColgan*.[10]

> It is fundamental, of course, that the corporation has a personality distinct from that of its *shareholders*, and that the latter *neither own the corporate property nor the corporate earnings. The shareholder simply has an expectancy in each, and he becomes the owner of a portion of each only when the corporation is liquidated by action of the directors or when a portion of the corporation's earnings is segregated and set aside for dividend payments on action of the directors in declaring a dividend . . . the dividends . . . represent a yield of the wealth invested in his legally recognized property interest, the shares of stock. Thus . . . the source of the income is the corporate stock, the legally created property interest owned* by [the shareholder] and without which he would not receive this benefit. The shares of stock are the immediate source of the income to the recipient. . . . It is this fundamental differentiation which underlies the well-established principle that 'the property of the shareholders in their respective shares is distinct from the corporate property.
>
> (Emphasis added.)

The California Supreme Court in *Miller v. McColgan* relied on the United States Supreme Court ruling in *Rhode Island Hospital Trust Co. v. Doughton*.[11]

> The owner of the shares of stock in a company is not the owner of the corporation's property. He has a right to his share in the earnings of the corporation, as they may be declared in dividends arising from the use of all *its* property. In the dissolution of the corporation he may take his proportionate share in what is left, after all the debts of the corporation have been paid and the assets are divided in accordance with the law of its creation. But he does not own the corporate property. . . . The interest of the shareholder entitles him to participate in the net profits earned by the bank in the employment of *its* capital, during the existence of its charter, in proportion to the number of his shares; and, upon its dissolution or termination, to his proportion of the property that may remain of the corporation after the payment of its debts. This a distinct independent interest or property, held by the shareholder like any other property that may belong to him.
>
> (Emphasis added.)

Since shareholders have no ownership rights in the corporation in which they own shares, they are not investors in the corporation. They are investors in the shares of the corporation that they own and from which they have an expectation (not a right) to receive dividends and share in the profit of the corporation in the employment of *its* capital.

For those who may need further convincing, consider this. When you own your own business, you put money into that business expecting to earn a profit, i.e., you invest in the business. If you enter into a partnership, either initially or by purchasing another partner's share, you put money into the partnership expecting to earn a profit, i.e., you invest in the partnership and own a percentage of the partnership, as evidenced by an account in the partnership reflecting your investment.

However, it was shown in Chapter 5 that shareholders are undeniably not owners of the corporation. If you own shares of stock, you do not own $x \div n\%$ of the corporation. If shareholders do not own the corporation, they are not investors in the corporation. Shareholders as investors in a corporation is merely a social construction not based on any legal principle. Shareholders, by the laws of property, are not and cannot be investors in the corporation.

The social construction of directors as agents and trustees

The social construction of directors as agents of shareholders

As noted earlier, federal and state judicial decisions have explicitly decreed that directors are the agents of shareholders. The arguments concerning directors as agents of shareholders need not be repeated here.

This theory of directors as agents of shareholders has been reinforced by economists, beginning with Jensen and Meckling (1976).

> Since the relationship between the stockholders and manager of a corporation fit the definition of a pure agency relationship it should be no surprise to discover that the issues associated with the "separation of ownership and control" in the modern diffuse ownership corporation are intimately associated with the general problem of agency.[12]

The problem is, of course, as the reader now knows, the relationship between the stockholders and managers (i.e., directors) of a corporation does *not* fit the definition of a pure agency.[13] Thus, the social construction of directors as agents of stockholders is contrary to the law of agency. Nevertheless, theories of the firm inform and undergird corporate law and have "sunk into the fabric of academic corporate law" (Bratton, 1989).

While, by statute, directors have a fiduciary duty to the corporation (however undefined that may be), the fiduciary duty of directors to shareholders was shown in Chapter 5 to be the result of making shareholders principals, contrary to agency law. If shareholders are not principals, directors are not agents, and therefore, directors owe no fiduciary duties to shareholders.

The social construction of directors as trustees of shareholders

Directors have been judicially and socially constructed as trustees of shareholders. The arguments concerning directors as trustees of shareholders need not be repeated here.

Just as constructing directors to be agents of shareholders necessarily transforms shareholders into principals, constructing directors to be trustees of shareholders necessarily transforms shareholders into beneficial owners. The construct of shareholders as beneficial owners was discussed earlier. This section focuses on the flip side of the coin, directors as trustees of the "beneficial owners."

But first, if directors are trustees of shareholders' property (money), who is the trustor? As seen in Chapter 3, to establish a trust requires a trustor to transfer property (money) to the trustee. But the shareholder does not transfer money to the director-trustee. She "transfers" it to the corporation when she purchases shares in an IPO. Furthermore, the trustor cannot be the beneficial owner. None of the factors required to create a trust are present when a person purchases shares either from the corporation in an IPO or in the market.

If directors are trustees of shareholders, shareholders must be beneficial owners. But, as discussed earlier, shareholders cannot be beneficial owners; therefore, directors cannot be trustees.

More problematic is the fact that directors have been constructed by judicial declarations as owing a fiduciary duty as trustees to shareholders. The judicial declarations have also been reinforced by economists and legal scholars.

While, by statute, directors have a fiduciary duty to the corporation (however undefined that may be), the fiduciary duty of directors to shareholders was shown in Chapter 5 to be the result of making directors trustees, contrary to trust law. If directors cannot be trustees, directors owe no fiduciary duties to shareholders.

Our understanding of corporations, directors, owners of shares, and investors in shares and their relationships with each other have been formed by centuries of common law and judicial and social (mis)construction. Yet the formation of our understanding of corporations, directors, owners of shares, and investors in shares and their relationships with each other was not done systematically but based on unjustified premises and unproven assumptions. As a result, we are left with a social construction of corporations, directors, owners of shares, and investors in shares completely contrary to property law, agency law, and corporate statutory law.

In the case of corporations, common law principles constructed shareholders as owners of corporations and directors as agents and trustees of shareholders. Some of those principles were codified into statutes; others were not, but all were assimilated into judicial decisions.

The dominant culture of shareholders as owners of corporations and principals of directors grants to shareholders a class status and power not supported by law.

Chapter summary

Twenty-seven years ago, Green (1993) argued that the significance of the metaphor of shareholders as the owners of the corporation and the principal-agent fiduciary relationship of shareholders and directors is undeniable and continues to shape society. It is even more significant today than it was in 1993.

Shareholders believe and accept that they own the corporation, that they are investors in corporations, and that directors are their agents. Directors believe and accept that shareholders own the corporation and that they are the agents and trustees of shareholders. The judicial declarations that shareholders own corporations and that directors are the agents and trustees of shareholders have been reinforced by economists and legal scholars to such an extent that society as a whole believes and accepts them. None of this has any validity in law.

State legislatures are not blameless. The reluctance of state legislatures to clarify corporate law is evident in statutes that fail to recognize the impossibility of shareholders owning corporations according to the laws of private property, or fail to acknowledge that directors are not agents or trustees of shareholders according to agency law and trust law, contributes to the social (mis)construction of the relationships between directors, owners of shares, and investors in shares. The social construction of shareholders as owners of the corporation with directors as their agents or trustees confers upon shareholders a class status and the power associated with that class status that have no basis in law, with both the class and the power of the class created by the social construction founded on contradictions. Furthermore, the social construction of directors as the agents or trustees of shareholders imposes a duty on directors that violates agency law and trust law.

Mizruchi and Hirschman (2010) argue that selective interpretations of Berle and Means were disseminated into academic disciplines that developed a socially constructed character in which the selective interpretations that fit the collectively accepted views became the prevailing interpretation.

While academia alone was not responsible (judges and lawyers bear much of the responsibility), the contribution of academia to the social construct of corporations, and thus of directors, owners of shares, and investors, was a significant factor in the establishment of the orthodox canon, with those who opposed the orthodoxy that shareholders owned corporations and directors were agents of shareholders were, like Galileo and Copernicus, ignored if not castigated outright. The orthodox canon became an ideology that Baker (2005) defines as "a view of the world from the perspective of a ruling class" and "a set of perspectives which reflect the interests of particular social groups."

The ideology thus signifies Bourdieu and Passeron's (1990) symbolic power. Veblen (1923) recognized this almost a century ago.

> In recent times absentee ownership has come to be the main and immediate controlling interest in the life of civilised men . . . absentee ownership has visibly come to be the main controlling factor in the established order of things . . . [and] has now plainly come to be *the prime institutional factor that underlies and governs the established order of society*.

Notes

1   This is not intended to discount the social life of other living organisms, but the focus here is only on *homo sapiens*.

2 The Wizarding World is a fantasy media franchise and shared fictional universe based on the Harry Potter novels by J. K. Rowling.
3 County of Santa Clara v. Southern Pac. R. Co. People of The State of California, 118 U.S. 394 (1886).
4 Merriam-Webster. www.merriam-webster.com/dictionary/primacy.
5 Not to be confused with the "nexus of contracts" theory of the theory of the firm.
6 Malone v. Brincat, 722 A.2d 5, 8 (Del. 1998).
7 Malone v. Brincat, 722 A.2d 5, 8 (Del. 1998).
8 Applebaum v. Avaya, Inc., 812 A.2d 880 (2002).
9 Investment. www.investopedia.com/terms/i/investment.asp.
10 Miller v. McColgan, 17 Cal.2d 432 (CA, 1941).
11 Rhode Island Hospital Trust Co. v. Doughton, 270 U.S. 69, 81, 46 S.Ct. 256 70, L.Ed. 475 (1926).
12 Neither Jensen nor Meckling were lawyers, so their inaccurate analysis of agency law can be excused.
13 "Manager" must be taken to mean "director" since shareholders have no relationship to officers or anyone further down the ladder of authority.

Bibliography

Cases

Applebaum v. Avaya, Inc., 812 A.2d 880 (2002).
County of Santa Clara v. Southern Pac. R. Co. People of The State of California, 118 U.S. 394 (1886).
Malone v. Brincat, 722 A.2d 5, 8 (Del. 1998).
Miller v. McColgan, 17 Cal.2d 432 (CA, 1941).

Authors

Baker, C.R. (2005). What is the meaning of "the public interest"? Examining the ideology of the American public accounting profession. *Accounting, Auditing & Accountability Journal*, 18(5), 690–703.
Berger, P.L., & Luckmann, T. (1966). *The social construction of reality*. New York: Random House.
Berle, A.A., & Means, G.C. (1991). *The modern corporation and private property* (2nd ed.). New York: Routledge.
Bourdieu, P. (1993). *The field of cultural production: Essays on art and leisure* (R. Johnson, Ed). New York: Columbia University Press.
Bourdieu, P., & Passeron, J-C. (1990). *Reproduction in education, society and culture* (2nd ed.) (Richard Nice, Trans). Thousand Oaks, CA: Sage Publications.
Bratton, W.W. (1989). The new economic theory of the firm: Critical perspectives from history. *Stanford Law Review*, 41, 1471–1527. Retrieved from https://scholarship.law.upenn.edu/faculty_scholarship/833.
Green, R.M. (1993). Shareholders as stakeholders: Changing metaphors of corporate governance. *Washington and Lee Law Review*, 50(4), 1409–1421. Retrieved from https://scholarlycommons.law.wlu.edu/wlulr/vol50/iss4/4.
Huber, W.D. (2018). The Supreme Court's subversion of the constitutional process and the creation of persons *ex nihilo*. *International Journal for the Rule of Law, Courtroom Procedures, Judicial Linguistics & Legal English*, 2(1), 53–72. Retrieved from https://papers.ssrn.com/sol3/papers.cfm?abstract_id=2841825.

Huber, W.D. (2020). *Economics, capitalism, and corporations: Contradictions of corporate law, economics, and the theory of the firm*. London: Routledge.

Jensen, M.C., & Meckling, W.H. (1976). Theory of the firm: Managerial behavior, agency costs and ownership structure. *Journal of Financial Economics*, 3, 305–360. doi: 10.1016/0304-405X(76)90026-X.

Mattessich, R.V. (2013). *Reality and accounting: Ontological explorations in the economic and social sciences*. London: Routledge.

Mizruchi, M.S., & Hirschman, D. (2010). The modern corporation as social construction. *Seattle University Law Review*, 33(4), 1065–1108. Retrieved from https://digitalcommons.law.seattleu.edu/cgi/viewcontent.cgi?article=1011&context=sulr.

Searle, J. (1995). *The construction of social reality*. New York: The Free Press.

Searle, J. (2010). *Making the social world: The structure of human civilization*. London: Oxford University Press.

Veblen, T. (1923). *Absentee ownership and business enterprise in recent times: The case of America*. New York: B.W. Huebsch.

8 Power and the cultural reproduction of directors, owners of shares, and investors in shares

Introduction

It is axiomatic (i.e., it is not only accepted as true without proof, but also cannot be proven untrue) that corporations have economic and political power.[1] But directors, owners of shares, and investors in shares also have power, which is derived from the institutionalization of the contradictions of corporate law.

Culture is what one must know or believe in order to function in a manner consistent with the members of the society to which she belongs. Without culture, human society would not exist. Culture is the institutionalized response to society's socially constructed reality. It is a set of control mechanisms used to impose meaning on experience (Geertz, 1973).

Culture as a control mechanism denotes power; i.e., control must be maintained by those who have the power to do so. Power is a social construct and is culturally reproduced through pedagogical acts (Bourdieu & Passeron, 1990).

Power is a social construct. As a social construct, power is inseparable from political constructs. It is also inseparable from culture. Power is an essential and fundamental force in all social relationships, and how power is perceived is an important element of culture and serves culturally relevant goals (Torelli & Shavitt, 2010). The social construct of power creates and maintains culture, and in turn, the social construct of power is reproduced by culture which necessarily includes the power of directors, owners of shares, and investors in shares.

Mizruchi and Hirschman (2010) argue that selective interpretations of Berle and Means (1992) were disseminated into academic disciplines which then developed a socially constructed character in which the selective interpretations that fit the collectively accepted views became the prevailing interpretation. An indisputable example of the selective interpretation of Berle and Means being disseminated into academic disciplines is Berle's statement in the preface to the revised edition that "directors . . . are not agents of the stockholders" (p. xxi). Yet the entire theory of the firm is built on the assumption that directors are agents of stockholders.

While academia alone was not responsible (judges and lawyers share much of the responsibility), the contribution of academia to the social construct of corporations, and thus of directors, owners of shares, and investors in shares, was a significant factor in the establishment of the orthodox canon that shareholders owned corporations and directors were agents of shareholders, and those who opposed the orthodoxy were ignored.

Much attention has been given to the power of corporations in legal, economic, sociological, and political literature, as established by their social constructions built on the contradictions of property law, agency law, and corporate law. Much less attention has been given to the cultural reproduction of the power of corporations and none given to the cultural reproduction of the power of directors, owners of shares, and investors in shares.

The previous chapter discussed the social construction of directors, owners of shares, and investors in shares. This chapter discusses the power and cultural reproduction of directors, owners of shares, and investors in shares – the progeny of the institutionalization of the contradictions of property law, agency law, and corporate law, which protects and reinforces class divisions and defines the parameters of the power struggle between shareholders and directors as well as between shareholders and society.

The power I discuss in this chapter is not that of corporations but of directors, owners of shares, and investors in shares vis-à-vis not just corporations, but society. As discussed in Chapter 7, the relationship of shareholders, directors, owners of shares, and investors in shares to each other and to the corporation has been socially constructed to portray relationships that do not, and cannot, exist legally but for the contradictions in corporate law. That social construction of power reverberates throughout society.

Culture and the reproduction of power

Cultural power is symbolic power. Symbolic power is exercised when the dominant power is capable of imposing meaning as legitimate while concealing the power relations that are the basis of its power (Bourdieu & Passeron, 1990; Bourdieu, 1993). Thus, culture is a control mechanism by which the dominant power imposes meaning on experience (Geertz, 1973).

Ideology is inherent in cultural power. Ideology is defined as "a system of ideas and ideals, especially one which forms the basis of economic or political theory and policy; The set of beliefs characteristic of a social group or individual."[2] Ideology is a set of perspectives that reflects the beliefs of particular social groups (Baker, 2005). Ideology thus reflects Bourdieu's symbolic power, and as symbolic power, it is transmitted via pedagogical acts.

Owners of the shares of a corporation have been transformed into owners of the corporation, and investors in shares have been transformed into investors in the corporation, something even Dumbledore couldn't accomplish.[3] That transformation has effectively conferred upon and reproduced a cultural power on shareholders built on a contradictions and invalid assumptions.

Corporations, like governments, are created by statute, as opposed to the common law creation of partnerships by simple agreement. While governments are created by constitutions (the United States or each of the 50 states) or charters from a higher level of government (cities created by charters from state governments), the principle is the same as corporations that are created by statutory authorization. The constitutions or charters of governments confer on the respective governments certain legal powers, i.e., legal rights, subsequently enforced by the police power of the state.

The legal act of creating a corporation pursuant to state law automatically creates directors and, once the directors issue shares, creates owners of shares, and investors in shares. The statutes, along with the corporate charters or articles of incorporation, confer on corporations certain legal powers (rights), such as the right to sue and to buy, own, and sell property. The legal and economic power of corporations is unquestionable.

The act of creating directors, owners of shares, and investors in shares also creates legal powers (rights) and duties of directors, owners of shares, and investors in shares. Yet the powers of directors, owners of shares, and investors in shares is not only legal, but also cultural, as a result of their social construction built on the contradictions of property law, agency law, and corporate law that reverberate throughout society.

In order to understand the cultural reproduction of power, it is necessary to recall from Chapter 7 that the creation of institutional facts is a matter of imposing a class status with those facts and, with that status, power. "In general, the creation of a status-function is a matter of conferring some new power" on the class (Searle, 1995). Of course, maintaining the class status naturally maintains the power of the class status.

Attempting to cast shareholders as owners of and investors in the corporation is merely an attempt to clothe shareholders with a power they would not legally have but for the institutionalization of the contradictions of corporate law.

The pedagogy of law schools and the pedagogical acts of the judiciary merely serve to reinforce the false narrative. "In law schools economic approaches have informed competing theories that emphasized principal agent relationships, transaction costs, the 'nexus' of contracts, or property rights as central to understanding the nature and purpose of the business enterprise" (Orts, 2013).[4]

As long as the culture of shareholders as owners of the corporation, directors as agents of shareholders, and shareholders as investors in the corporation continues to be reproduced by pedagogical acts – law schools, judicial decisions – then the same contradictions will continue to dominate society.

The cultural power of shareholders was reinforced by Friedman's dictum "The corporate responsibility of corporations is to maximize shareholder wealth" (paraphrased). When a noted economist says the duty of corporations is to maximize profits (shareholder wealth), it has a great influence on both shareholders and society. They actually believe it and accept it.

The first institutional fact is the corporation. The creation of a corporation thus imposes a status function, and therefore power, on the corporation. Concurrent with the creation of a corporation (with a slight time lag) is the creation of directors and shareholders, the second institutional fact, along with their status functions and power.

The cultural reproduction of symbolic power

There are, of course, different types of power – military power, for example. Culture does not reproduce military power. Rather, military power reproduces itself. Symbolic power is reproduced by culture. Culture is the institutionalized response to society's socially constructed reality. It is a set of control mechanisms, and therefore an expression of power, used to impose meaning on experience (Geertz, 1973).

Symbolic power is culturally reproduced through pedagogical activities that transmit institutional meanings (Bourdieu & Passeron, 1990; Bourdieu, 1993). Pedagogical activities occur in a classroom or by other means. In the case of legal relationships, that transmission is accomplished by court rulings, which, when they are issued by the highest court of a particular jurisdiction, are authoritative even when they contradict common or statutory law.

Symbolic violence

Bourdieu's (1993) concept of symbolic violence, while much more complex, basically holds that symbolic violence is committed by the establishment of a canon, a universally valued cultural inheritance established in order to guarantee the continued reproduction of its legitimacy by those with power to do so. The mere fact of transmitting a message in a pedagogic communication imposes a social definition. In the case of corporations, shareholders, and directors, the established canon is shareholders own corporations and are investors in corporations, and directors are their agents.

The social definition, i.e., the social construction, of shareholders as owners of the corporation with directors as their agents confers upon shareholders a class status and, with the class status, the power associated with the class, with both the class and the power of the class created by the social construction founded on contradictions. "If shareholders are treated as corporation 'owners', their dominant position is validated with respect to firm governance" (Chassagnon & Hollandts, 2014).

Chapter summary

In this chapter, it was shown that the cultural power and the cultural reproduction of the power of shareholders, directors, owners of shares, and investors in shares have been created and reinforced on the foundation of the social construction of the contradictions of property law, agency law, and corporate law. It is those contradictions that keep those in power, in power.

Notes

1 For those who question the political power of corporations, in 2010 the United States Supreme Court ruled in *Citizens United v. Federal Election Commission* (558 U.S. 310), that corporations are allowed to donate to political campaigns.
2 Oxford English Dictionary. www.lexico.com/en/definition/ideology.

3 Dumbledore is the headmaster of Hogwarts School of Witchcraft and Wizardry in the Wizarding World from the Harry Potter books.
4 The "nexus of contracts" is examined in *Economics, Capitalism, and Corporations: Contradictions of Corporate Law, Economics, and the Theory of the Firm.*

Bibliography

Cases

Citizens United v. Federal Election Commission, 558 U.S. 310 (2010).

Authors and publications

Baker, C.R. (2005). What is the meaning of "the public interest"? Examining the ideology of the American public accounting profession. *Accounting, Auditing & Accountability Journal*, 18(5), 690–703.

Berle, A.A., & Means, G.C. (1991). *The modern corporation and private property* (2nd ed.). New York: Routledge.

Bourdieu, P. (1993). *The field of cultural production: Essays on art and leisure* (R. Johnson, Ed). New York: Columbia University Press.

Bourdieu, P., & Passeron, J-C. (1990). *Reproduction in education, society and culture* (2nd ed.). (Richard Nice, Trans). Thousand Oaks, CA: Sage Publications.

Chassagnon, V., & Hollandts, X. (2014). Who are the owners of the firm: Shareholders, employees or no one? *Journal of Institutional Economics*, 10(1), 47–69. doi: 10.1017/S1744137413000301.

Geertz, C. (1973). *The interpretation of cultures*. New York: Basic Books.

Mizruchi, M.S., & Hirschman, D. (2010). The modern corporation as social construction. *Seattle University Law Review*, 33(4), 1065–1108. Retrieved from https://digitalcommons.law.seattleu.edu/cgi/viewcontent.cgi?article=1011&context=sulr

Orts, E.W. (2013). *Business persons: A legal theory of the firm*. London: Oxford University Press.

Searle, J. (1995). *The construction of social reality*. New York: The Free Press.

Torelli, C.J., & Shavitt, S. (2010). Culture and concepts of power. *Journal of Personality and Social Psychology*, 99(4), 703–723. doi: 10.1037/a0019973.

9 Reconstructing corporations, directors, owners of shares, and investors in shares

Introduction

Having deconstructed corporations, directors, owners of shares, and investors in shares in the previous chapters, they must now be reconstructed. This chapter proposes reconstructions of corporations, directors, owners of shares, and investors in shares that is consistent with principles of property law, agency law, and statutory corporate law.

As they are legal entities, reconstructing corporations legally would require revising the corporate statutory laws of each jurisdiction: an exercise in futility, not something reasonably possible in the foreseeable future and perhaps not completely necessary. Corporations can, and must, be judicially reconstructed to be consistent with property law, agency law, and corporate statutory law. Furthermore, corporations can, and must, be socially reconstructed.

Directors, owners of shares, and investors in shares have judicial and social constructions. However, the social, as well as the judicial, constructs of corporations, directors, owners of shares, and investors in shares and their relationships have been perverted. The judicial and social construction of directors, owners of shares, and investors in shares and their relationships must be reconstructed to conform to property law and agency law. There is, of course, overlap, and one certainly cannot exist without the others. However, each is considered separately in order to place each one in the proper context and perspective.

Reconstructing corporations

First and foremost, judges must cease and desist from treating corporations as being owned by shareholders. Whether corporations are legal persons or not, a subject examined in the next chapter, is not determinative of whether corporations are owned by shareholders. The owner of a corporation is determined solely by property law and corporate statutory law, and according to property law and corporate statutory law, shareholders do not and cannot own the corporation.

Corporations thus have no owners, which makes them autonomous "legal persons," which in turn makes them dangerous since, without owners, they are relatively free of many of the social constraints that operate in society as a whole. Their excesses can only be reined in by courts and legislatures, both of which have proven reluctant to resist the established orthodox canon.

Are ownerless corporations in the best interest of society? "In any society it is an irrefutable fact that the society must allocate scarce goods and resources" (Geertz, 1973). The allocation of scarce resources is accomplished by the owners of the resources of production, which are now corporations. But deciding what is in society's best interest is a political process. Friedman (1970) states, "[T]he basic reason why the doctrine of 'social responsibility' involves the acceptance of the socialist view that political mechanisms, not market mechanisms, are the appropriate way to determine the allocation of scarce resources to alternative uses." Yet there is a difference between the market mechanism as the appropriate way to determine the allocation of scarce resources and the political process for determining what is in the best interest of society. Friedman himself admits that using its resources to engage in activities designed to increase its profits is only acceptable when the corporation "stays within the rules of the game, which is to say, engages in open and free competition without deception or fraud." But it is only the political process that decides on the "rules of the game," not the market.

When courts rule, contrary to the property law, agency law, and corporate statutory law, that corporations are owned by shareholders, "the rules of the game" are skewed not just in favor of shareholders against other "players" in "the game" (Velasco, 2010), but also in favor of corporations that labor under the false assumption that they have a duty to maximize profits and shareholder wealth.

When ownership of corporations by shareholders is removed from the equation, the balance of rights is more equitable. Balancing rights is a political process, and corporate law is an expression of the political process. Property law and corporate statutory law do not make shareholders the owners of corporations. When courts rule that shareholders own corporations, the political process is subverted, and the institutionalization of the contradictions guarantees their social construction.

Rulings that uphold shareholders as owners of corporations misplace corporate duties and responsibilities and affect how society socially constructs corporations and their relationships to shareholders. If shareholders own corporations, corporations have duties to shareholders not owed to non-shareholders, as enshrined by the Friedman (1970) doctrine: "There is one and only one social responsibility of business – to use its resources and engage in activities designed to increase its profits." Friedman explains what he means by responsibility: "A [director] is an employee of the *owners of the business*. He has direct responsibility to his employers." (Emphasis added.) It is abundantly clear from the Friedman doctrine that corporations have a duty to increase their profits for the owners of the corporation – the shareholders.

Friedman's doctrine is thus based on the (false) assumption that shareholders own the corporation. But what if shareholders do not own the corporation? Friedman's doctrine falls apart on two fronts. First, if shareholders do not own the corporation, the corporation then has no duty to the owners to use its resources and engage in activities designed to increase its profits for its owners. This in turn leads to two consequences. One, the corporation has no duty to increase its profits at all, at least not beyond what is necessary to sustain its operations in perpetual existence. Two, the corporation has no duty to owners for anything because there are no owners.

Second, if corporations have no duties to owners to use their resources and engage in activities designed to increase their profits for their owners, then the corporation's responsibilities are not controlled by what it owes to owners. A corporation's potential duties to non-owners take on greater weight and importance.

While judges must cease and desist rendering opinions that rest on the assumption that shareholders own corporations, legal scholars and economists must abandon their theories that shareholders own corporations.

Reconstructing shareholders

Corresponding to the reconstruction of corporations is the reconstruction of shareholders. Since shareholders have been considered as more than just owners of shares, i.e., as owners of the corporation, reconstructing shareholders is considered separately. Owners of shares are discussed later.

First, as with reconstructing corporations, judges must cease and desist from treating shareholders as owners of corporations. As discussed in Chapter 1, property owners have rights *vis-à-vis* the rest of the world; e.g., the right to use their property, the right of exclusion, etc. Those rights stem first from common law and second from statutory property law. Owning property also gives the property owner the right to appoint or hire agents and trustees who may sell the property and who administer the property for a beneficiary. Shareholders have none of those rights over the corporation in which they own shares because they do not own the corporation.

It is widely, although not exclusively, accepted by courts that shareholders do not own the assets of the corporation, but it is just as widely, although not exclusively, accepted by courts that shareholders own the corporation. Rulings that shareholders own corporations have no legal theoretical basis. Such rulings distort the law and the relationships between corporations and shareholders and grant rights to shareholders that they are not legally entitled to.

Second, legal scholars and economists must abandon their theories that shareholders own corporations.

Reconstructing directors

First, judges must cease and desist from ruling that directors are agents of shareholders. Without question, directors are agents of the corporation and owe certain duties to the corporation. But when judges rule that directors are agents of shareholders, they impose on directors fiduciary duties to shareholders that directors cannot owe according to the laws of agency. Such rulings contradict the laws of agency and cannot be legally justified.

Second, judges must cease and desist from ruling that directors are trustees of shareholders. When judges rule that directors are trustees of shareholders, they impose on directors duties to shareholders that directors cannot owe according to the laws of trusts. Such rulings contradict the laws of trusts and cannot be legally justified.

Equally important, legal scholars and economists must abandon legal and economic theories built on agency theory. Such theories are built on contradictions of property law and agency law. Legal and economic scholarship that sustains invalid legal principles has done nothing to advance our knowledge and understanding of corporations and their relationships to shareholders and directors.

Reconstructing owners of corporations

Judges, legal scholars, economists, and society must distinguish between owners of corporations and owners of shares of the corporation. Shareholders are, of course, loath to admit they do not own the corporation in which they own shares. But the simple fact that they own shares does not make them owners of the corporation. Shareholders own shares. Period. Nothing more.

Owners of shares have rights. Those rights are governed by corporate statutory law, the articles of incorporation of the corporation in which they own shares, and the class of stock of the corporation in which they own shares, which dictate such things as their voting rights and dividend rights. The articles of incorporation and the class of stock do not make owners of shares owners of the corporation. Thus, the rights of owners of shares are more limited than they would be if they owned the corporation.

Legal scholars and economists must abandon their theories of the corporation that rest on shareholders being owners of the corporation.

Reconstructing investors in shares

As proven in the previous chapters, the total property of the corporation, i.e., the total assets, is not owned by the shareholders. The property (assets) is owned by the corporation. The liabilities are owed by the corporation. If the total assets are owned by the corporation, and the liabilities are owed by the corporation, then the net assets are owned by the corporation. Since the equity of the corporation is the net assets, it is the corporation that owns the equity of the corporation. If the corporation owns the equity, the equity is not owned by the shareholders. If the shareholders do not own the equity, they are not investors in the corporation since investment requires ownership rights.

Shareholders are not investors in the corporation. They are investors in the shares. Therefore, judges must cease and desist ruling that shareholders are investors in corporations. Ruling that shareholders are investors in the corporation gives shareholders rights that they are not legally entitled to according to the laws of property and corporate statutory law.

Legal scholars and economists must abandon their theories of the corporation that rest on shareholders being owners of the corporation.

Chapter summary

This chapter emphasized the need to reconstruct corporations, shareholders, directors, owners of shares, and investors in shares, both legally and socially. Corporate law defines the relative rights and duties of corporations, directors, and shareholders and mediates the contractual and bargaining relationships among directors and shareholders (Baysinger & Butler, 1985). But the current legal construction of corporations, shareholders, directors, owners of shares, and investors is distorted, based on contradictions between property law, agency law, trust law, and statutory corporate law.

I call on judges to cease and desist ruling that corporations are owned by shareholders, that directors are agents or trustees of shareholders, and that shareholders are investors in the corporation rather than investors in shares. Federal courts must use state law when ruling on corporations so there is very little flexibility in federal courts. If state courts rule that shareholders own corporations, directors are agents of shareholders, and shareholders are investors in the corporation, federal courts must follow suit.

I call on economists and legal scholars to abandon theories of the firm that are built on contradictions of property law, agency law, trust law, and statutory corporate law.

Veblen (1923) wrote,

> absentee ownership [of corporations] has visibly come to be the main controlling factor in the established order of things [and] has now plainly come to be *the prime institutional factor that underlies and governs the established order of society*. At the same time and in the same degree it has, as a matter of course, become the chief concern of the constituted authorities in all the civilised nations.

If absentee ownership is the prime institutional factor that underlies and governs the established order of society and has become the chief concern of the constituted authorities in all the civilized nations, then ownerless corporations are an even greater concern.

Bibliography

Baysinger, B.D., & Butler, H.N. (1985). Corporate governance and the board of directors: Performance effects of changes in board composition. *Journal of Law, Economics, & Organization*, 1(1), 101–124. Retrieved from www.jstor.org/stable/764908.
Geertz, C. (1973). *The interpretation of cultures*. New York: Basic Books.
Friedman, M. (1970, Sept. 13). The social responsibility of business is to increase its profits. *New York Times Magazine*, p. 2.
Veblen, T. (1923). *Absentee ownership and business enterprise in recent times: The case of America*. New York: B.W. Huebsch.
Velasco, J. (2010). Shareholder ownership and primacy. *University of Illinois Law Review*, (3), 897–956. Retrieved from https://heinonline.org/HOL/LandingPage?handle=hein.journals/unilllr2010&div=27&id=&page=.

Part IV

Corporatehood, the corporation as a legal person, and the theory of the firm

For over a century and a half, corporations have been considered to be "legal persons" in the United States with rulings by the United States Supreme Court beginning before the Civil War that recognized corporations as legal persons. (They were considered as fictitious persons or artificial persons, particularly in Europe, for much longer.) Chapter 10 is concerned with the corporation as a legal person, also referred to as "corporate personhood." Chapter 11 then briefly highlights the fallacious assumptions of the nature of the firm and the theory of the firm, topics explored in greater depth in *Economics, Capitalism, and Corporations: Contradictions of Corporate Law, Economics, and the Theory of the Firm.*

10 Corporatehood and the corporation as a legal person

History and origin of the corporation as a legal person

The history and origin of corporations fill volumes. But only a brief excursion into the history and origin of corporations is necessary to establish the context of the modern doctrine of the corporation as a legal person and its relevance to directors, owners of shares, and investors in shares, particularly in the United States. The corporation as a legal person is a social construction.

The term "corporation" comes from considering a business firm as a "body corporate" and the "joint-stock company" from a form of business where investors of capital received transferable shares in the firm (Gevurtz, 2011).

A "legal person" is simply an association or organization of more than one person that is recognized in law as having separate and distinct legal rights. A neighborhood book club, for example, is not a legal person. It has no legal rights as a club. There was a time in English and American legal history, for example, that married women had no separate and distinct legal rights. They were not recognized as legal persons. Under the doctrine of *coverture*, a married woman could not own property, control her own earnings, or even be the guardian of her underage children upon the death of her husband.[1] But, as seen in Chapter 5, corporations have separate and distinct legal rights and thus are legal persons.

Unless otherwise noted, this section is adapted from Seymour, Jr. (1903).

The corporation as a "legal person" had its origins centuries ago in common law. Seymour cites an anonymous author in the *Encyclopedia Britannica* that defines a corporation as "an association of persons which the law treats in many respects as if it were itself a person."

Seymour traces the elementary beginnings of the corporation to ancient times with Roman law and religious corporations, in particular the Roman Catholic Church, for the purpose of holding title to property.[2] The elementary corporate system was carried over into England after the Norman Conquest in 1066. The concept of the corporation as a person, according to Seymour, was first mentioned by Pope Innocent IV in the 13th century, although its importance was not "discovered" until the end of the 15th century (the dates are somewhat uncertain); he stated, "the corporation is a person; but it is a person by fiction and only by fiction."

Corporations existed because three or more persons united for a common purpose, which made it necessary to determine by what right such associations acquired the power to act as one person for the purpose of owning property. The corporate system, although common law, became codified in civil law in the sense that the king could create a corporation by issuing a royal charter. The corporation created by the charter could do only what the king had granted it the power to do in the charter. Although created by royal charter, only the Parliament could terminate a corporation.

> By the early part of the sixteenth century the *Persona Ficta* [fictitious person] was firmly embedded in the laws of England.
>
> (Seymour, citing Lord Coke)[3]

In 1819, just 30 years after the ratification of the United States Constitution, in *Trustees of Dartmouth College v. Woodward*, Supreme Court Chief Justice Marshall considered a corporation as existing only in law. Specifically,

> An aggregate corporation, at common law, is a collection of individuals, united into one collective body under a special name and possessing certain immunities, privileges and capacities in its collective character which do not belong to the natural persons composing it. Among other things, it possesses the capacity of perpetual succession, and of acting by the collected vote or will of its component members, and of suing and being sued in all things touching its corporate rights and duties. It is, in short, *an artificial person, existing in contemplation of law* and endowed with certain powers and franchises which, though they must be exercised through the medium of its natural members, are yet *considered as subsisting in the corporation itself as distinctly as if it were a real personage.*
>
> (Emphasis added.)[4]

Corporations as we know them began to assume greater importance in the middle of the 17th century, necessitated by new discoveries and the colonization of North and South America and Asia, which required large amounts of capital investment. The advantages of incorporation became increasingly recognized for carrying out the risky ventures associated with exploration and colonization where the promoters were unwilling to risk more than a limited amount of capital.

Gevurtz (2011) describes the impact of the English East India Company on the development of the modern corporation. The English East India Company was formed in 1600. Initially, joint stock in the English East India Company lasted only for a specific voyage. After the voyage was successfully completed, the profits would be distributed among the investors. Eventually, the joint stock became permanent for the funding of continuing operations, and investors who did not want to wait until completion of a specific voyage were able to sell their shares, which gave rise to stock markets. After the founding of the English East India Company, the Dutch East India Company was formed. The success of the English and Dutch East India Companies, in turn, spurred the formation of joint-stock companies by other European countries.

According to Blackstone, it was by that time established that the creditors of the corporation should look only to the corporation's assets for satisfaction of their claims.[5] Thus, it was unquestionably established in law that corporations had a separate legal existence, and there existed at that period no liability of the shareholders other than what might attach to their original contribution.

At the beginning of the 19th century, corporations began multiplying more rapidly as a consequence of the English industrial revolution.

Corporatehood and the corporation as a legal person in the United States

The English system of corporations naturally carried over into the American colonies, and thus the United States, beginning in 1789 with the adoption of the U.S. Constitution.

In the United States, only the individual states have power over corporations – formation, governance, and termination. The federal government only has power over corporations when federal law is involved, such as under the securities acts or if it involves interstate commerce. The Tenth Amendment of the Constitution states, "The powers not delegated to the United States by the Constitution, nor prohibited by it to the States, are reserved to the States respectively, or to the people." Power over corporations was not delegated to the United States by the Constitution except insofar as interstate commerce is involved. Article I, Section 8 of the Constitution states, "The Congress shall have Power. . . . To regulate Commerce with foreign Nations, and among the several States, and with the Indian Tribes."

In the United States, the issue of the corporation as a person arose initially in disputes concerning taxation and the jurisdiction of courts over corporations for purposes of lawsuits and taxation.

The corporation as a legal person in judicial opinions

The corporation as a person is generally considered to begin officially with the U.S. Supreme Court's ruling in *County of Santa Clara v. Southern Pac. R. Co. People of The State of California*,[6] a case arising in 1886.

> The Court's Santa Clara decision is considered as the watershed moment in American legal history for the personification of the corporation in its own right and can be considered the beginning of corporate personhood as we understand it today, namely in terms of the application of the Bill of Rights to corporations.
>
> (Kaeb, 2015)

However, the *Santa Clara* ruling was not actually a ruling in the normal sense of the word. Several actions were brought in the state of California for the recovery of certain county and state taxes claimed to be due from the Southern Pacific Railroad Company and the Central Pacific Railroad Company under assessments made by the California State Board of Equalization upon their respective franchises, roadways, roadbeds, rails, and rolling stock. The issue on appeal to the Supreme Court in *Santa Clara* was whether the defendant was deprived of equal protection under the laws when it was taxed by the state of California.

Chief Supreme Court Justice Waite is reported to have said prior to oral argument that

> The court does not wish to hear argument on the question whether the provision in the Fourteenth Amendment to the Constitution, which forbids a State to deny to any person within its jurisdiction the equal protection of the laws, applies to these corporations. We are all of opinion that it does.

The ruling in *Santa Clara* that corporations are persons entitled to rights under the Fourteenth Amendment did not actually appear in the text of the case, but only in the headnotes prepared by the court reporter (Piety, 2015). Yet it has been treated as precedent for over 130 years.

The Fourteenth Amendment to the Constitution was adopted in 1868 after the Civil War ended in 1865. It states,

> All persons born or naturalized in the United States, and subject to the jurisdiction thereof, are citizens of the United States and of the State wherein they reside. No State shall make or enforce any law which shall abridge the privileges or immunities of citizens of the United States; *nor shall any State deprive any person of life, liberty, or property, without due process of law; nor deny to any person within its jurisdiction the equal protection of the laws.*
> (Emphasis added.)[7]

But *Santa Clara* was not actually the first case to rule that corporations are persons. Two decades prior to *Santa Clara*, prior to the adoption of the Fourteenth Amendment, the Supreme Court had also considered corporations to be persons. In *Louisville, Cincinnati & Charleston R. Co. v. Letson* (1844),[8] the court held that "*a corporation created by a state . . . seems to us to be a person*, though an artificial one." (Emphasis added.)

In *Louisville, Cincinnati & Charleston R. Co.*, the Supreme Court was confronted with the question of the jurisdiction of federal courts to hear a lawsuit when one of the members of the defendant corporation was the state of South Carolina. It must be kept in mind that *Louisville* was decided prior to the adoption of the Fourteenth Amendment. Several quotes are worth repeating in their entirety because they express the applicability of agency law and limited liability as well as the social construction of corporations.

> A corporation, or to speak in the more accurate and scientific language of the continental [European] jurists, a "juridical person," is, as I have said, a

creature of the law, known to it under a given name, whose essence is in that name, and *the social identity it implies* – whose capacities are defined in its charter – whose will is expressed under its seal – whose unity is affected by no change in the parts that compose it – and whose existence survives the deaths of its members.

(Emphasis added.)

It is true that *a corporation acts by the agency of natural persons, but no principle is more familiar than that the acts of an agent, acting within the limits of his agency, are referred to the principal, and regarded as the acts of the principal only, and not of the agent.* A corporation sues and defends suits by attorney. He is the natural person by whom the personal acts of suing and defending are done, yet nobody ever imagined that he is the party to the suit.

(Emphasis added.)

Surely if anything is settled beyond all controversy, it is that an individual member of a corporation, or any number of members less than the whole united under the corporate name, and in the corporate character, cannot be sued on a contract of the corporation.

But it is affirmed that in a corporation all the parts are not the whole. Nothing is more true than that a corporation aggregate, consisting of a given number of individuals, is in legal contemplation, for all purposes of administration, rights, obligations, and procedure, a different thing from the aggregate of the individuals composing it. The legal entity, the corporation, is a different thing from the natural persons, the members, but it is nevertheless true, that the corporation includes all the members, and that any one of them is just as much a part of the corporation as any other. . . . But nothing is more certain, indeed nothing has been more strenuously insisted on by the learned counsel themselves, than that the members of a corporation are not individually bound by the obligations of the corporation.

But even that was not the first. The *Dartmouth College* decision defined the corporation for the American bar for much of the 19th century. Decided when corporations were first emerging as a regular vehicle for economic enterprise, the court held that a corporation was an artificial person that owed its existence more to government than to its incorporators and, as a creature of positive law, had only the rights and privileges that obtained from the government's grant.

Noteworthy is the Supreme Court's 1908 ruling in *Ponce v. Roman Catholic Apostolic Church*[9] because it acknowledged that the ancient and medieval origins of modern corporate law even applied to not-for-profit religious corporations.

The Roman Catholic Church has been recognized as possessing legal personality by the treaty of Paris with Spain of 1898 and its property rights solemnly safeguarded. In so doing the treaty followed the recognized rule of international law which would have protected the property of the church in Porto

[sic] Rico subsequent to the cession. The *juristic personality* of the Roman Catholic Church and its ownership of property was formally recognized by the concordats between Spain and the papacy and by the Spanish laws from the beginning of settlements in the Indies. Such recognition has also been accorded the church by all systems of European law from the fourth century of the Christian era."

(Emphasis added.)

In 1946, the Supreme Court ruled in *Schenley Distillers Corp. v. United States*,[10] a case involving the Interstate Commerce Commission's order that held the appellant was a contract carrier,

While corporate entities may be disregarded when they are used to avoid a clear legislative purpose, they will not be disregarded where those in control have deliberately adopted the corporate form in order to secure its advantages and where no violence to the legislative purpose is done by treating the corporation as a *separate legal person.*

(Emphasis added.)

In *Dole Food Co. v. Patrickson*,[11] a 2003 case arising under the Foreign Sovereign Immunities Act of 1976 involving injury from exposure to chemicals, the Supreme Court took special notice that

As a corporation and its shareholders are distinct entities, see, e.g., *First Nat. City Bank v. Banco Para el Comercio Exterior de Cuba*, 462 U.S. 611, 625, a corporate parent which owns a subsidiary's shares does not, for that reason alone, own or have legal title to the subsidiary's assets; and, it follows with even greater force, the parent does not own or have legal title to the subsidiary's subsidiaries.

First Nat. City Bank v. Banco Para el Comercio Exterior de Cuba, which the Supreme Court cited as precedent, held that *"Separate legal personality* has been described as 'an almost indispensable aspect of the public corporation.'"

State supreme courts have also ruled that corporations are legal persons. In New York, for example, even though the case was not a business-related case,[12] the New York Court of Appeals stated in *Byrn v. New York City Health & Hospitals Corp.*, *"What is a legal person is for the law, including, of course, the Constitution, to say*, which simply means that upon according legal personality to a thing the law affords it the rights and privileges of a legal person."

The New York Court of Appeals, in *People ex rel. Bank of Commonwealth v. Commissioners of Taxes & Assessments*,[13] ruled in 1861 that a corporation is a legal person. But equally important is its recognition that it is the *corporation* that owns the corporation's equity, not the shareholders.

This theory only needs to be analyzed in order to demonstrate is illusory character. A just conception of the meaning of terms is the first requisite. *The word "capital"* is unambiguous. It signifies the actual estate, whether in money or property, which is owned by an individual or a corporation. In reference to a corporation, it *is the aggregate of the sum subscribed and paid in, or secured to be paid in, by the shareholders,* with the addition of all gains or profits realized in the use and investment of those sums, or, if losses have been incurred, then it is the residue after deducting such losses. *The corporation as a legal person, is the owner or proprietor of this capital,* and there is not a corporation aggregate in the world which ever owned any else except the franchise of being a corporation. The term "stock" is, perhaps, sometimes used with less precision. It may occasionally be employed to denote the same thing as capital. If that were its meaning in the statutes, of course the argument of the Supreme Court in this case would not have even a verbal criticism to rest upon. But, whenever it means anything different from the capital of a corporation, it can refer to nothing else that the interests of the shareholders or individuals. Such interests are called "stock," and the sum total of them is appropriately enough called the "stock" of a corporation. Those interests are the resulting estates of private persons, which flow from the nature of corporate organizations. In some respects, they resemble a chose in action, and thus are so treated in the relation of husband and wife and in other relations. More accurately, I think, they may be called equitable estates, which entitle the holders to share in the income of the capital, which is legally vested in and managed by the corporate body. The material point now is, that corporations themselves never own what is sometimes called their own stock. *They have the power and capacity to create and issue stock, but when created and issued it always belongs to the individual to whom it is issued.*

(Emphasis added.)

Here, unlike the Delaware corporate law, which declares that stock is personal property of the shareholder, it is the highest court in New York that states shares are owned by the shareholder, which necessarily makes shares personal property.

In 2016, the Delaware Supreme Court ruled in *Genuine Parts Co. v. Cepec,*[14] a case involving due process and the registration of a foreign corporation for jurisdiction purposes, that Delaware had jurisdiction over the defendant. The court cited, rather than judicial precedent, the *Harvard Law Review.*

At one time, a corporation was considered a creature of the state of incorporation; it was legally recognized only in the state of incorporation and therefore subject only to the corporation laws of that state. Modern commercial needs have caused this conception of the corporation to yield to the "natural entity" theory, which conceives of a corporation as a legal person, with rights virtually equivalent to those of a natural person."

(Notes, 2002)

The corporation as a legal person in legal scholarship

A Nexis Uni search of " 'corporations' and 'legal person'" turned up 2,907 separate law review articles from 1974 to the present, with an exponential increase from 1993. Most are not relevant, but the number merely mentioning the two terms together is impressive. (A search for "corporations" and "fictitious person" or "artificial person" was not performed.)

Horwitz (1985) suggests that *Santa Clara*[15] is thought to be a dramatic example of judicial personification of the corporation, which radically enhanced the position of the business corporation in American law.

Petrin (2013) argues that the firm should be defined not by its legal nature, but rather by its function. The question, therefore, should not be "What are firms?" but "Why do we have firms?" and "How do they affect us?" Yet, assuming those questions can be answered, the answers must be framed by what they are legally. The questions are no different than asking "Why do we have government, and how does government affect us?" The question "What is government?" frames the answers to why we have government and how government affects us. Petrin, like many others, has it backwards.

Piety (2015) rejects the suggestion that corporate personhood is not important. Corporate personhood matters, she believes, because it "tilts" the outcomes. Insisting that corporate personhood does not matter is equivalent to saying "Pay no attention to the man behind the curtain!" as the Wizard of Oz told Dorothy.

Pollman (2011) argues that corporate personhood should be understood as nothing more than acknowledging the corporation's rights and ability to own property.

As I recommended elsewhere, "corporatehood" is a more appropriate term to refer to a corporation. There is simply no need to refer to the corporation as a "legal person" or to the "corporate personhood."[16]

Relevance of the corporation as a legal person to the theory of the firm

The concept of a corporation as a legal person is important in many contexts: for example, extending constitutional protections against unwarranted searches and seizures. But the corporation as a person does not define a corporation's legal rights and duties. Corporate statutory law, along with property law, agency law, and trust law, defines a corporation's legal rights and duties.

As seen in Chapter 5, a corporation has the power to buy, own, use, and sell property and to sue and be sued, among others. But a corporation has those powers whether or not it is a legal person. That is, corporations are considered legal persons because they have those powers. Corporations do not have those powers because they are legal persons. It is thus, in that respect, more accurate to refer to "corporatehood" than to "corporate personhood." (See Huber, 2017.)

The corporation as a legal person must be considered in the context of the theory of the firm because it presents questions that are not easily answered by the theory of the firm because the theory of the firm either ignores the law (at best) or twists the law (at worst). (I will ignore the metaphysical question of whether one person can own another person, prohibited by the Fourteenth Amendment, when that other person is merely a legal person.)

The corporation as a legal person and the separation of ownership and control

There is a tension at the very least between the proposition that shareholders own corporations but do not control them and the corporation as a legal person. Since the corporation is a separate legal person, it obviously must be controlled by someone. Why does corporate statutory law place directors in the position of controlling the corporation? Because shareholders do not own the corporation. If shareholders owned the corporation as partners own the partnership, then the shareholders would control the corporation the way partners control a partnership. Partnership law makes partners both owners and controllers of the partnership. Thus, if the corporation is a legal person separate from its shareholders, there can be no separation of ownership and control because no one owns a corporation. The corporation is not separate from itself. Furthermore, corporate statutory law places directors in control of the corporation as a legal person.

Although the Delaware General Partnership Act makes a partnership a legal entity separate from its owners,[17] it also defines a partnership as "the association of 2 or more persons (i) to carry on as co-owners a business for profit."[18] In fact, partners pay income tax on their share of the partnership income whether or not it is distributed. Shareholders do not pay income tax on corporation income. But nowhere does the Delaware General Corporation Law, the Model Business Corporation Act, or the New York Business Corporation Law make shareholders the "co-owners" of the corporation. It makes shareholders the owners of shares, nothing more.

There is no separation of ownership and control because there is no ownership. The corporation is a legal person and thus has no ownership.

The corporation as a legal person and agency and trust law

We must now contend with the problems presented by the corporation as a legal person and agency law and trust law.

How does a corporation as a legal person, a separate legal entity, correspond to the doctrine of directors as agents of shareholders? Directors are, it is argued, agents of shareholders, i.e., of real persons.[19] Yet directors are by law agents of the corporation, a legal, fictitious person.

If directors are agents or trustees of shareholders, then first, agency law or trust law must apply, and second, as a consequence of applying agency law or trust law to directors, fiduciary duties are imposed on directors by various courts (recalling from Chapters 2 and 3 that the principles of the two are diametrically opposed to each other). However, agency law or trust law can only be applied to shareholder-director relationships if directors are actually agents of shareholders as individuals. Yet

> The notion that the corporation is an associated group of individuals is misguided and at odds with objective reality. . . . Corporations are accurately viewed not as associations of citizens, but rather as distinct legal entities in their own right that have been formed under statute and authorized by law to act as autonomous "persons" with full legal responsibility. It is this view of the corporation that provides the analytical justification for allowing corporations to enter into contracts and be sued in their own right. On this account, the corporation can – and must – be distinguished analytically from its shareholders.
>
> (Macey & Strine, 2019)

If a corporation can – and must – be distinguished analytically from its shareholders, then directors cannot be agents or trustees of shareholders.

Chapter summary

This chapter discussed the corporation as a "legal person" ("fictitious," artificial") in judicial rulings and in legal scholarship and the problems presented by the corporation as a legal person and directors being agents of the shareholders.

Notes

1 Women and the Law. www.library.hbs.edu/hc/wes/collections/women_law/.
2 This would, of course, have been after Emperor Constantine issued an edict that protected Christians in the Roman Empire in 337 CE.
3 Sir Edward Coke (1552–1634), *Institutes of the Laws of England*, 7 volumes, published posthumously (London: E. & R. Brooke, 1794).
4 Trustees of Dartmouth College v. Woodward, 17 U.S. 518 (1819).
5 Sir William Blackstone (1773–1780), *Commentaries on the Laws of England*, 4 volumes, 1765–1770.
6 County of Santa Clara v. Southern Pac. R. Co. People of The State of California, 118 U.S. 394, S.Ct. 1132, 30 L.Ed. 118, (1886).
7 U.S. Constitution, Fourteenth Amendment.
8 Louisville, Cincinnati & Charleston R. Co. v. Letson, 43 U.S. 497 (1844).
9 Ponce v. Roman Catholic Apostolic Church 210 U.S. 296, 28 S. Ct. 737, (1908).
10 Schenley Distillers Corp. v. United States, 326 U.S. 432, 66 S. Ct. 247, 90 L. Ed. 181, (1946).
11 Dole Food Co. et al. v. Patrickson et al., 538 U.S. 468 (2003).
12 Byrn v. New York City Health & Hospitals Corp., 31 N.Y.2d 194, 286 N.E.2d 887, 335 N.Y.S.2d 390, (1972).
13 People ex rel. Bank of Commonwealth v. Commissioners of Taxes & Assessments, 23 N.Y. 192, (1861).
14 Genuine Parts Co. v. Cepec, 137 A.3d 123, (2016).
15 County of Santa Clara v. Southern Pac. R. Co. People of The State of California, 118 U.S. 394, S.Ct. 1132, 30 L.Ed. 118 (1886).

16 Huber, W.D. (2018). Law, language, and corporatehood: Corporations and the U.S. Constitution. *International Journal for the Rule of Law, Courtroom Procedures, Judicial Linguistics & Legal English*, 1(2), 78–110.
17 Delaware General Partnership Act, § 15–201(a).
18 Delaware General Partnership Act, § 15–202(a).
19 Even if a corporation is a subsidiary of another corporation, the shareholders of the parent company are still people.

Bibliography

Cases

Byrn v. New York City Health & Hospitals Corp., 31 N.Y.2d 194, 286 N.E.2d 887, 335 N.Y.S.2d 390 (1972).

County of Santa Clara v. Southern Pac. R. Co. People of The State of California, 118 U.S. 394, S.Ct. 1132, 30 L.Ed. 118 (1886).

Dole Food Co. et al. v. Patrickson et al., 538 U.S. 468 (2003).

First Nat. City Bank v. Banco Para el Comercio Exterior de Cuba, 462 U.S. 611 (1983).

Genuine Parts Co. v. Cepec, 137 A.3d 123 (2016).

Louisville, Cincinnati & Charleston R. Co. v. Letson, 43 U.S. 497 (1844).

People ex rel. Bank of Commonwealth v. Commissioners of Taxes & Assessments, 23 N.Y. 192 (1861).

Ponce v. Roman Catholic Apostolic Church 210 U.S. 296, 28 S. Ct. 737 (1908).

Schenley Distillers Corp. v. United States, 326 U.S. 432, 66 S. Ct. 247, 90 L. Ed. 181 (1946).

Trustees of Dartmouth College v. Woodward, 17 U.S. 518 (1819).

Authors and publications

Gevurtz, F.A. (2011). The globalization of corporate law: The end of history or a never-ending story? *Washington Law Review*, 86(3), 475–523. Retrieved from https://papers.ssrn.com/sol3/papers.cfm?abstract_id=2026610##.

Horwitz, M.J. (1985). Santa Clara revisited: The development of the corporate theory. *West Virginia Law Review*, 88, 173–225. Retrieved from https://heinonline.org/HOL/LandingPage?handle=hein.journals/wvb88&div=17&id=&page=.

Huber, W.D. (2017). Law, language, and corporatehood: Corporations and the U.S. Constitution. *International Journal for the Rule of Law, Courtroom Procedures, Judicial Linguistics & Legal English*, 1(2), 78–110. Retrieved from https://papers.ssrn.com/sol3/papers.cfm?abstract_id=2835563.

Huber, W.D. (2018). The Supreme Court's subversion of the constitutional process and the creation of persons *ex nihilo*. *International Journal for the Rule of Law, Courtroom Procedures, Judicial Linguistics & Legal English*, 2(1), 53–72. Retrieved from https://papers.ssrn.com/sol3/papers.cfm?abstract_id=2841825.

Kaeb, C. (2015). Putting the "corporate" back into corporate personhood. *Northwestern Journal of International Law & Business*, 35(3), 591–643. Retrieved from https://scholarlycommons.law.northwestern.edu/njilb/vol35/iss3/3/.

Macey, J., & Strine Jr., L.E. (2019). Citizens United as bad corporate law. *Wisconsin Law Review*, 3, 451–530. Retrieved from https://scholarship.law.upenn.edu/cgi/viewcontent.cgi?article=3009&context=faculty_scholarship.

Notes. (2002). The internal affairs doctrine: Theoretical justifications and tentative explanations for its continued primacy. *Harvard Law Review*, 115(5), 1480–1501. doi: 10.2307/1342553.

Petrin, M. (2013). Reconceptualizing the theory of the firm – from nature to function. *Penn State Law Review*, 118, 1–53. Retrieved from https://papers.ssrn.com/sol3/papers.cfm?abstract_id=2225447.

Piety, T.R. (2015). Why personhood matters. *Constitutional Commentary*, 30(361), 101–128. Retrieved from https://papers.ssrn.com/sol3/papers.cfm?abstract_id=2594539.

Pollman, E. (2011). Reconceiving corporate personhood. *Utah Law Review*, 4, 1629–1675. Retrieved from https://papers.ssrn.com/sol3/papers.cfm?abstract_id=1732910.

Seymour Jr., E.B. (1903). The historical development of the common-law conception of a corporation. *The American Law Register*, 51(9), 529–551. Retrieved from https://scholarship.law.upenn.edu/cgi/viewcontent.cgi?article=6409&context=penn_law_review.

11 The theory of the firm

Introduction

A physicist, an engineer, and an economist are stranded in the desert. They are hungry. Suddenly, they find a can of corn. They want to open it, but how?

The physicist says, "Let's start a fire and place the can inside the flames. It will explode, and then we will all be able to eat."

"Are you crazy?" says the engineer. "All the corn will burn and scatter, and we'll have nothing. We should use a metal wire, attach it to a base, push it, and crack the can open."

"Both of you are wrong!" states the economist. "Where the hell do we find a metal wire in the desert? The solution is simple: Let us assume we have a can opener."

(Source unknown)[1]

What economists and legal scholars say with respect to the nature and theory of the firm is in essence no different than the old economics joke – make assumptions contrary to facts: "Let us assume directors are agents of shareholders." What both legal scholars and economists have said implicitly (implicit because they rarely state explicitly the bases for their assumptions (Coase, 1937)) is "Even though property law, agency law, and corporate law say that shareholders do not own the corporation, and directors are not agents of shareholders, let us assume that shareholders do own corporations, and directors are agents of shareholders. Then we can build an entire theory around those assumptions."

The origin of "nature of the firm" is attributable to Coase (1937), who considered a "firm" to consist of "the system of relationships which comes into existence when the direction of resources is dependent on an entrepreneur," rather than the price mechanism. He defined "entrepreneur" as "the person or persons who, in a competitive system, take the place of the price mechanism in the direction of resources."

The modern theory of the firm can be found beginning with Jensen and Meckling (1976), who attempted to integrate agency law and property law with the theory of finance to develop a theory of the ownership of the firm. In reality, the term "theory of the firm" is itself much older. Boulding (1942) gave an historical account of *The Theory of the Firm in the Last Ten Years*.[2] Unlike Boulding, however, the modern theory of the firm espouses agency theory and agency costs and has become the orthodox canon of corporate law in both law and economics.

Whether in law or economics, the theory of the firm rests on what has become a sacred chant for economists and legal scholars alike – the separation of ownership and control – with directors as agents of shareholders its inviolate creed. Law and economic novitiates are trained in a catechismal manner to chant the mantra every morning: "Corporations are characterized by separation of ownership and control" and "Directors are agents of shareholders." (Of course, I speak hyperbolically. They don't actually have to chant it *every* morning.)

Nevertheless, 80 years ago, Coase (1937) admitted that "economic theory has suffered in the past from a failure to state clearly its assumptions." Little has changed. When considering the nature and theory of the firm, those assumptions are for the most part implicit, or in the few instances when the assumptions are explicit, they are not supported by any analysis, or even mention, of property law, agency law, or corporate statutory law but amount to nothing more than mere assertions. It's as if property law, agency law, and corporate law are not relevant or don't even exist. But whether implicit or explicit, property law, agency law, trust law, and statutory corporate law prove beyond debate or question that those assumptions are wrong and have no validity in property law, agency law, trust law, or corporate statutory law.

The nature of the firm and the theory of the firm are intricately intertwined yet have been treated separately in the literature (but with emphasis on the theory of the firm). The nature of the firm and the theory of the firm are dealt with in greater depth in *Economics, Capitalism, and Corporations: Contradictions of Corporate Law, Economics, and the Theory of the Firm*, which also addresses in depth economic, finance, investment, and accounting issues, among others. This chapter is limited to identifying the basic assumptions of the nature and theory of the firm and how corporate law invalidates those assumptions.

As explained in the prologue,

> notions of "firm" and "corporation" are very often confused in the literature on the theory of the firm. In this paper . . . the corporation is a legal entity entitled to operate in the legal system and in particular to own assets, to enter into contracts and to incur liabilities. . . . The firm is the economic activity developed as a consequence of the cluster of contracts connecting the corporation owning these assets to various holders of resources required in the firm's operations
>
> (Robé, 2011, p. 1)

In previous chapters, I have referred only to "the theory of the firm" rather than "the nature of the firm." I have necessarily, for the purposes of this book, considered the firm and the corporation to be merely different terms to describe the same object – the corporation – since there can be no "economic activity developed as a consequence of the cluster of contracts connecting the corporation owning these assets to various holders of resources required in the firm's operations" in the absence of the existence of the corporation as a "legal entity" and the legal relationships created by its existence as a legal entity. The economic activity and cluster of contracts can be considered the dependent variables, with the legal status of the corporation the independent variable.

Since "the nature of the firm" and "the theory of the firm" have been treated separately in the literature, they will likewise be considered separately in this chapter.

The nature of the firm

The "nature of the firm" is attributable to Coase (1937), who considered a "firm" to consist of "the system of relationships which comes into existence when the direction of resources is dependent on an entrepreneur," rather than the price mechanism. But Coase's mistake was that he, like those who followed him, had it backwards, placing the cart before the horse, so to speak. Coase thought it "convenient if, in searching for a definition of a firm, we first consider the economic system as it is normally treated by the economist." Coase's purpose was to bridge what he saw as a gap in economic theory – the assumption that resources are allocated through the price mechanism and the assumption that the allocation of resources is dependent on the entrepreneur. He defined "entrepreneur" as "the person or persons who, in a competitive system, take the place of the price mechanism in the direction of resources."

But the definition of the firm is dependent on its system of relationships between the corporation, the shareholders, and directors, which comes into existence prior to the corporation directing any resources in the economic system. In other words, the firm can only be defined by its system of relationships between the corporation, the shareholders, and directors.

In Coase's framework, the normal, i.e., competitive, economic system works itself. That is, it is under no central control.[3] Supply adjusts to demand, and production adjusts to consumption by the price mechanism. The allocation of resources of production (traditionally referred to as factors of production) is determined by the price mechanism. Coase assumes that the distinguishing mark of the firm is the supersession of the price mechanism.

Although Coase presumably was aware of Veblen's 1923 proposition of the separation of ownership and control, he failed to incorporate it into his theory of the nature of the firm, or even to acknowledge it. Coase also ignored Berle and Means's work, published only five years earlier, firmly establishing the theory of the separation of ownership and control.

The theory of the firm

Jensen and Meckling (1976) are considered the pioneers of the modern theory of the firm with their study of the relationship between shareholders and CEOs, which has been widely adopted by both economists and legal scholars who consider the firm a "nexus of contracts" (Meurer, 2004).[4] Nevertheless, Meurer suggests that legal scholars confuse the relationship between the principal-agent theory and the theory of the firm. Although corporate law scholars frequently cite Coase (1937), according to Demsetz (1991), Coase did not actually develop a theory of the firm (Meurer, 2004).

The separation of ownership and control is the lynchpin of the theory of the firm, which most economists consider to have begun with Berle and Means's 1932 publication of *The Modern Corporation and Private Property*. Yet the separation of ownership and control can be traced at least as far back as Veblen (1923).

The separation of ownership and control in the modern corporation, along with its concomitant agency theory, retains a central position in the economic theory of the firm (Demsetz, 1983). As the lynchpin of the theory of the firm, the theory of the separation of ownership and control inevitably leads to the theory of agency. Yet Berle (a lawyer) and Means did not actually discuss agency theory and the theory of the firm. That was the work of non-lawyers – the economists. Since Coase's article *The Nature of the Firm*, both economists and legal scholars have devoted considerable attention to the theory of the firm (Bainbridge, 2003).

The theory of the firm in economics

The theory of the firm was developed in economics and subsequently infiltrated legal theories of the corporation.

Jensen and Meckling (1976) are frequently credited with initiating the modern theory of the firm with *The Theory of the Firm: Managerial Behavior, Agency Costs and Ownership Structure*. Yet, this, too, is disputed. Boulding (1942), for example, reviewed *The Theory of the Firm in the Last Ten Years*. Foss (2000) cites Boulding (1942) as tracing an "explicit recognition of the theory of the firm to Chamberlin (1933) and Robinson (1933)." However, the theory of the firm at that time, according to Foss, had been subordinated to price theory. Chamberlin and Robinson did not base their theory of the firm on the separation of ownership and control and agency theory, but on equilibrium theory and industrial organization (competition and monopoly). Jensen and Meckling's modern theory of the firm bears little resemblance to that of Chamberlin and Robinson.

Jensen and Meckling attempted to integrate elements from agency theory, property rights, and finance to develop a theory of the ownership structure of the firm and called upon Adam Smith to support their theory. They criticize previous theories of the firm as being theories of markets rather than actual theories of the firm. They considered the relationship between stockholders and managers of a corporation as corresponding to the definition of a pure agency relationship, and therefore the issues associated with the separation of ownership and control were "intimately associated with the general problem of agency."[5]

Jensen and Meckling defined an agency relationship as "a contract under which one or more persons (the principal(s)) engage another person (the agent) to perform some service on their behalf which involves delegating some decision making authority to the agent." They explain how agency costs generated by a corporation lead to a theory of "the ownership (or capital) structure of the firm." Agency costs are defined as costs generated by the contractual arrangements between the owners of the corporation and the top management of the corporation and relate agency costs to the separation of ownership and control. To Jensen and Meckling, the absentee owners of the corporation are the shareholders. The problem, of course, is that shareholders elect directors. Shareholders do not hire "top management" and bestow upon them decision-making authority. Top management are hired by the board of directors.

Fama and Jensen's 1983 paper *Separation of Ownership and Control* attempts to "explain the survival of organizations characterized by separation of 'ownership' and 'control' – a problem that has bothered students of corporations from Adam Smith to Berle and Means and Jensen and Meckling." In classical entrepreneurial firms (sole proprietorships, small partnerships, and close corporations), the decision makers are also the "residual risk bearers." However, in what Fama and Jensen refer to as "large open corporations" (i.e., publicly traded), there is a "nearly complete separation . . . of decision control and residual risk bearing" since residual risk bearers "delegate their decision control rights to other agents."[6]

Fama and Jensen's "decision control agents" take the form of a board of directors. The exercise of decision control rights by the board "helps to ensure separation of decision management and control" from residual risk bearers, i.e., the stockholders. Furthermore, "separation and specialization of decision management and residual risk bearing leads to agency problems between decision agents and residual claimants. This is the problem of separation of ownership and control that has long troubled students of corporations."

Foss (2000) observed that

> Few practitioners and observers of economics would disagree with the proposition that the theory of the firm has become a favorite preoccupation of the modern economist . . . the theory of the firm in the sense of the body of theory that addresses the *existence*, the *boundaries* and the *internal organization* of the firm – has only picked up steam relatively recently. Thus, whereas the economics and business administration journals had close to no contributions on the theory of the firm only 25 years ago, today top economics journals, including those with a non-specialist orientation, such as *The American Economic Review* or *The Journal of Political Economy*, in close to each issue has at least one paper that deals with aspects of the theory of the firm.
>
> (Emphasis in original.)

The theory of the firm in law

Jensen and Meckling's attempt to integrate elements from agency theory, property rights, and finance to develop a theory of the ownership structure of the firm failed miserably. They showed no understanding of agency theory, property rights, or ownership of the firm. Nevertheless, their lack of understanding agency law, property law, or ownership of the firm did not prevent their work from being among the most widely cited papers in economics and finance literature, generating tenure for many law and economics faculty.

The economic theory of the firm in law focuses on the separation of ownership and control of the firm, as highlighted by Berle and Means; agency theory; and corporate governance, which is basically the power and primacy of shareholders (Velasco, 2010) vs. the power and primacy directors (Bainbridge, 2003; Reich-Graefe, 2011). "Corporate law scholars are really more concerned about developing a framework for analyzing governance of the corporation. . . . Corporate law addresses conflicts between managers and shareholders, and between controlling and minority shareholders" (Meurer, 2004).

"When law and economics scholars peer inside a business organization and distinguish managers from the firm, they use the principal-agent framework" (Meurer, 2004). That is because, according to Meurer, "Corporate law scholars have not been troubled by their limited understanding of the nature of firm, because it probably does not seem especially relevant to questions about the relationships between top management, the board of directors, and shareholders."

It is that lack of questioning that has led law and economics scholars to base the theory of the firm on unsupportable assumptions since, by definition, the ownership of the firm is a legal question, and it is the law the determines who owns what and how it is owned. (As discussed in previous chapters, there is no legal ownership of the firm.) It is necessary to understand principal-agent relationships and property rights because the ownership of the firm is a legal question. But even legal scholars forget, intentionally ignore, or at least downplay the importance of the law in determining the ownership of the firm. Legal scholars' and judges' obeisance to the theory of the firm is staggering. The separation of ownership from control "has dominated the approach of modern legal scholarship and education regarding relationships within the corporate form" (Baysinger & Butler, 1985).

"[I]n law schools, economic approaches have informed competing theories that emphasize principal-agent relationships, transaction costs, a 'nexus' of contracts, or property rights as central to understanding the nature and purposes of the business enterprise" (Orts, 2013). As seen in Chapter 5, in addition to corporate law, property law and agency law govern corporations, corporate ownership, and the relationships between corporations, shareholders and directors. "Laws pertaining to the *creation of agency relationships*, *organizational contracts*, and *private property* count as an additional set of foundations needed for the construction, growth, and management of firms" (Orts, 2013, emphasis in original).

Baysinger and Butler (1985) comment that "law and economics writers restated corporate law in the new theory's terms and successfully reoriented legal discourse on corporations. The new theory already has sunk into the fabric of academic corporate law" and observed that, in law schools, the disciples of the theory of the firm "moved aggressively for equal academic status (including representation among the drafters of the American Law Institute's Corporate Governance Project)." Other commentators saw the stage set for "activist law, by controlling the legal forms provided to the parties, can shape the way they use their legal freedom to plan their activities."

Masten (1993) wanted to "explore in depth the . . . question of whether it even makes sense to talk about the firm as a distinct organizational form" (p. 196). To answer his own question, rather than examining property law, agency law, contract law, and corporate law, his paper was "devoted to exploring the status of the employment relationship in the legal system and a comparison of corresponding doctrines of commercial contract law" (p. 196), which have very little, if anything, to do with the legal basis of the firm, i.e., the corporation.

It is perhaps doubly ironic that Masten himself ignores the legal basis of the corporation, given that he explicitly points out the irony that economics ignores the legal structure of the firm. "Ironically, economists have either downplayed or rejected outright the role of law in defining the firm [both of which are correct], divorcing the economic concept from the 'legal fiction.'"

Meurer (2004) states that shareholders are the nominal owners of the firm who delegate the authority to operate the firm to directors. But he and others who hold similar views of shareholders' delegation of authority are quite incorrect. First, shareholders do not own the firm, nominally or otherwise. Second, shareholders do not delegate authority, a requirement for principal-agent relationships. The authority of directors is not by shareholder delegation, but by corporate statutory law. Directors have authority prior to shareholders even existing.

Walker (2016), echoing Berle and Means, states "Investor-owned firms are the most common form of ownership for large-scale enterprises in most of the world." A firm's owners are those who have a "right to control the firm and the right to appropriate the firm's profits [the] residual earnings" Hansmann (1996). But, as seen in Chapter 5, shareholders neither own the firm nor are able to appropriate its profits. That is, shareholders have no ownership rights over the firm and have no income rights. The only thing shareholders own is a certain bundle of rights, as defined by the shares and the articles of incorporation. Furthermore, the directors, by law, control (manage) the corporation. The directors, by law, are agents of the corporation, not of the shareholders.

Bainbridge (2003) asks, "What do shareholders own?" He answers his own question,

> Traditional scholars contend that shareholders own the firm itself. In contrast, agency cost-oriented scholars typically contend that shareholders own the residual claim to the corporation's assets and earnings. In either case . . . directors and officers are mere agents of the shareholders.

But both views – that shareholders own the firm and that directors and officers are mere agents of the shareholders – are without legal support, as is the view that shareholders own the residual claim to the corporation's assets and earnings.

A claim, residual or otherwise, is a property right (a chose in action) which, as seen in Chapter 1, can only be enforced by legal action. Shareholders owning the residual claim to the corporation's assets and earnings would mean that shareholders could enforce, through legal action, claims against the corporation's assets and earnings. But shareholders cannot enforce, through legal action, claims against the corporation's assets and earnings. By property law and corporate law, shareholders have no rights to the corporation's assets or earnings.

Baysinger and Butler (1985) note that the relationship between directors and shareholders has been described as analogous to that of an agent to his principle or a trustee to his beneficiary. As a consequence, directors of a corporation owe fiduciary duties "to the corporation (i.e., stockholders)." But corporations are not the stockholders. It is universally maintained by courts of all jurisdictions that corporations are legal entities separate from the stockholders, going so far as to declare corporations are "legal," "fictitious," or "artificial" persons, as discussed in Chapter 10.

Furthermore, Baysinger and Butler confuse directors elected by shareholders with managers, who are not elected by shareholders. They state, "The many dispersed owners of corporate stock delegate authority to a small group of *hired managers* who in turn formulate and implement corporate-level strategies." (Emphasis added.) This is incorrect on at least two counts. One, shareholders do not own corporations. Two, shareholders do not hire managers; directors hire managers. Shareholders elect directors, not managers.

Chapter summary

This chapter briefly examined the nature of the firm and the theory of the firm. While there is significant overlap, they are also considered somewhat distinct in the literature. One thing they share in common is their proclivity to ignore agency law, property law, and statutory corporate law in formulating legal and economic theories of the firm while simultaneously proclaiming their purpose is to integrate agency law, property law, and finance theory. The theory of the firm is grounded in Berle and Means's thesis of the separation of ownership of the corporation from control of the corporation. From the separation of ownership of the corporation from control of the corporation comes agency theory and agency costs, which form the basis of the theory of the firm.

This chapter highlighted the basic errors in the assumptions of the theory of the firm and the invalidity of the conclusions based on the erroneous assumptions. Directors are not agents of shareholders; there are therefore no agency costs, and directors have no fiduciary duty to shareholders to maximize profits or shareholder wealth.

It is incredible that economists and legal scholars, not to mention the judiciary, continue to maintain any theory of the firm when the theory of the firm has no legal or logical basis, being contradicted by property law and agency law.

Interestingly, Baird and Henderson (2008), both of the University of Chicago School of Law, are emphatic that

> Legal principles that are *almost* right are often more mischievous than those that are completely wrong. . . . An almost-right principle invites sloppy thinking, vague generalities, and a general distortion of the otherwise sound ideas that lie close by. An example of an almost-right principle that has distorted much of the thinking about corporate law in recent decades is the oft-repeated maxim that directors of a corporation owe a fiduciary duty to

the shareholders. . . . People who should know better paint themselves into embarrassing corners trying to reaffirm the principle"

(pp. 1309, 1312, emphasis added)

Chassagnon and Hollandts (2014) concur that "economists have distorted the legal nature of the firm."

Notes

1 There are several variations to the joke, but the intent of versions in all is clear – assumptions contrary to facts.
2 Boulding considers that the works of Chamberlin (1933) and Robinson (1933) "mark the explicit recognition of the theory of the firm as an integral division of economic analysis upon which rests the whole fabric of equilibrium theory." The modern theory of the firm rests on the separation of ownership and control and agency costs.
3 This can be compared to Smith's invisible hand.
4 The nexus of contracts theory is explored more extensively in *Economics, Capitalism, and Corporations: Contradictions of Corporate Law, Economics, and the Theory of the Firm.*
5 As explained in Chapter 5, it is incorrect to link shareholders with "managers" when the term "managers" means anyone other than the board of directors since shareholders have no relationship to non-director managers.
6 Fama and Jensen also considered other large organizations such as large not-for-profit corporations and large partnerships, which also have issues of "separation of ownership and control" even though there are no owners in not-for-profit corporations. Partnerships, of course, do have owners.

Bibliography

Bainbridge, S.M. (2003). Director primacy: The means and ends of corporate governance. *Northwestern University Law Review*, 97(2), 547–606. Retrieved from http://heinonline.org/HOL/Page?handle=hein.journals/illlr97&div=19.

Baird, D.G., & Henderson, M. (2008). Other people's money. *Stanford Law Review*, 60(5), 1309–1344. Retrieved from https://chicagounbound.uchicago.edu/cgi/viewcontent.cgi?article=8043&context=journal_articles.

Baysinger, B.D., & Butler, H.N. (1985). Race for the bottom v. climb to the top: The ALI project and uniformity in corporate law. *Journal of Corporation Law*, 10(2), 431–463. Retrieved from https://heinonline.org/HOL/LandingPage?handle=hein.journals/jcorl10&div=20&id=&page=.

Berle, A.A., & Means, G.C. (1991). *The modern corporation and private property* (2nd ed.). New York: Routledge.

Boulding, K.E. (1942). The theory of the firm in the last ten years. *The American Economic Review*, 32(4), 791–802. Retrieved from www.jstor.org/stable/1816760.

Chamberlin, E. (1933). *The theory of monopolistic competition.* 8th ed. Cambridge, MA: Harvard University Press.

Chassagnon, V., & Hollandts, X. (2014). Who are the owners of the firm: Shareholders, employees or no one? *Journal of Institutional Economics*, 10(1), 47–69. doi: 10.1017/S1744137413000301.

Coase, R.H. (1937). The nature of the firm. *Economica*, 4(16), 386–405. Retrieved from www.jstor.org/stable/2626876.

Demsetz, H. (1983). The structure of ownership and the theory of the firm. *Journal of Law and Economics*, 26(2), 375–190. Retrieved from www.jstor.org/stable/725108.

Demsetz, H. (1991). The theory of the firm revisited. In O.E. Williamson & S.G. Winter (Eds). *The nature of the firm: Origins, evolution, and development* (pp. 159–178). London: Oxford University Press.

Fama, E.F., & Jensen, M.C. (1983). Separation of ownership and control. *Journal of Law Economics*, 26(2), 301–326. Retrieved from www.jstor.org/stable/725104.

Foss, N.J. (2000). The theory of the firm: An introduction to themes and contributions. In N. Foss (Ed). *The theory of the firm: Critical perspectives on business and management*, 4 vols. London: Routledge.

Hansmann, H. (1996). *The ownership of enterprise*. Cambridge: The Belknap Press of Harvard University Press.

Jensen, M.C., & Meckling, W.H. (1976). Theory of the firm: Managerial behavior, agency costs and ownership structure. *Journal of Financial Economics*, 3, 305–360. doi: 10.1016/0304-405X(76)90026-X.

Masten, S.E. (1993). A legal basis for the firm. In O.E. Williamson & S.G. Winter (Eds). *The nature of the firm: Origins, evolution, and development* (pp. 196–212). London: Oxford University Press.

Meurer, M.J. (2004). Law, economics, and the theory of the firm. *Buffalo Law Review*, 52(3), 727–755. Retrieved from https://digitalcommons.law.buffalo.edu/buffalolawreview/vol52/iss3/8.

Orts, E.W. (2013). *Business persons: A legal theory of the firm*. London: Oxford University Press.

Reich-Graefe, R. (2011). Deconstructing corporate governance: Director primacy without principle? *Fordham Journal of Corporate and Financial Law*, 16, 465–506. Retrieved from https://ssrn.com/abstract=1971300.

Robé, J-P. (2011). The legal structure of the firm. *Accounting, Economics, and Law – A Convivium*, 1(1), 1–85. doi: 10.2202/2152-2820.1001.

Robé, J-P. (2019). The shareholder value mess (and how to clean it up). *Accounting, Economics, and Law—A convivium*, 9(3), 1–27. doi: 10.1515/ael-2019-0039.

Robinson, J. (1933). *The economics of imperfect competition*. 2nd ed. London: Macmillan.

Veblen, T. (1923). *Absentee ownership and business enterprise in recent times: The case of America*. New York: B.W. Huebsch.

Velasco, J. (2010). Shareholder ownership and primacy. *University of Illinois Law Review*, (3), 897–956. doi: 10.2139/ssrn.1274244.

Walker, P. (2016). *The theory of the firm: An overview of the economic mainstream*. London: Routledge.

Epilogue

The past

Velasco (2010) recognized that the issue of the ownership of a corporation is necessary in order to understand the nature of the corporation and corporate law. The ownership of a corporation is an important consideration in the allocation of rights within the corporation and between corporations, shareholders, and directors. The issue of ownership of a corporation shapes corporate law and directs the purpose of corporations.

Summary of chapters

Chapter 0 established the "ground floor" of Anglo-American law: jurisdiction, common law, and contract law. Jurisdiction determines whether a court can hear a case and whether it can issue rulings for a particular case. Jurisdiction is important in corporate law in the United States because there are basically 50 separate jurisdictions corresponding to each state that govern corporate law that are not identical but that have substantial similarities.

Property laws, agency laws, trust laws, and partnership laws are founded on common law and contract law, meaning that originally they were not statutory but court-made principles. Trust law and partnership law in particular have been have been codified to varying degrees.

On the other hand, corporate law is basically statutory, in the sense that, originally, corporations were created with charters made by some sort of "royal decree" but, in modern times, were created by legislation as opposed to court-made principles. However, although statutory in nature, corporate law is an amalgamation of contract law, property law, agency law, and trust law and is therefore founded on and interpreted by common law principles, particularly when the statutory law is ambiguous or does not otherwise define the rights and duties of the parties.

Chapter 1 reviewed basic property and property law. Ownership of corporations, shares, and corporate assets can only be determined by property law applied to corporate law. Failure to understand or properly apply principles of property law to questions of the ownership of corporations, shares, and corporate assets has resulted in contradictory court rulings between property law and corporate law within the same jurisdiction.

Courts have ruled that shareholders own corporations as a property right when property law does not permit the ownership of corporations by shareholders. Bolstered by faulty analysis by economists, courts have ruled that shareholders are "residual owners" and have "residual claims" (although what they are residual claimants of is not entirely clear), which is a property right. But property and statutory corporate law do not permit shareholders to be residual owners or claimants since shareholders have no claims against the corporation or its earnings.

The requirements to create an agency relationship were discussed in Chapter 2. Courts have ruled that directors are agents of shareholders and, therefore, have a fiduciary duty to shareholders. However, such rulings are contradicted by both agency law and corporate statutory law. According to the principals of agency law, principals appoint or hire agents. In corporations, directors exist prior to shareholders. Corporate statutory law creates directors; shareholders do not create directors. Therefore, since directors cannot be agents of shareholders, directors owe no fiduciary duty to shareholders, contrary to court rulings.

Courts have ruled that directors are trustees of shareholders and, therefore, have a fiduciary duty to shareholders. Courts have also ruled that shareholders are beneficial owners of corporations. However, such rulings are contradicted by trust law. As discussed in Chapter 3, in order to create a trust relationship between directors and shareholders, shareholders would have to transfer legal title to their property to the directors. But shareholders do not transfer legal title of their property to the directors. They transfer legal title of their property (cash) to the corporation when they purchase shares in an IPO. Thus, a trust relationship between directors and shareholders is precluded by trust law, and therefore, directors owe no fiduciary duty to shareholders, contrary to court rulings. Furthermore, shareholders cannot be principals, residual claimants, and beneficial owners *at the same time*!

Partnerships and partnership law were discussed in Chapter 4 in order to compare and contrast partnerships and partnership law with corporations and corporate law. Partners own the partnership and are mutual agents of each other and of the partnership. Partners share in partnership profits in proportion to their capital contributions to the partnership.

Chapter 5 reviewed in depth the statutory law of corporations, shareholders, and directors and the principles of common law of property, agency, and trusts as applied to corporations, shareholders, and directors.

Corporations are created by state statutes, but courts have applied common law to interpret corporate law and the relationships between corporations, shareholders, and directors. Courts have ruled shareholders are owners, beneficial owners, or residual owners of corporations. Courts have ruled directors are agents or trustees of shareholders. All such rulings pertaining to shareholders and directors are contradictory.

State statutes, not shareholders, create the directors of corporations prior to the existence of shareholders. Directors create shareholders when they issue shares. Therefore, directors cannot be agents of shareholders. Shareholders transfer money to the corporation when they purchase shares in an IPO. Therefore, directors cannot be trustees. Since directors cannot be agents or trustees of shareholders, they owe no fiduciary duty to shareholders.

Shareholders do not own the corporation. They own the shares of the corporation. Shareholders, therefore, have very limited rights. Shareholders' rights are only those rights that attach to the shares, not the rights of ownership of the corporation. Since shareholders have no ownership rights in the corporation, they are not investors in the corporation. Shareholders are investors in shares only.

The contradictions of corporate law were summarized and organized in Chapter 6. Courts have ruled shareholders own corporations, which contradicts property law and corporate statutory law. Courts have ruled shareholders are investors in corporations, which contradicts property law. Courts have ruled directors are agents or trustees of shareholders, which contradicts agency law and trust law.

Chapter 7 described the social construction of shareholders, directors, owners of shares, and investors in shares. The social construction of corporations, shareholders, directors, owners of shares, and investors in shares reflects, and is reflected by, the contradictions expressed in judicial constructions. The social construction of shareholders as owners of corporations and of directors as agents or trustees of shareholders bestows on shareholders a class status and corresponding power not supported by law.

Chapter 8 described the power and the cultural reproduction of the power and class status of shareholders, directors, owners of shares, and investors in shares through pedagogical acts in court rulings and academic venues, including classrooms and research.

Chapter 9 called for reconstructing corporations, shareholders, directors, owners of shares, and investors in shares by first calling on courts to cease and desist from ruling shareholders own corporations, that shareholders are investors in corporations, and that directors are agents or trustees of corporations. Second, it called for economists and legal scholars to abandon theories of the firm based on shareholders as owners of corporations or investors in corporations and directors as agents or trustees of corporations.

Chapter 10 considered the corporation as a legal person. The corporation has been considered an "artificial person," "fictitious person," and "legal person" for centuries as a method of owning property. The corporation as a legal person was officially recognized by the United States Supreme Court in 1886, following the Civil War. The corporation as a legal person is a pure common law concept. It is not statutory.

Chapter 11 briefly discussed the theory of the firm and the inherent flaws of the theory. The theory of the firm is founded on the propositions that shareholders own corporations and directors are their agents. Thus, the theory of the firm is contradicted by property law, agency law, and corporate statutory law.

Summation of the past

The previous chapters were summarized here in order to create a forest of the trees, where the whole is greater than the sum of its parts. By assembling past judicial rulings and academic research from previous decades, we can better understand the current state of corporate law and its contradictions.

As if by default, past judicial rulings have resorted to ruling that shareholders own corporations, shareholders are investors in corporations, and directors are agents or trustees of shareholders with no analysis of property law, agency law, or trust law and no thought about how their rulings are contradicted by property law, agency law, and trust law, proof of the old saying that those who ignore the past are destined to repeat it.

They have been in subsequent judicial rulings and academic research by economists and legal scholars in a cyclotronic effect, each reinforcing the other. And that brings us to the present.

The present

In spite of the fact that several researchers have brought to our attention that shareholders do not own corporations and directors are not agents of shareholders, the theory of the firm refuses to die a dignified death. Courts, lawyers, legal scholars, and economists are disinclined to forsake a theory that has no validity in law. There is a reluctance to acknowledge that the law does not make shareholders owners of corporations or directors their agents. Such acknowledgment is a surrender of shareholders' class status and power in society. All the contradictions propagated by past judicial and social constructions of shareholders and directors produced in the past decades continue to the present.

This is not to suggest there has been or is an overt conspiracy between judges, economists, and legal scholars, but when Berle and Means argued there is a separation of ownership and control, and Jensen and Meckling introduced the agency theory of the firm, it set the stage for an ideological conflict between shareholders and directors fed by a wave of economists vying for tenure by "contributing to the literature" and reinforced by Friedman's doctrine of maximizing shareholder wealth.

Every study, paper, book, or article, whether theoretical or empirical, whether legal or economic, that is based on shareholders owning either the corporation or corporate property, directors being agents of shareholders, or directors having a fiduciary duty to shareholders is meaningless. The "contributions to the literature" that promote the separation of ownership and control and the agency theory of the firm are the intellectual equivalent of snake oil and perpetuate legal fallacies that serve not only to divert our attention away from solving the social, political, and economic dislocations introduced into society by ownerless corporations, but also to reinforce the social construction of corporations, shareholders, directors, owners of shares, and investors in shares that has created a "false consciousness" in society in general and shareholders in particular.

Posner (2014) states, "economics is a powerful tool for analyzing a vast range of legal questions." But the reverse is also true. Law is a powerful tool for analyzing a vast range of economic questions. It does little good to develop economic analyses of the firm if the analyses are contradicted by law.

Posner goes on to say that most lawyers and law students "have difficulty connecting economic principles to concrete legal problems." But again, the opposite is true. Economics and economics students have difficulty connecting legal principles to concrete economic problems.

While it may be true that laws were developed to solve economic problems, those laws cannot then be ignored by developing economic theories that are contradicted by the very laws that were developed to solve economic problems.

The future

How do you actually own a corporation? Obviously, it is not tangible property since it exists only in law. Since it exists only in law, it is equally obvious that a corporation is intangible, like a government or a church (i.e., the religious body, not the building called a "church"). But more than that, a corporation is not property any more than a government is property or a church or a not-for-profit corporation is property. A government is a legal person that can own property but is not property itself. A church is a legal person that can own property but is not property that can be owned.

A profit motive is insufficient to make shareholders the owners of corporations. A not-for-profit corporation is a legal person by virtue of its being a corporation just as a for-profit corporation is a legal person. Not-for-profit corporations are every bit a "nexus of contracts," especially large not-for profit corporations, as are for-profit corporations. Yet not-for-profit corporations are not owned, even when they have members. Why should the presence of a profit motive determine that a corporation is something to be owned?

Therefore, the first step in undertaking a reconstruction of corporations, both judicially and socially, is to acknowledge that corporations have no owners, and that makes them dangerous to society because owners of shares have been endowed with power judicially and socially that they do not have legally; namely, to force directors to maximize their profits above all else.

To mitigate the dangers posed to society by ownerless corporations, corporations, directors, owners of shares, and investors in shares must be reconstructed judicially and socially so that their rights, duties, and responsibilities are actually consistent with property law, agency law, and corporate statutory law.

When corporations, directors, owners of shares, and investors in shares are reconstructed by courts to be consistent with property law, agency law, and corporate statutory law, rather than in contradiction of property law, agency law, and corporate statutory law, they can then be socially reconstructed to align with judicial constructions.

What is the result of judicially reconstructing corporations, directors, owners of shares, and investors in shares? First, the economics of the firm, based on property law, agency law, and corporate statutory law, can be better understood. The economic power of corporations can be more equitably distributed across more than owners of shares and investors in shares.

Reconstructing corporations, shareholders, directors, owners of shares, and investors in shares realigns the rights and responsibilities of corporations, shareholders, directors, owners of shares, and investors in shares, as well as their relationships with each other and society. In realigning the legal rights, responsibilities, and relationships of corporations, shareholders, directors, owners of shares, and investors in shares, their rights, responsibilities, and relationships are rebalanced more equitably. The rules of "the game," as Friedman calls it, will no longer be distorted by judicial constructions of corporate law that are contradicted by property law, agency law, and trust law.

What is the result of socially reconstructing corporations, shareholders, directors, owners of shares, and investors in shares? Since their legal rights and responsibilities are rebalanced, their relative social and cultural power is likewise rebalanced more equitably. For example, since owners of shares are not legally constructed as owners of the corporation, their power is greatly reduced. Since directors are not legally constructed as agents of shareholders, their duties to shareholders are greatly reduced.

New theories of the firm that are not based on shareholders as owners, fiduciary duties of directors to shareholders, or an agency relationship between directors and shareholders must be developed. But any future economic theory of the firm must stay within the parameters of property law, agency law, and corporate statutory law.

Not only will it be necessary to develop new legal theories of the corporation; new laws will have to be enacted. Since there are no owners of a corporation, there is sufficient justification for federal intervention to enact laws that require corporations to operate more responsibly in matters pertaining to society and the environment. Since a publicly traded corporation has no owners, it must therefore be subject to greater public oversight and control. It is the responsibility of legislators in all jurisdictions to amend their corporate laws accordingly and of courts to cease issuing opinions that are based on shareholders owning either the corporation or corporate property, directors being agents of shareholders, or directors having a fiduciary duty to shareholders.

Summary

My purposes in writing this book were (1) to reveal the contradictions in property law, agency law, trust law, and corporate law; (2) to fill in the gap left by Berle and Means's failure to engage in a rigorous analysis of property law and agency law in relation to corporations, shareholders, and directors; (3) to supplement the claims of those who correctly understood that shareholders are not owners of corporations and that directors are not agents of shareholders with the proofs that they omitted; and (4) to expose the false premises on which the economic theory of the firm is based.

I submit that I have accomplished my purposes. I have provided sufficient evidence that economic theories of the firm are contradicted by property law, agency law, trust law, and corporate statutory law, which, in turn, contradict each other.

I have proven that, as a matter of law, shareholders do not and cannot own corporations; shareholders do not and cannot own either the property of the of the corporation or the equity of the corporation; there is no separation of ownership and control; there are no shareholder principals, and there are no director-agents or director-trustees there are no fiduciary duties owed by directors to shareholders; and shareholders are not investors in corporations.

For those who persist in advancing the economic theory of the firm based on shareholders as owners of the corporation and investors in the corporation, and directors as agents of shareholders, the burden of proof is now on them to refute the legal proof I have provided herein. I submit that the evidence is incontrovertible.

Bibliography

Posner, R.A. (2014). *Economic analysis of law* (9th ed.). New York: Wolters Kluwer.

Velasco, J. (2010). Shareholder ownership and primacy. *University of Illinois Law Review,* (3), 897–956. Retrieved from http://dx.doi.org/10.2139/ssrn.1274244.

Index of Authors and Publications

Index of Publications, Cases, and Statutes

Index of Subjects

Printed in the United States
by Baker & Taylor Publisher Services